THE MEGA MAGA MIND MELTDOWN

THE ULTIMATE MIND GUIDE TO AMERICA'S ODD RIGHT

VOL. I

BY

S.J. BREDE

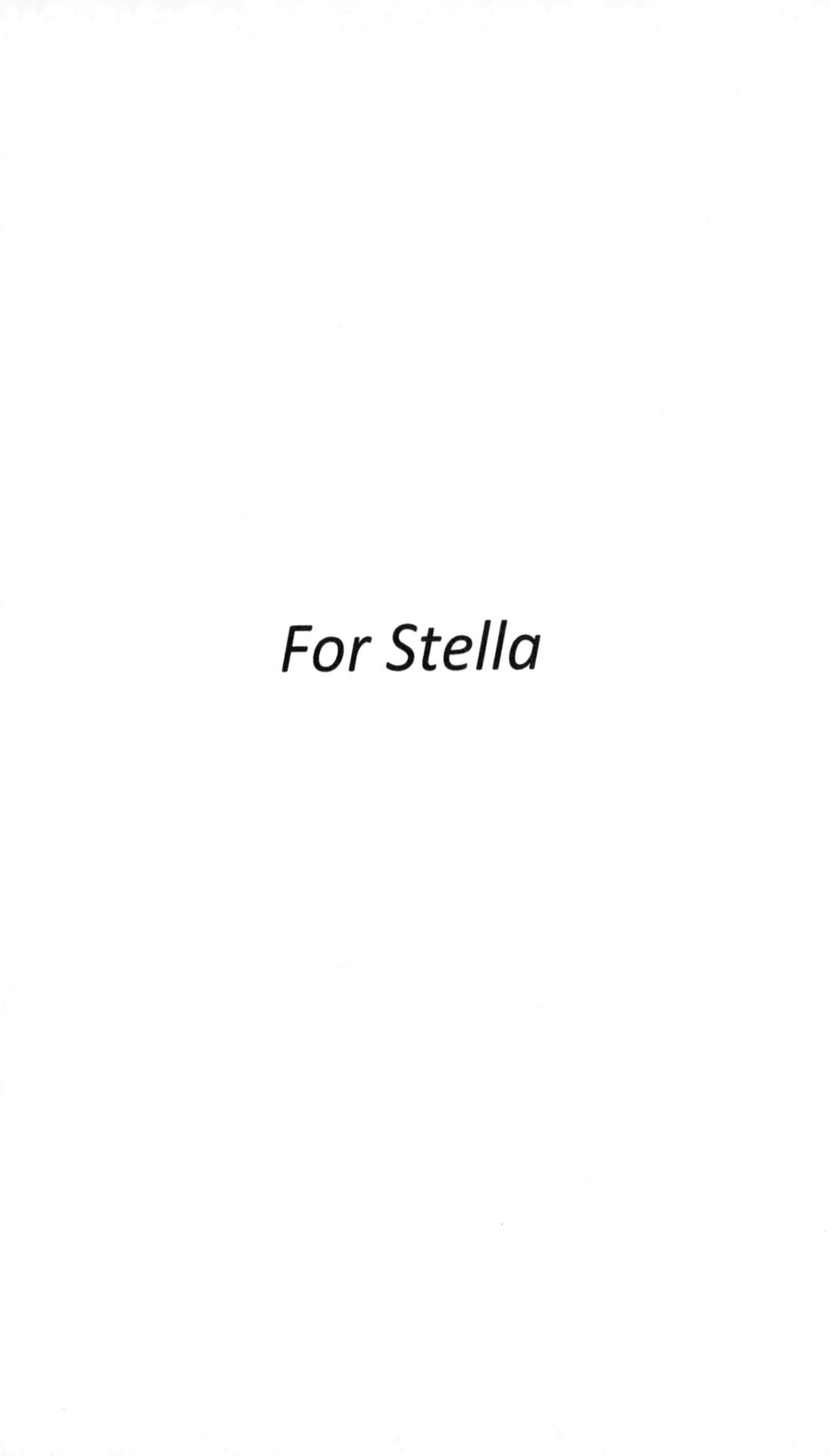

For Stella

Table of Contents

VOLUME II

Bullshitting

The Ballad of Bullshitter Jeff

A Tale of Two Trumps

The Bullshitter's Playbook

John Barron. A Report.

Childhood and Youth

Spreading His Wings

Coming into His Own

A Star is Born

Discoveries

The Later Years

The Bullshitter's Pawns and Prey

An (Incomplete) Damage Report

Behind the Bullshitter's Mask

The Emotional Emptiness of the Embezzler

The Path of the Bullshitter

They live! Among Us.

Drying Out a Parasite

Circular Reasoning

"Checkmate, mate!"

O

One of the doubtlessly most flummoxing experiences for any debater believing in reason and logic comes when crossing rhetorical swords with a fundamental Christian on the validity of their religion's *"incontrovertible truths"*. In fact, many openminded proponents of logic-based argumentation already left such debates with a metaphorical bloody nose as well as literal blood on their minds. All of whom having fallen into the same, age-old trap of a particularly bold case of *Circular Reasoning* employed by believers in an omnipotent douchebag for at least as long back as Abraham's premeditated, murderous attack on his own son's life.

Undeniably, *Circular Reasoning*, (also called *circular logic*, Lat.: *circulus in probando:* "circle in proving"), can claim millions of loyal and enthusiastic fans in politics, the judiciary, in finance, business, entertainment, and even in the military. Yet, no other social group has taken to this specific mind-twister like a duck to water just as strongly as religious leaders and believers.

Ironically, monotheists' almost canonical employment of this debate-technique when their belief comes under scrutiny in fact suggests it as a textbook-example for the deviousness of *Circular Reasoning* and its underlying rhetorical mechanism. Once stripped of all the usual, accompanying embellishments, obfuscations, and distractions, (normally serving an important role in the scheme), the God-fearer's essential *Circular Reasoning*-argument when debating an inexperienced sceptic comes down to the following example.

Believer: "Everything the Bible says comes directly from our unfailing God!"

Sceptic: "But how can you be sure about this?"

B: "Because it says so in the Bible, of course."

S: "And why do you believe what the Bible says?"

B: "How could I not? The Bible is infallible!"

S: "Ah. But how can you know this with absolute certainty?"

B: "Didn't you listen? Because everything the Bible says comes directly from our unfailing God, heathen!"

(Cue audio: Forehead repeatedly hitting wall. Sirens in the distance.)

Experts making it their profession to study all sorts of bamboozling like to call these hoodwinking mindbenders *logical fallacies*. Once people manage to wrap their head around the functional principle of this fallacious logic, most come to the sobering realization that any reason-relying debater has as much a chance of winning such lopsided debates as of fitting a camel through a needle's eye. Put bluntly, hence, the game is rigged before it begins.

By arguing from the firm base of his *logical fallacy*, your meek Christian counterpart made his first move already long before you as the starry-eyed logic-lover have uttered your first *"But …"*. The true extent to which you have been outsmarted becomes obvious by imagining a game of chess in which your opponent is allowed to place an additional piece on the board that comes without any rules attached, free to move how, where, and whenever its player deems it opportune.

While you came to the board assuming both of you will play by the same basic and universally accepted rules, your Christian counterpart produces his illogical and random super-piece, the *"indubitable existence of an almighty, unfailing god"*, to place it squarely on the board as if this piece would be just a regular, generally accepted part of the game.

To add insult to injury, alas, you actually dug your own grave already the moment you made the decision to play, since by entering the debate you unwittingly gave your consent to the rules determined by your opponent, including his use of the god-piece, thus forfeiting any option for bringing the game back on a sound footing. To now opt out, after discovering the misshapen figure on the board, will only allow your adversary to claim easy victory because you are apparently not much convinced of your chances regarding the pieces you control, (e.g., scientific, historical, philosophical, logical arguments), only proving further that your Karate is weak and therefore wrong, (constituting another *logical fallacy* all on its own).

Ultimately, at this point you will have no above-the-board move left to you, since agreeing to discuss the existence of God while allowing your adversary to utilize "God-given proof" (aka the Bible) as valid "evidence", the believer's stance on the matter has become a legitimate debate point, allowing him to bring this super-piece to the board and into his line of argumentation. Hence, in this case, *"the only winning move is not to play."* (*"War Games"*, 1983).

Hiding Circular Reasoning in Plain Sight

Fortunately, though, the Christian *logical fallacy* demonstrated in the curt example above is generally well known nowadays, to a large extent thanks to such eloquent atheist debaters as the unforgettable Christopher Hitchens as well as Richard Dawkins, Lawrence M. Krauss, and Sam Harris. Serious critics of religion are therefore aware of the trap and prepare their refutations accordingly. (Incidentally, Hitchens and Harris demonstrate in numerous YouTube-videos how to perfectly execute *Circular Reasoning*-counterstrikes).

Unfortunately, alas, having rendered this concrete *logical fallacy* mostly inefficient had almost no effect on the ongoing effectiveness of other *Circular Reasoning*-traps still abundantly in use today. Moreover, detecting the utilization of *Circular Reasoning* remains a difficult endevor, particularly with *logical fallacies* hidden underneath expertly crafted jumbles of distracting filibusters, obfuscating phrases, false comparisons, misused synonyms, reinterpreted word-meanings, and other rhetoric auxiliaries. One of which being among the most effective invisibility cloaks when attempting to hide *logical fallacies* in broad daylight.

This specific obfuscation makes use of nothing less than mankind's instinctive subservience to higher authorities. More precisely, once again we are duped by our inherent readiness to accept any claim to authority, for as long as the claimant displays the correct symbols and signs we have come to expect from an authority in the respective field of expertise.

Next to an authority's outward appearance, (e.g., all types of uniforms, impressive modes of transportation, bodyguards, et.al.), their place of employment, (e.g., Harvard, MIT, White House, etc.), and their titles, (PhD, professor, minster, CEO, et.al.), people also pay particular attention to an authority's choice of words, style of expression, and phrasing. After all, a white coat, a stethoscope, and a bunch of expensive pens in the breast pocket go only so far in identifying a medical doctor, quickly losing their validity as proof of genuineness when the white coat-wearer starts talking in some linguistic style more at home with the *Sons of Anarchy* or *Breaking Bad* than *Grey's Anatomy* or *Emergency Room*.

Having grown up in the fold of modern society, we all have come to expect a certain, specific enunciation, choice of words, and mode of expression from the different authorities present in all areas of life today. Naturally, such deeply ingrained conditioning attracts conmen like a dung-heap draws flies. Hence, confidence tricksters are making it their principal duty to study specific enunciations and word-choices of authorities of different professions in order to emulate the characteristic style right down to the last detail. With people in other professions demanding a convincing appearance such as lawyers, CEOs, or politicians, often also being naturally talented in adopting an ideally suited rhetoric mode depending on the respective type of audience.

Just how easily people are taken in by self-proclaimed authorities simply hitting the right tone that resonates with preconditioned expectations was demonstrated by scientific methodologist Hugh G. Gauch in his book *"Scientific Method in Brief"*, (Cambridge University Press, 2012). In his work, Gauch provides a descriptive example to show why a non-logical argumentation based on made-up or misrepresented facts, i.e. *Circular Reasoning*, is often difficult to detect for average listeners or viewers.

Demonstrating the impact of different phrasing and word-choices on the credibility-level of an argument, Gauch first takes a basic fact – *"Objects lighter than water will float"* – to nonsensically use this statement as explanation for itself as demonstration of *Circular Reasoning*.

"Whatever is less dense than water will float, because whatever is less dense than water will float."

Certainly, any self-proclaimed physics-authority stating this pearl of wisdom on TV and in front of a studio-audience most likely elicits first a stunned silence to be quickly followed by a general outbreak of snorts and laughter right before the station cuts hastily to commercials.

In stark contrast to the statement in the second part of Gauch's example. Once again, Grauch takes the exact same fact – *"Objects lighter than water will float"* –, and again "explains" this fact with nonsensical *Circular Reasoning*. However, this time he hides the snake biting its own tail underneath coils of fancy rhetoric.

"An object X possessing lesser density than water will factually float, since objects determined to own this specific attribute will, under normally existing circumstances, not sink below the surface of liquid water."

A studio-audience's reaction to this statement will assumedly look rather different from the previous one. Sure, anyone thinking the above sentence through for two seconds will unavoidably arrive at *"WTF?!"*. Yet, any snorts and derisive laughter will most likely fail to materialize this time around and neither will the producer reflexively hit the button to cut to commercials.

In comparison to an inept physicist-imposter, it is not difficult to imagine what a talented conman with a knack for rhetorical chicanery can accomplish by utilizing well-disguised *Circular Reasoning* when given preparation-time and a topic slightly more demanding than the properties of a rubber-duck in liquid water.

Hiding fallacious *Circular Reasoning* in plain sight by glossing it over with pseudo-highbrow rhetoric has allowed more people a lucrative career than anybody wants to know seriously. However, this constitutes just one option for obfuscating logical fallacies. Another one being at least equally effective is merely replacing scientific claptrap with authoritarian big talk to presently lead about 65 million Americans successfully on a merry chase.

The Impenetrable Circles of Lies

They say a fish rots from the head down. And never more so than in a scam-organization like that led from inside the White House. No question, Don the Con remains the uncontested *Circular Reasoning* master in the art of giving a gullible 35% of American voters the run-around. But then, Donald Trump's apparent penchant for biting his own tail argumentatively will come as no big surprise after he went on the record dozens of times on radio and television in past decades while applying the same, trusted *Circular Reasoning*-formula, "*A is true because B is true, and B is true because A is true*", albeit in ever new variations.

A particularly clear example for Donald J. Trump's unparalleled audacity of brazenly applying *Circular Reasoning* in support of an unsubstantiated claim has been recorded in 2015 during the infamous pre-presidential election-interview with CNN's Chuck Todd, with Trump claiming to have personally witnessed *"hundreds of Muslims in New Jersey cheering and celebrating"* [the attacks on 9/11]. Chris Cillizza, former author of politics-blog *The Fix* at the *Washington Post* meticulously recounted the interview in his blog-article from November 30, 2015, titled, "***Donald Trump's dangerously circular logic***".

This is an excerpt.

DONALD TRUMP: *"Chuck, I saw it on television. So did many other people. And many –"*

CHUCK TODD*: "In Jersey City –"*

TRUMP: *"– many people. I said hundreds. In the area. I –"*

TODD: *"– you saw in Jersey City? Okay."*

TRUMP*: "– heard Patterson. Excuse me. I've heard Jersey City. I've heard*

Patterson. It was 14 years ago. But I saw it on television. I saw clips. And so did many other people. And many people saw it in person. I've had hundreds of phone calls to the

Trump Organization saying, "We saw it. It was dancing in the streets." [...] "I saw it at the time. I stick by it. Hundreds of people have confirmed it. You look at @realdonaldtrump, where I have millions and millions of people on there, between Facebook and Twitter. I have ten million people between the two of them. You look at that. And I'm getting unbelievable response of people that said they saw it. Now –"

TODD: *"But if you repeat something? Wait a minute."*

TRUMP: *"– you know, just go a step further. All over the world at the time it was reported that Muslims were celebrating the downing."* [...] TODD: *"But you're repeating, Mr. Trump."*

TRUMP: *"So, there is a problem here, Chuck, of hatred that is unbelievable."*

TODD: *"But Mr. Trump, this didn't happen in New Jersey. There were plenty of reports. And you're feeding that stereotype."*

TRUMP: *"Chuck, it did happen in New Jersey. I have hundreds of people that agree with me."*

TODD: *"But they want to agree with you –"*

[...]

To summarize, Trump's *Circular Reasoning* here follows these three easy steps:

1. Trump maintains that his Claim A - *"There were hundreds of Muslims cheering on 9/11"* - is true.
2. Trump follows up with his Claim B: Hundreds of people agree with him on social media that his Claim A is true.

3. Trump concludes from his own two prior claims that, since (unverified) Claim B is true, (unverified) Claim A must be true as well.

Chris Cillizza commented in his article: "Trump's argument boils down to this: I don't care what published fact-checks say. I have heard from people on Twitter who tell me they saw the same thing I did. Trump uses the social media response he gets to the outrageous claims he makes as justification that those claims are correct." [...]

Remember the Christian chess-player from the beginning? The guy had his Circular Reasoning perfected by inserting the allegation "God and Bible are real and infallible" as a "given" into the debate. Any attempt of debating him while he holds his successfully implemented super-chess piece in hand cannot result in any fruitful discussion since he has an unassailable base to which he always can return to spin the same circle anew for a thousand times should you allow it.

For Donald Trump and his Trumpaganda-brigade on the other hand, the crux of the matter lies in not owning such an unprovable, yet widely accepted "god-piece" to base their house of cards on, as much as they would love to. In this case, it is actually true for a change that nothing can beat a god even if only as an unsubstantiated allegation big enough to serve as the foundation of a Circular Reasoning on which billions of believers build their whole lives.

Leaving the question of the "secret" behind Donald Trump's appeal to preconditioned authority-cravers such as the religious right. Put differently, how are Trumpagandists preventing their house of lies from crashing down without a foundation as impermeable to scrutiny as the "sky-dictator"-pipe dream shared by billions of monotheists? The answer is as ancient as it is simple. As any cult-leader, big-time conman, successful dictator, and professional narcissist will gladly admit under sufficient pressure, in case of being unable to fall back on an already existing highest authority and his/its accompanying belief-system that can be easily hijacked, the go-to solution constitutes the creation of an own quasi-deity and its flanking, tailor-made belief-system.

While Soviet dictator Joseph Stalin got his religiously preconditioned followers quasi delivered on a silver-platter, Donald Trump needed first to box his base into shape out of the raw material unquestionably lying around, only waiting to be picked up and moulded into the Trump-lump known as the Trump-base. By presenting this gullible minority with an "Only I can fix it!"-figure who had "proven" his natural authority for years by yelling "You are fired!" at hapless reality-TV show contestants, the strategists behind Don the Con's political success had an easy job in convincing their figure-head to strike the appropriate pose of "strong leader" to win over easily impressed authority-seekers who had felt "disenfranchised" by the first Black President.

Trump grew visible into his role as the second coming of Christ in the eyes of his congregation during his time in the Oval Office and if there would be a Book of Trump in the Bible, it would no doubt contain the "Highest Authority's" most important directives to his disciples, coalesced into Trump-commandments such as:

- "Thou shalt fear those of different heritage and of an appearance unlike your own and strike them with great hatred and cruelty."

- "Thou shalt not trust in your own eyes and ears but accept as the whole and only truth solely what I, thy Savior, promulgate."

- "Thou shalt not care for a system of democratic checks and balances but place your trust entirely in the omnipotence and omniscience of Me, your Lord and Savior, and in My perfect gut-feeling decisions."

- "Thou shalt not ask what your Lord and Savior can do for you, but what you can do for your Lord and Savior (Your favorite President, Me)."

- "Thou shalt neither ruminate nor recalculate, neither doubt nor question what your King of Kings giveth you so freely but be content and rejoice for it cometh from your Lord, thus being inherently a tremendous win for you and this nation under Trump."

The success of these and similar Trump-centric directives for the most part rides undeniably on the prior conditioning of millions of staunchly religious conservatives who readily converted nonetheless to a personality cult whose leader demonstrated on countless occasions severest moral shortcomings, additional to an utter lack of business acumen, human compassion, common sense, and basic intelligence. This apparent ease of transition as well as Trumpism-converts' complete unawareness regarding the incommensurateness of the teachings of their "old" savior Jesus Christ with the dictates of their new Orange Overlord perfectly demonstrate the subversive power of *Circular Reasoning, Arguments from Authority*, and *Closed World Assumptions*.

From devout GOP-Senators to the last bible-thumping village-conservatives, Trumpism-converts merely re-purposed the template of this other sect they have already been intimately familiar with, including the uncritical acceptance of a "god-piece", and applied its principles one-to-one to their new *Emperor with New Clothes* who bears apparently an almost uncanny resemblance to Jesus Christ.

Although, this tendency to embrace one's own, mindless infatuation in the face of a "charismatic" leader is nothing new in American culture. After all, it is no mere coincidence that all the largest and most deranged Christian cults originate in the *Land of Boundless Possibilities*, from Joseph Smith's *Mormons,* to Charles Taze Russell's *Jehovah's Witnesses,* to L. Ron Hubbard's *Scientology*, to name just the most infamous ones.

Any reliable American history-book, often found somewhere close to the family-Bible at home, provides ample disclosure on the uniquely close relations between Americans and their dozens of Christian denominations throughout the centuries. For generations, a vast majority of the American population has relentlessly been subjected to the admonitions of missionaries, vicars, ministers, chaplains, prelates, priests, pastors, and preachers from every church, religion, sect, and cult plying their tax-exempt trade in the United States.

Incidentally, the one and only country worldwide with a constitution explicitly decreeing the separation of church and state represents also the only nation in the Western hemisphere where any politician not constantly professing his deep religiosity and love of God does not even have the ghost of a chance of winning an election.

When it comes to susceptibility to religious great promises and potential saviors, the United States are unique among Western nations in being able to claim a place right up at the top of the list of zealot states, together with most fanatically Islamic countries. No wonder, hence, that the part of the American population having grown up under the unblinkingly vigilant, all-seeing eyes of an almighty, omniscient, and easy to anger super-daddy is taking to any self-styled worldly "savior" like an altar boy to the mass wine.

While the USA indeed constitute a "promised land" for populists, mountebanks, conmen, and grandstanders knowing how to harvest the ingrained gullibility of zealots and religion-bred ignoramuses, it might be at least a quantum of solace to non-believers that human history is full of civilizations whose populations had been thoroughly soft-boiled over time by some religious cult. In defense of such enthralled communities it needs to be said that most of these lost societies simply did not know any better at the time, therefore allowing a small group of professional tall tale-tellers to "interpret" natural phenomena as the will of the gods or of God, to read the future from the intestines of birds or human sacrifices, and to declare themselves the sole, unchallengeable, and unquestionable source of all godly wisdom and worldly justice.

The point at which the cultists decidedly gained the upper hand and controlled the political side of things usually also marked the beginning of the end for zealot-infected civilizations. Today, only a few millennia later, the populace's learned adoration of "decisive, God-sent leaders" has long since crossed the line between religion and politics and finds its most prominent target-figures today not so much in churches but rather in various seats of government, from the Russian Kremlin to the Turkish Presidential Palace and the American White House.

By necessity, this reorientation of reverence also brings about a replacement of the rank and file with religious preachers taking a backseat to the professional mouthpieces of modern politics, of whom the best can teach the Pope some *Circular Reasoning*-tricks for selling unsubstantiated allegations as "honest truth" to the masses. In fact and all fairness, even Putin's state-controlled media and personal mouthpieces cannot hold a candle to the Trumpaganda-propagators in the West Wing when it comes to pulling the wool over the eyes of Trump's admittedly outstandingly gullible followers.

Not that former chief-witch Kellyanne Conway, head-ghoul Stephen Miller, and clueless claptrap-gabbler Kayleigh McEnany would do in any way, shape, or form a particularly good job, of course. Rather on the contrary, given that a clear majority of Americans had a decidedly negative impression of their new commander-in-chief and his administration at the beginning of his term and has become more steadfast in its initial opinion after four years. The "secret" of the Trumpaganda-brigade's success with

Trumpists therefore does not lie in their predominantly dilettantish practice of their professions but in the unparalleled level of wilful ignorance prevalent in most Trumpists, allowing Miller, McEnany, and their minions an unprecedentedly easy access to the hearts, minds, and souls of these preconditioned believers. This wilful ignorance, in combination with a hefty dose of *Cognitive Dissonance Avoidance*, habitual *Circular Reasoning* and the occasional *Dunning-Kruger Effect*, makes religious Trumpublicans not just exceptionally susceptible to all kinds of conspiracy theories from flat-earthers, anti-vaxxers, and moon-landing deniers all the way to anti-maskers, virus-deniers, and QAnus-madhatters, but also leaves them wide open to the ordinary, unimaginative, and vicious propaganda pieces of the Trump-administration.

The toxic concoction of learned blind belief with its *Circular Reasoning*-defense, its instinctive avoidance of information contradicting this core-belief, and the erroneous assumption of "being in the know" also explains partially why Evangelicals are sticking with an immoral narcissist who has obviously never read the Bible, is twice divorced, and evidentially is a serial adulterer to boot. Moreover, the "champion of the religious right" is known to have ridiculed his pious Vice-President, to swear in the presence of religious leaders, get spanked by porn stars, grab women by the pussy, and to generally live a life that would prompt even the famously tolerant Jesus Christ to gag in revulsion. And still, the hard core of trumpist America will unabashedly swear on the family-Bible that Donald John Trump, good friend of the deceased Mr. Jeffrey Epstein and on tape boasting about his pussy-grabbing technique, (*"You know I'm automatically attracted to beautiful—I just start kissing them. It's like a magnet. Just kiss. I don't even wait. And when you're a star, they let you do it. You can do anything. Grab 'em by the pussy. You can do anything."*), is standing clearly right up there next to Jesus regarding Christian values, morale, and decency.

Such a level of blind infatuation in combination with the Trump-base's self-proclaimed, openly displayed affinity to authoritarianism, (*'We need a strong law and order leader'*; *'George Floyd got what he deserved'*; *"Lock her up!"*; *"Blue Lives Matter"*, et.al.), should constitute a shrilling alarm-signal for all citizens still interested in the actual state of American democracy. Unfortunately, too many non-trumpist Americans tend to shrug off the radical tendencies of their red-hatted friends, colleagues, family-members, and neighbors with a disinterested *"Eh, what can you do?"*, as if supporting an openly anti-democratic and justice-perverting egomaniac with publicly admitted authoritarian tendencies would be no more egregious than pouring first the milk and then the cereals in the bowl.

The general numbness and widespread disinterest displayed by many Americans in the face of a rising tide of totalitarianism with its millions of sources just on the other side of the dinner-table, office-desk, or garden-fence, can trace its origins back similarly to the deeply rooted religiosity permeating the country for well over two-hundred years by now. The Trump-base's spiritual trailblazers, aka Evangelicals and their predecessors, have been an integral part of American culture and history from the very beginning, with the nondelusional part of the citizenry having long since learned to handle zealots either with velvet gloves or to give them a wide berth lest they sic torch- and pitchfork-wielding mobs, respectively nowadays their lawyers, on them. Until today it remains fact that only a politically suicidal candidate or officeholder could be reckless enough to question or critizise, let alone attack the God-fearing crowd's motivation and rationale behind their apparent inclination for authoritarian leaders with totalitarian ambitions, in other words with an all-seeing, all-knowing, all-controlling Highest Authority offering protection and prosperity to his loyalists, believers, and supporters, while punishing all who critizise, question, or attack his person, doctrines, commandments, or decisions.

Naturally, this problem is neither exclusively American nor unique to the present era. History provides abundant examples for authoritarian rulers and dictators who took advantage of their religious countrymen, with one of the most brutal examples from less than a century ago proving just how easily, rapidly, and completely such an exploitation can be executed when a huge and deeply religious population becomes suddenly subjected to a new, charismatic leader taking the reins of government in his steely hands.

Concretely, when becoming General Secretary in 1922, Joseph Stalin, the fiercely anti-religious new leader of a young U.S.S.R. masterfully utilized the deeply ingrained religiosity of the Russian people at the time to establish a new personality cult with himself as quasi-godlike savior and leader. Stalin knew of his people's inherent desire to believe in and follow a highest authority and hence decided ingeniously against simply abolishing religion to leave a dangerous vacuum. Instead, the dictator razed the country's churches and executed its priests while simultaneously offering the population an enticing alternative in the form of himself as their new god, communism as their new religion, and the communist party as their new church.

With a massive propaganda-campaign and an all-pervasive stick-and-carrot-policy – where the stick could not have been more brutal while accepting the carrot meant, willingly or unwillingly, to become Stalin's partner in horrendous crime – Stalin redirected the Russians' centuries-old faith in one specific higher authority, i.e. the God of the Russian-Orthodox Church, forcefully towards the new religion of the Communist Party of the Soviet Union (CPSU) and above all of the *"Great Leader, General Secretary, "Generalissimo, Man of Steel, Brilliant Genius of Humanity, Great Architect of Communism, Gardener of Human Happiness, and Dear Father"*, (all real titles), the one and only Joseph Vissarionovich Stalin.

No question, there remains a tremendously wide gap between Stalin's Soviet Union and Trump's United States, most apparent in the incomparable brutality and cruelty of Stalin's Gulag-riddled Russia versus merely overcrowded, underfunded, and profit-driven U.S.-prisons, or in the complete absence of democracy and genuine rule of law in the erstwhile U.S.S.R. compared to the more subtle anti-democratic process instigated by the 45th President and his inner circle. Nonetheless, Trump's and Stalin's approaches share at least one basic common denominator, albeit one of vastly differing dimensions. While separated by space, time and a galaxy of disparate circumstances, both the United States since 2017 and the Soviet Union between 1920 and 1953 have seen their leaders utilizing their religious people's inherent willingness to succumb to higher and highest authorities.

Trump's shtick of impersonating the strong, decisive, and infallible Authority appealing to authority-craving believers has been his discernible strategy at countless rallies, whenever yelling at reporters under the running rotors of Marine One, and in the most outlandish manner at his short-lived daily press-conferences amidst the Corona-crisis. Indisputably with great success, too, regarding the continuous support of a base that includes an above-average percentage of bleach-drinking, hydroxychloroquine-hoarding, *"Sacrifice-the-Weak"*-promoting and, most perplexing, suddenly *"My Body. My Choice!"*-proclaiming conservatives.

Add a good pinch of *Circular Reasoning* to Trump's authority-shtick and the result is the tried and tested recipe for successfully reeling in almost any gullible citizen who has either never learned of, is incapable of, or is wilfully ignorant of independent thinking. A clientele that once again includes a large percentage of the Trump-base, as the following examples indicate, summing up some of the arguments of Trumpists on television between 2015 and 2020:

- *"I don't vote for the Democrats because they won't win. They can't win. Because nobody will vote for them."*
- *Trump is the best president America ever had! Why? Because he is the best president in history, that's why."*
- *"Trump never tells lies. I know this because Trump said so. And that is the truth because Trump never tells lies."*
- *"Illegal immigration is illegal."*
- *"The news is fake because so much of the news is fake."* (Donald J. Trump, Feb. 2017)

Although run-of-the-mill Trumpists presumably will never cease to surprise the world with ever more dumbfoundingly simpleminded *Circular Reasoning* examples, the shadowy figures currently holding the strings of the red-hatted marionettes and their predecessors throughout the ages have taken the once simple concept of *Circular Reasoning* to whole new levels of devious cleverness. In the never-ending battle over the prerogative of reality-interpretation, the original *Circular Reasoning*-formula *"A is true because of B and B is true because of A"* has thusly sprouted several specialized variations, called *Closed World Assumption, Open World Assumption, Whitewashing over one Rail,* and the ubiquitous *What-Aboutism,* each designed to expertly dupe an interviewer, debate-adversary, or audience and to get away with it scot-free.

Closed World Assumption
"Period!"

From a ridiculous, yet no-nonsense point of view, any *Closed World Assumption* (CWA) constitutes nothing but the "assumption", (of which the trickster needs to convince his audience), that whatever is not irrefutably *known* to be true *must* therefore be false.

"I don't know personally if Trump already knew in February about the lethal dangers of the Coronavirus. A recording can be faked to promote just another of these "Gotcha"-books. And since there is no rock-solid proof, everything points to just another made-up lie by the fake-news media."

Incidentally, behavioral scientists have classified the *Closed World Assumption*-prevarication as a well-engineered, formal false-logic system to be actively employed by habitual liars and deceivers to give the impression of a "logical" (i.e. fallacious) conclusion, while truth-deniers and apologists utilize CWAs passively and more straightforward in order to deny any knowledge of a truth that is starring everyone else in the face.

Hence, *Closed World Assumptions* offer two different ways to lead a bamboozled audience to accepting an unproven or false assertion as true. In the first variation, the deceiver insists that an opposing assertion that disproves his own statement has not (yet) been proven to be 100%

true and must therefore "logically" be false. Frequently, this line of CWA-argumentation is used by monotheists to attack scientific theories by indignantly pointing out that scientists can only come up with *"theories"* which as such cannot have any lasting significance.

The apologists conveniently omit here, or worse, are not even aware of, however, that the word *"theory"* is used by scientists for all scientific conclusions, since a basic premise of all sciences purports that at any time new evidence can turn up and either support, negate, alter, or add to existing conclusions. Differently put, all scientists have made it their professional obligation to always keep an open mind, thus allowing new information to improve any existing models.

Theists misuse this scientific mindset by misinterpreting the word *"theory"* as synonymous to *"not known"*, pretending this to be enough of an argument to successfully debunk for example the *theory of evolution*. Particularly enthusiastic fans of this CWA-fallacy can also be found among conspiracy theorists, by the way, for example when asserting that nobody can prove with 100% certainty that there is no hidden Nazi-base on the dark side of the moon and that therefore there obviously must be a hidden Nazi-base on the dark side of the moon.

But religion and conspiracy theories are not the only areas in which CWAs thrive. One of the most fruitful fields on which CWAs bloom constitutes, of course, the political arena. In this context, one of the best examples for the above mentioned first variant of CWA has been provided in the long-forgotten times prior to the new era rung in by a microscopic virus. Older readers may still remember the time when the 45th President of the United States, Donald J. Trump, had been impeached just a few weeks ahead of the first American Corona-cases becoming public knowledge. This impeachment-trial on January 16, 2020 had been preceded by almost two years of Robert Mueller's Special Counsel Investigation culminating in the publication of the official investigation report.

During the months of the Mueller-probe, a never-ending stream of scoops and revelations pointing at severe wrong-doings by Trump and his cronies kept the world on the edge of its seat, while the Trumpministration's reaction to any bad news was always the same. Don the Con and his band of misfits retreated grudgingly one step after another, although every time only once their previously made allegations had been irrefutably disproven, following the CWA-premise that if something has not been proven to be 110% correct, it must be false.

In this manner, erstwhile press-secretary Sarah Huckabee Sanders, her forgettable successor, Trump's inner circle, and the denier-in-chief himself could be observed tumbling and stumbling ever further backwards, from an initial *"No collusion!"*, to *"Okay, maybe collusion, but collusion is not a crime"*, to *"Fine, maybe collusion is a crime, but the President had nothing to do with it"*, to *"Alright, maybe the President had something to do with it, but a President can't be indicted"*.

Once the Mueller-report had been published the same game began anew, first with Trump claiming to have been *"completely exonerated"*, soon followed by, *"Okay, there has been some misconduct, but still: 'no collusion'"*, all the way to the impeachment-trial where MoscowMitch saved Trump's soggy ass once again.

While this first version of CWA is thus ideally suited for "credibly" refuting negative allegations or statements attacking the own position, claiming *"if it is not proven to be right beyond any doubt, it clearly must be wrong"*, the second variation of *Closed World Assumptions* works the other way around, with the bamboozler using a widely accepted misconception for convincing the audience of the correctness of own assertion's correctness. The following quoted tweet provides an example of this tactics.

"So last year 37,000 Americans died from the common Flu. It averages between 27,000 and 70,000 per year. Nothing is shut down, life & the economy go on. At this moment there are 546 confirmed cases of Coronavirus, with 22 deaths. Think about that!"
– (Donald J. Trump, Twitter, 03/09/2020)

Translated, in this tweet the U.S.-President equates the *Coronavirus* with the common flu, a brazen lie widely disseminated right from the beginning of the pandemic by Trump himself as well as trumpist business-, and economy-experts, medical charlatans, and FOX News alike. Subsequently, the dangerous lie has been readily accepted and spread further by millions of Trumpists from California to Florida, Indiana to Louisiana, and Texas to Michigan.

Only two days after Trump's tweet, none other than Dr Anthony Fauci had to set the record straight by explaining:

"This is 10 times more lethal than the seasonal flu". Unsurprisingly, though, the words of the Head of Infectious Diseases at the National Institutes of Health fell on deaf ears with Trumpists devoted to Trump's version of the truth, roundly falling for the second variant of the *Close World Assumption* in which a true-sounding "fact" (*"Corona is like the flu"*) is used to justify or legitimize another assumption (*"therefore we don't need a lockdown"*).

By brazenly insinuating that, *"everybody knows that X is true, therefore Y must be true as well"*, CWA-perpetrators are creating a logical fallacy and rely on the gullibility of an audience-majority to disregard the simple mind-fuck, *"It's true because it's known to be true."* Incidentally, this fallacious line of argumentation has a long tradition in the Trumpministration, beginning on day one with the uncontested pinnacle of CWA-employment, former press-secretary and Melissa McCarthy-doppelgänger Sean Spicer uttering the legendary words: *"This was the largest audience to ever witness an inauguration. Period!"*

Open World Assumption
"I don't recall!"

O

In contrast to CWAs, *Open World Assumptions* (OWA) constitute an argumentation-tool in almost anyone's box of little tricks. While adults are by no means above deploying this gambit, OWAs can mainly be observed with the small human beings who are readily inclined to adorn an expensive wallpaper with every rainbow-color available in the crayon-box. When subsequently interrogated about their heinous act, many devious little perpetrators tend to profess complete ignorance, (spuriously) assuming that by simply pretending to not recall the incident they will be let off the hook. (It won't).

However, far from being unique to the world of diaper-clad mini-villains, the same logical fallacy has also a firm place in the adult world, only in a more dressed-up and formalized manner. In this case, the same non-sensical line of argumentation will frequently be expressed with the sentence: *"I don't recall"*, as could be regularly observed in Senate hearings with members of the Trumpministration when grilled by Elizabeth Warren, Kamala Harris, or Sheldon Whitehouse.

The basic premise of the *Open World Assumption* states that a (professed) lack of knowledge generally will not be considered a lie. In other words, that what is not known to be true is unknown and therefore cannot be judged to be wrong or false. At first glance, this *Open World Assumption*-premise may appear as a rather feeble-minded strategy, no doubt. Nonetheless, some of the highest-ranking Trumpministration-officials based their defense before a Senate sub-committee solely on this OWA-strategy, claiming: "*I have no knowledge or recollection of the issue. Since having no knowledge does not equal falsity, I am clearly innocent.*" Or translated into plain English: "*As long as I don't confess to anything, everything is possible, and nothing can be pinned on me!*"

Who will not remember in this context former US-Attorney General Jefferson Beauregard Sessions, III., eternalizing the OWA-strategy on live television while sitting in front of the House Judiciary Committee in November 2017? When asked by Representative Hakeem Jeffries (D-NY) whether he realizes that he had already replied at least 20 times with, "*I don't recall*", America's highest-ranking lawman replied without batting an eye, "*I have no idea*". Viz, "I don't recall".

To take Rep. Jeffries' question literal as opposed to the reproach it was clearly meant to be fitted seamlessly into AG Sessions' overall attitude on that day. The namesake of Confederate President Jefferson Davis was oozing a smug assertiveness while facing the House committee members, bolstered by the knowledge of his "*I have no idea what you're talking about*"-defense was working perfectly. Moreover, the old and sly legal fox Sessions was certainly aware of the psychological effect of his "cluelessness" on representatives and TV-audience alike, letting an interviewee to appear increasingly more innocent and credible the more often he professes his lack of knowledge. After the twentieth *"I don't recall"*, even sceptical audience-members will involuntarily begin to doubt the committee-members' allegations since, clearly, the poor man does not remember any of the alleged events, strongly suggesting a growing probability that the "callous" Democratic interrogators' accusations have little or no basis in fact.

Once these first seeds of doubt have been successfully sown, Jefferson Beauregard and other utilizers of the *"no idea!"*-variation of Open World Assumptions can generally rely on one of the most fundamental legal principles known to mankind, that is the *presumption of innocence* or *"not guilty until proven otherwise"*. Any righteous and law-abiding citizen priding themselves on a proper sense of right and wrong will involuntarily side with the accused when sufficient doubt about his or her guilt has been aroused. In this state of mind, laymen-audiences can be readily convinced to follow the accused OWA-utilizer on the last leg of his scheme, accepting the logical fallacy-employer's underlying assertion that, *"Any predicate that cannot be proven to be true must therefore be obviously false"*.

In case of the devout Christian, Eagle Scout, and Doctor of Jurisprudence Jefferson Beauregard Sessions III., his audacious usage of *Open World Assumption*-tactics worked out flawlessly on this day in the House Judiciary Committee. Democratic committee-members were left only with no-legged dog Sessions' brazen denials, translating in plain English to, *"Look, I don't remember talking with any Russian officials about campaign-matters. Hence, I did not talk with any Russian officials about campaign-matters. Can y'all prove me wrong? What, my testimony is the only way to gather evidence on that matter? Well, as I said, I don't recall. So, obviously there's nothing there to recall. Now, if you excuse me. Good day to y'all and fuck you very much."* Exit to the right.

Whitewashing Over One Rail

"They are killing us!"

O

"The Mexican legal system is corrupt, as is much of Mexico. Pay me the money that is owed me now - and stop sending criminals over our border." - Tweet by @realDonaldRrump, 2:47 AM – Feb. 25, 2015.

"You look at countries like Mexico, where they're killing us on the border, absolutely destroying us on the border. They're destroying us in terms of economic development." - Donald Trump during his Super Tuesday victory speech, March 1, 2016.

"Everybody is talking about the protesters burning the American flags and proudly waving Mexican flags. I want America First - so do voters!" - Tweet by @realDonaldRrump, 4:06 PM - May 2, 2016

"I've been treated very unfairly by this judge. Now, this judge is of Mexican heritage. I'm building a wall, OK? I'm building a wall. I am going to do very well with the Hispanics, the Mexicans." - Donald J. Trump in an interview with CNN on June 3, 2016.

Trump's statements above boldly illustrate the *Circular Reasoning*-variation *Whitewashing Over One Rail* allowing an aggressor to appear as the "genuine" victim in a dispute. Donald Trump's tweets and utterances display explicitly such attempted spins, for instance when the original aggressor tries repeatedly to establish the "fact" that Mexicans are optionally "*corrupt*", "*criminals*", "*destroyers*", or "*killers*", as well as "*flag-burners*" and "*unfair*". Simultaneously, the 45th President also employs the second lever this *Circular Reasoning*-variant provides, allocating the role of the "actual victim" to someone else, in this case to the United States and the American people.

The strategy of portraying oneself or one's peer-group directly or indirectly as the victims or "good guys" in a conflict and frequently called *Whitewashing Over One Rail*, constitutes a trademark of authoritarian regimes in their overwhelmingly successful attempts to "unite" the masses behind the common cause of defeating an "aggressor".

From the very beginning, Trump and the Trumpministration singled-out Mexico and the Mexican population to function as this unifying "aggressor" as well as an exemplary ethnic and national group representing the complete non-Caucasian part of the world that was out to rob "real" Americans of their innocent daughters' virginity, as well as their jobs, wages, social benefits, suburban paradises, "patriotic" traditions, and the American Way of Life.

Once the *Circular Reasoning*-assertion of "*Mexicans and refugees equal illegal, evil criminals*" had been firmly established in Trumpists, Donald Trump extended his *Closed World Assumption* to the next seemingly logical level, insinuating that the Trumpministration was merely defending the vulnerable American population against imminent, vicious attacks from hundreds of thousands of brown-, and black-skinned Hispanic-, African-, and Arabic-looking illegals. In effect, the official Trumpaganda-doctrine drew a discernible, society-permeating line of barbed wire between the Trump-identified "aggressors" on the one side and one specific group on the other side, having been suspiciously absent from Trump's list of undesired criminals, i.e., white Americans. Hence allowing conservative circles to conclude "logically" that the multi-colored and -cultured "hordes" must constitute the criminal scum of the earth and that by implication they themselves must be the achromatic "victims" of the villains' viciousness, making them obviously the "good guys" in this equation.

Furthermore, as Hollywood and the Great American Narrative are teaching the world since 1945, victims of criminals and bullies can usually count on being assigned the role of heroic underdogs with the implication that the underdog represents the "good guy" who finds him- or herself solely in a predicament because they have been "*too nice for too long*".

Following this train of thought, once Trumpists identify with the role of valiant underdogs, the resulting "logical" conclusion appears to be that it is only fair and square to "fight back" with a vengeance against the "*barbaric hordes storming our border*", where the phrase "*our border*" predominantly refers not to Trump's infamous border wall per se but to the invisible border surrounding the small bubble-world of "white America".

In stark contrast, citizens of Native American, African, Arabic, Asian, or Hispanic heritage - for instance the judge of Mexican descent who ruled against Trump in the *Trump University* case - are to be regarded as *agent provocateurs* not to be trusted and at best grudgingly tolerated as long as they do not "overstay their welcome" and overstep any elusive "white rules". Since, who else would keep the world running inside the white demarcation line, clean Caucasian Christians' hotels, houses, pools, and gardens, dry-clean their suits and costumes, cook their exotic lunch, dinner, and take-away, babysit their kids, drive their taxis and Ubers, and fill the ranks in essential jobs like nurses, paramedics, firemen, police officers, garbage collectors, soldiers, cashiers, and delivery drivers.

In the *Circular Reasoning*-bubble of Trumpists' *Closed World Assumption*. dividing the world into *good guys* (white) and *bad hombres* (black and brown), it has now become as easy as shooting exhausted illegal immigrants in the Texan desert to proclaim themselves the victims of an "obvious aggressor" and to *Whitewash* their genuine role of callous xenophobes and sociopaths *Over* the *One Rail* of Donald Trump's continuously presented, fallacious "proof" ("*massacres by MS-13*", "*cornsacks full of drugs thrown over border-fences*", "*floods of disease-infected criminals*", et.al.), to justify their own inhumanity. With the additional cherry on top of in this way having "proven" to themselves that they are "on the right side of history" and in effect allowing Trumpists the wholeheartedly embraced conclusion of representing the very definition of "*the good American*".

What-Aboutism

"But, but … but what about them!"

In the cold light of day, any deliberate attempt by politicians to use *Circular Reasoning* – whether based on an *Open* or a *Closed World Assumption* – as a means to deceive and mislead the populace must be regarded as committed fraud or worse, since a frauded victim remains afterwards usually far from convinced that fraud is actually cool and the proper thing to do, while the lie underpinning any *Circular Reasoning* will not only contort the target's perception of objective reality but will fester and bloom into an accepted "fact" in the victim's mind. Moreover, each accepted lie grooms the recipient further, to swallow the next fallacy ever more willingly. Consequentially, once a Trumpist's reality-perception is firmly bend out of whack, the gullible Trumpublican will gladly adopt any subsequent fallacies as own opinions to be repeated ad nauseam in conversations, thus spreading the lie ever further.

Since the maddening impossibility of counter-arguing *Circular Reasoning* does not originate, as might be suspected, in its circular structure per se but rather in its underlying *Closed* or *Open World Assumption,* any effort to debunk an allegation justified by *Circular Reasoning* begins and ends with the successful disassembly of said underlying *Closed* or *Open World Assumption,* either by disproving the assertion beyond any reasonable doubt or by tricking or forcing the Circular Reasoner into admitting the fallacy of their foundational allegation.

In a practical example, the trumpublican argument that *"a general lockdown is vastly exaggerated"* will be frequently based on Donald Trump's long-standing (and, as Trump knew since February 2020, also utterly false) premise that, *"Corona isn't worse than the common flu"*. Any counter-argumentation with reasonable chances for success will hence first of all need to shoot down this false equation with irrefutable facts before even beginning to discuss various degrees of lockdown, mortality rates, overflowing ICUs, European statistics, or the term actual connotation of the term "exaggerated". In other words, the circular wall right-wingers build around their fallacious allegations will not be breached for as long as the counter-debater continues to overlook or accept the *Circular Reasoning*-underlying false premise. Hence, a common mistake and sure-fire recipe for frustration in debating Trumpists consists in arguing against the rightist's conclusion brought forward in the form of their (false) assertion, e.g., *"The Virus is a hoax!"*; *"America is worldwide No. 1 in testing"*; *"Everyone who wants a test can get a test"*; et.al. Debaters will achieve better results when disregarding the false allegation (*"Masks are useless!"*), instead presenting unignorable, understandable, and verified data to debunk the false root-assumption, (*"The virus gets through the mask"*; *"The mask is worse for my health than the virus"*; *"The mask takes away my freedom"*; *"There is no virus!"*, (although in the last case, simply walking away remains the best solution).

For another example, Democrats frequently tend to argue against Trump's border wall by citing the exorbitant costs, thus leaving their flanks wide open for *"Build the wall!"*-fanatics to charge them with the argument: *"We can talk about the costs for concrete walls, or steel slats, or call it what you want, as long as the American people are protected against the monsters on the other side!"* Put differently, while Democrats in Congress are holding sheets up in the air with latest numbers, graphs, and statistics, Republicans are displaying an oversized printout with the picture of a fantasy-monster looming threateningly over an all-American family. Pop-quiz: What image elicits the stronger emotional reaction with the gullible part of American voters?

Incidentally, while in the minds of most Americans the microscopic virus *Sars-CoV-2* has supplanted even most pressing non-virus-related problems currently facing the world, those problems have not miraculously disappeared, of course. Millions of displaced and helpless men, women, and children fleeing from war, oppression, hunger, murder, mutilation, and life-threatening poverty still continue to be more concerned about surviving the next night than about being "finally" allowed again to go to the hairdresser for a new perm or to get their nails freshly done or to go mask-less to the liquor store for their boxed wine. Still, the *Closed World Assumption* made by Trumpists and Trumpublicans that is, *"Immigrants are an insidious, treacherous, and murderous danger to America, therefore we need a physical wall on the southern border!"*, remains for the most part uncontested.

Despite all officially known facts and data roundly disproving this fallacy, no influential media-channel or grassroots-movement has yet come up with a concerted effort to thoroughly debunk the fearmongering notion of *monster-*

migrants and a *necessary* border wall. Serious critics will need to considerably sharpen and emotionalize their arguments against the fallacious assertion of a *"danger from the other side"* and initiate a widespread shakeup encouraging people to actively taking sides against this nefarious and devastating narrative and leaving pro-Wallers no more escape route to return to the falsehood at the base of this *Closed World Assumption.*

To successfully facilitate this outcome, though, courageous debaters will not only need to outsmart and debunk all above-mentioned *Circular Reasoning*-variations but furthermore will be forced to face an additional *Closed World Assumption*-variant tremendously popular with Trumpists on every rung of the societal ladder, viz *What-Aboutism.* An ubiquitous argumentation-strategy of half-crazed alt-righters like Alex Jones, Tucker Carlson, Laura Ingraham, and other Trumpnatics such as verbal *Pirro-maniac* Jeanine, Jim *"Gym"* Jordan, or Matt *"Gasmask"* Gaetz as well as any run-of-the-mill Trumpist Karen and Kevin,.

In a nutshell, the whole *What-Aboutism* "strategy" boils down to no more than a basic defense most often used by diminutive kindergarten-attendees when accused of some wrong-doing, usually voiced in a whiny tone and constituting of variations of the claim: *"But Billy also did it!"*, with the more sophisticated variation running along the lines of, *"But what Billy did is so much worse!"*

Adult toddler-brains such as Ingraham, Jones, Hannity, or Donald J. Trump himself not only adopted this tactic of the average four-year old almost unmodified but made it also acceptable in (im)polite society, as has been infamously shown by their constant whining of, *"But what about Hillary's e-mails!?"*. The picture painted by Trump and de facto his sycophantic finger-paint eaters on the blank canvases of Trumpists' minds displays nothing else but a giant finger pointing at Democrats, liberals, and progressives with the caption; *"They also did it!"*, respectively, *"What they did was so much worse than what we did!"*

Successful *What-Aboutists* know to ignore crucially relevant facts in their accusations, instead coming up with broad generalizations accompanied by the simple tactic of shouting and speaking over other debate-participants. While every nursery teacher will deal with this type of asocial behavior by reprimanding the little *What-Aboutist* for comparing apples with immigrants, however, most news-hosts, journalists, and politicians continue to allow grown-up *What-Aboutists* to get away unchallenged with the same toddler-trick. Far from calling the culprits out and subsequently shutting them up, so-called "adults in the room" engage with *"But what about ..."*-stammering Trumpists time and again in lengthy discussions on the veracity of their lopsided comparisons, while the only sensible reaction has proven to be taking out a page of any nursery teacher's book and giving the *What-Aboutist* a lengthy time-out on the naughty step.

Addressing the Brown Elephant in the Room

"We will make America loving again. Love it. Love it!"
– Donald J. Trump

O

Ever since the rise of the *Nationalsozialistische Deutsche Arbeiterpartei (NSDAP)*, viz the National-Socialist German Workers Party or in short: the *Nazis*, during the democratic *Weimarer Republik* in pre-World War II Germany, history-literate Americans continued wondering how one of the most educated people in the world at the time, living in one of the most modern sciences-, industries-, arts-, and literature-affectionate countries on Earth, could have so easily fallen for a failed Austrian postcard-painter turned political agitator displaying a decidedly devilish worldview, a laughably exaggerated demeanor, and a ridiculously styled moustache

To be clear, comparing the inhuman monster with his toothbrush-moustache to any living democratic leader remains rightfully a taboo today. For one, because the sheer excessiveness of such a comparison will constitute the probably gravest insult possible to any democratic politician. For another and even more important reason, though, because any comparison with Hitler and the Nazis will relativize and hence diminish the incomparably horrendous atrocities committed by the erstwhile WWI-private from Braunau, Austria, and his equally monstrous disciples.

Nevertheless, it would be foolish to misuse this taboo as an impervious wall in order to block out the many, vitally important insights to be learned from the circumstances having contributed to the rise to ultimate power of the only son of Austrian customs-officer Alois Hiedler.

Of course, neither the socially normalized malice and callousness prevalent in schools, families, offices, factories, and general society in the nascent age of industrialization nor the living-conditions in Germany in the era before the second World War can compare to the conditions in present-day America. Still, it would be negligent to ignore the fact that certain aspects of the Trumpministration bear an uncanny resemblance to the early days of the Nazi-movement in the 1920s. Just like the post-9/11 United States with *Patriot Act* and *Homeland Security*, with billion-dollar companies and billionaire-CEOs, with America's cultural hegemony, its electoral college and its weak system of checks and balances, so too was the German *Weimarer Republik* between the two World Wars a fragile democracy with long-ignored weaknesses, allowing determined politicians to undermine the state by abusing the system's soft spots and wiggle their way into highest positions. With the one major differences that the National Socialists (*Nazis*) have achieved their aim in record time compared to the Republican Party under Senate Majority Leader MoscowMitch McConnell, who incessantly worked for more than thirty years to perfectionate the GOP's strategy of anti-democratic obstructionism and clientele-politics.

Hitler's Hook, Line, and Sinker

Appeasement-advocates downplaying the seriousness of the dangers to American democracy under Donald J. Trump pointing out that, "*what happened in pre-Nazi Germany will never happen in the U.S. because we have a functioning democracy*", unfortunately commit a *Closed World Assumption* based on the faulty premise that the Nazi-party NSDAP had not been democratically elected. In actual fact, though, the NSDAP took lawfully part in the *Reichstag*-elections of July 1932, where it received 37.4% of all votes making it the dominant party in the new German parliament. As soon as the *Reichstag* (parliament) was in session, the elected Nazi-representatives and their coalition-partners participated democratically in the parliament's voting of a new, government-forming *Kanzler* (Chancellor) of Germany and by using their superior numbers elected the NSDAP's roistering party-leader Adolf Hitler to the office, accomplishing the hostile takeover fully in accordance with the established democratic process from A like *Arier,* (arian), to Z like *Zerstörung,* (devastation).

At the time of the 1932-elections, anti-Jewish propaganda had not yet blown up into society-permeating fanatism and hysterics, although the positions of the new Nazi-administration had already been made abundantly clear thanks to hundreds of thousands of torch-marching, stone-throwing Nazi-followers regularly flooding the streets of German cities like Berlin, München, (Munich), or Nürnberg, (Nuremberg), frequently chasing down, beating up, and lynching Jewish citizens as well as Nazi-opposing social democrats, socialists, and communists.

Contrary to popular belief, the agitator-in-chief, who endlessly practiced his gestures and mimics prior to speeches in front of a mirror, had not yet become the maniacal brawler prevalent in today's collective memory. Rather, the Hitler of the early 1930s followed a maxim adopted after his failed attempt of a *coup d'état* in 1923 in Munich, where he had led a frontal attack on the Bavarian government nicknamed later the "*Beer Hall Putsch*" that ended in a devastating failure for Hitler and his early-day fellow Nazis.

The Nazis' violent attempt to overthrow the Bavarian government had been met by a hail of bullets from the Bavarian police and had resulted in the deaths of several founding members of the Nazi-party as well as in a severe bullet-wound for Hitler and his subsequent arrest followed by a five-year prison-sentence, soon after being reduced to nine months imprisonment for the new star on the Nazi-firmament.

During his time in prison, where he began writing his infamous book "*Mein Kampf*", Hitler concluded that he had gone about the whole takeover-, of power-business all wrong and committed himself instead to a new strategy. Dismissing all attempts of seizing power by violent means, Hitler decided to fully embrace any politician's bread and butter-tactics of patiently plotting and scheming and to infiltrate the system and disassemble the state from within, before remodelling it to his liking. Assailing the state and its representatives full frontal only to be literally or figuratively gunned down once more had become an old-fashioned, 1920s-thing for Hitler, while the future belonged clearly to the man who could master the manipulation of the masses by utilizing propaganda to aim at the hearts and guts of the populace while bypassing the brains.

Only after this strategic 180°-turn began the unstoppable ascent of Adolf Hitler to a position of absolute power and textbook-dictator portrayed in countless documentaries. By inciting the masses with a carefully concocted mix of exaggerations, lies, "alternative facts" and baseless allegations delivered in frenetic and gesture-laden speeches, promising to make Germany great again after the lost World War, the aspiring *GröFaZ (Größter Führer aller Zeiten,* i.e., "greatest leader of all times"), turned the average soldier, baker, butcher, teacher, shop-owner, veteran, factory worker, unemployed, and disenfranchised citizen as well as most of their friends and families seemingly effortlessly into ballistic-going mobs who stormed the streets with aggressive chants and eruptions of violence against political opponents and Jews while brandishing the swastika-flag and the Hitler-salute.

The seeds of Hitler's malicious generalizations fell on fertile grounds with a populace already having felt unfairly treated by the *Treaty of Versailles* after World War I. As their new Chancellor, Adolf Hitler promised to right all the wrongs done to the unquestionably poor and down-trodden populace while targeting particularly Germans working in coalmines, steel-production, and the building industry and the millions of unemployed workers and disillusioned, disabled war-veterans found everywhere in the recession-plagued and utterly defeated country.

In his successful effort to utilize the most modern communication-technology at the time as ideal means to circumvent the established media, i.e. newspapers, and to reach the population instead directly, the tech-savvy *"Führer"* decreed the development and nationwide distribution of a cheap, stylish, and reliable radio-receiver. In answer to the dictator's demands, German engineers presented him with the so-called *"Volksempfänger"* (i.e., people's receiver, or radio for the people, similar to Volkswagen (VW), being the "people's car"). The heavily subsidized radio soon had a place in every German household, allowing the lawfully elected dictator to speak personally to the German people, further diminishing the need for a press that had anyway been almost completely forced-in-line by the time when the *Volksempfänger*, infamous forefather of television and Twitter, received its place of honor in German living rooms.

At this point in the mid-1930s, Hitler, Goebbels, Himmler, and the NSDAP had set the stage, the script had been written, all actors had been assigned their roles, and every stooge had his text memorized. By then, the audience had been sufficiently indoctrinated to easily ignore the gigantic plot-holes in the demonic *Closed World Assumption* upon which the complete *Herrenrasse*-farce had been based. To his accomplices behind the stage-curtain, the devilish author and director of the horrendous play the world was about to witness had issued one directive: *"Make the lie big, make it simple, keep saying it, and eventually they will believe it!"* And lo and behold, the target-audience of ill-educated German "patriots" totally loved the Big Show and continued cheering frenetically even after the theater was already engulfed in flames and the flesh melted from their bones.

Egregiously Erroneous Education

Countless books, treatises, TV-documentaries, scientific papers, novels, movies, and TV-series have attempted to lift a corner of the veil and catch a glimpse of the inexplicable conundrum of the phenomenon of mass-infatuation, delusion, and fanatic obedience in Nazi-Germany. Historical science-based publications concluded preponderantly that it has been in actual fact not merely one specific circumstance that had led to a totalitarianism-embracing German majority but an interaction of numerous factors ultimately leading to the moral downfall of a whole nation.

Most of these factors have proven to be far from unique to the German people of the time, instead lying dormant and ready to flame up in most if not all modern societies. One such aspect known to exist universally constitutes for instance the susceptibility of individuals to the empowerment experienced as a member of a group with a common cause, be it a political party, an army, a protest-movement, or a raging mob.

Other underlying reasons for the willing compliance with totalitarian leadership include widespread economic hardship and unemployment, insurmountable personal debts, a society-pervading fear of outside aggressors as well as cityscape-defining poverty, unsurprisingly making a populace thusly affected receptive to agitators promising to alleviate their sufferings. Another piece of the puzzle falls into place when regarding such populists' specific phrasing, tonality, and choice of words, resonating in particular with less-educated citizens, blue collar workers, and a rural population traditionally most likely to be economically left behind in industrialized nations. In the understanding of these demographics, the term *"plainspoken"* constitutes in fact a positive attribute of politicians, with short and memorable political slogans only enhancing these target-groups' affection for an agitator who *"talks like one of us"* and who *"understands us"*.

Finally, the probably most impactful and therefore also most controversially discussed factor contributing to people's susceptibility to populists, agitators, and political conmen is represented by the complicated topic of education respectively the lack thereof.

Though, the simple formula, *"The less educated, the more susceptible people are"*, is falling way short of linking specific levels of education to the degree of susceptibility shown in face of simplified "solutions" offered by authoritarian populists. Easy evidence for the unrelatedness of education and intelligence provide the countless people who unfortunately missed out on a broad and comprehensive education and yet outshine many university-educated minds in rational argumentation skills, general or specific knowledge, and overall mental brightness.

Moreover, if Germany during the *Weimar Republic* between the world wars has proven one educational premise then, that "traditional" chalk and talk teaching with teacher-delivered facts being unquestioned absorbed by obediently cowering pupils presents a sure-fire recipe for a generation of young adults filled with resentment, prejudices, and pent-up anger. At worst, the apparently "classically educated" young men and women will become perfect vessels empty of morale and conscience, easily to be filled with ideas of racism, nationalism, bigotry, and fanatism, and thus ideally prepared for their embrace of authoritarianism and dictatorship.

In its heydays in the 1920s, the Weimar Republic had been known the world over as the *Land der Dichter und Denker* ("the country of poets and thinkers"), with an almost uniquely high level of literacy and one of the most advanced industrialization-standards in the world, numerous revolutionary inventions under its belt, and a large array of famous scientists, philosophers, authors, politicians, engineers, and artists among its population. A mere decade later, the same population started a worldwide war.

The White Ribbon – A German Children's Story

Today, psychologists, sociologists, educational scientists, historians, and certain politicians realize that education consists of much more than book-knowledge, subject-specific know-how, good manners, and unquestioned obedience to authorities. The practical and terrifying result of such "good old times" when reactionary, traditions-, and authority-based education had been the norm, are uniquely captured in the shot in black-and-white movie, *"Das weiße Band – Eine deutsche Kindergeschichte"*, (*The White Ribbon*), that premiered at the 62nd Cannes Film Festival in May 2009 where it won the Palme d'Or, followed by the 2010 Golden Globe Award for Best Foreign Language Film.

The film portrays a village-community in the barren landscape of Northern Germany on the eve of World War I, where a puritanical pastor's draconical rule over his children and inexplicable deadly events paint a dark picture of adolescent life in an era a mere eleven decades ago. Almost imperceptibly at times the movie focusses on the village-children's stoical, seemingly phlegmatic acceptance of their parents' violent educational methods, with the camera sometimes fleetingly catching children-eyes set in expressionless faces, glinting with the dark fire of abysmal hatred, an emotion every present-day viewer feels towards the adults portrayed in this cinematic masterpiece.

From the perspective of 2020 it seems glaringly obvious how such tortured young souls grew up to become almost inevitably callous, empathy-lacking, loveless, adults, passing their trauma on to their own offspring. But in 1914, cane-, belt-, and cudgel-swinging parents had never heard of words like *"trauma"* or *"psychological scarring"*. Instead, it was the pastor or priest of the village who was the highest authority on "proper education" which included the teaching of absolute obedience to God and all authorities on the rungs below "Him", whether clerical, social, or political. Therefore, it was no particularly large step from a child's expressionless acceptance of the words *"This hurts me more than you, boy. And now bend over!"* to the obedient hollering of the words, *"Führer befiehl! Wir folgen!"* ("Führer command! We follow!")

Weimar, USA, 2020

While the flogging of offspring has lost much of its erstwhile social acceptance nowadays, parental cruelty has by now means disappeared from American children's rooms. In many cases, it became merely a "private family-issue" to be "discussed" behind closed apartment-, and home doors. More frequently, the educational method of physical brutality has been replaced by subtler methods of mentally and emotionally scarring punishment, with deliberate withdrawal of love, attention, and affection at the top of the list of mental cruelties.

Particularly "traditional" communities, where zealous conservatives continue to determine cultural and social values, are churning out generation after generation of young men from the same mould as 17-year-old double murderer Kyle Rittenhouse, who killed two human beings with his AR-15 in Kenosha, Wisconsin, on 8/25/2020. Such juvenile "patriots" tend to display an astounding level of pent-up anger, rage, and hatred and appear always giddy to unload their full violence-potential on anyone declared fair game by accepted authority-figures.

Many conservatively educated young men go through extensive conditioning until obedience to these authority-figures has become their first nature. When adding to this trained subservience the perpetually looming threat of an all-seeing, all-knowing, all-powerful celestial megalomaniac who might unleash his ungodly wrath at a whim by causing strokes, heart attacks, cancer, car-accidents, miscarriages, bankruptcies, and any other life-destroying event, will often result in frightened, angry, and vengeful individuals, eager to vent the pent up pressure on someone weaker than themselves and who, according to the indicatory authority-figures, is apparently bearing the responsibility for their own miserable life.

In a manner akin to the *Stockholm-Syndrome*, the populistic authorities instrumentalize the emotionally abused boys of yesteryear who turned into today's emotionally crippled adult as dispensable foot soldiers in their war for power and riches. Conservative education based on platitudes like *"Real men don't cry!"*, *"Beatings have made me a man!"*, or *"Only the strongest survive!"* will form characters who become ridiculously proud of their displayed toughness and manliness and love to prove their "worth" to the authoritarian elite by gunning down unarmed civilians in the name of "law and order", ostensibly achieving a "hero"-status among their reactionary community they would have otherwise never been able to obtain.

Since neither overly intelligent nor knowledgeable, neither eloquent nor smart, neither charming nor good-looking, successful, or interesting, "militia"-men and other gun-toting ignoramuses like Kyle R. turn to the only sources of power attainable for them. With the inevitable result of handing a thusly disadvantaged 17-year-old teenager an AR-15 semi-automatic rifle being the manifestation of illusions of grandeur, invulnerability, and god-like power. Gone are Kyle's fears of insignificance and of weakness once instilled by the threat of an almighty punisher and furthered by the authority-figures surrounding him. Gone are the little pimple-faced wannabe-soldier's insecurity and self-loathing, replaced by the power over life and death. Kyle may not be old enough to drink, but he is certainly old enough to kill "enemies of the state"! No wonder, that Kyle will therefore choose the only way a constantly suppressed individual like him has left to feel strong and significant, by appropriating the power inherent to all guns capable of taking lives.

Any attempts to infringe on Kyle's right to legally possess one of these emotional crutches and to use it as he sees fit must therefore inevitably result in one of the well-known, regular temper tantrums thrown by Kyle's elders in the NRA and the Republican Party. After all, every mother knows what will happen if she plucks the pacifier out of her baby's mouth. Naturally, this same toddler-mentality prevalent in gun-nuts and 2nd Amendment-cry-babies literally begs to be exploited by populists at any opportunity, (*"LIBERATE VIRGINIA, and save your great 2nd Amendment. It is under siege!"* – Donald J. Trump, Tweet, 04/17/2020), to drum up an army of potential killers ready to be deployed the moment the autocrat fears for his power, freedom, or life.

By simply replacing the name "Kyle" with the name "Fritz", or any other typical German first name of the time, the terrifying similarities between the situations in Germany in 1920 and America in 2020 become even more obvious. Fritz too grew up in constant fear of God and of his "betters". Fritz too lived in a perpetual state of powerlessness and insignificance until a "strong leader" provided him with a valve for his resentment and undirected hatred by pointing out whom he should hate, (*"Die Untermenschen"* – "the sub-humans"), and for whom he should fight, (*"Für Führer, Volk und Vaterland"* – "For Leader, People, and Fatherland").

Fritz too found a new home in the movement of his new Leader where he was among like-minded friends, finally giving him a sense of relevance, significance, belonging, and a modicum of power. Fritz too wallowed in his Leader's appreciation for the inhuman acts of violence he committed in the name of the movement against those who appeared to be "different", viz the *Untermenschen* and their supporters. And Fritz too declared his undying loyalty to his Leader and vowed together with millions of fellow fanatics to follow the Leader's commands to the very end.

And the rest is history.

Principiis obsta – Or: Nip It Right in the Bud

At the height of the Nazi-dictatorship, German resistance against the regime had been decimated to some single activists and only a handful of scattered cells, most notable among them *"Die weiße Rose",* ("The white Rose"), led by siblings Hans (1918 – 1943) and Sophie (1921 – 1943) Scholl, who were decapitated on February 22, 1943 by the Nazi-guillotine, as were more than 77,000 other Germans who defied the Nazis in one way or the other.

After Europe's and Germany's liberation from the Nazis. it took another 20 years before the influence of surviving Hitler-followers in West-Germany's post-war society had been finally and decisively neutralized. A new generation then began to look back on the atrocities of their fathers and grandfathers and started to reappraise Germany's recent history with unsparing honesty and relentless openness. In these days, a quote of the ancient Roman poet Ovid became the unofficial state motto of West-Germany: „*Principiis obsta*" – "*Wehret den Anfängen!*", (literally, "Fight the beginnings", or colloquially, "Nip it in the bud").

From the early 1970s on, school-children at first in West-Germany and later in a reunified Germany at least hear once per week some account related to the horrendous crimes committed by Germans who had only a few decades before walked the same streets, lived in the same houses, and spoke the same language, many of whom had been their own fathers, grandfathers, or great-grandfathers. Young German students quickly understand the ultimate lesson underlying this intensive analysis of their country's dark past, condensed in the words, *"Wehret den Anfängen!"*

This society-permeating perspective may well be one of the reasons why Germany today is prone to rather err on the side of caution when it comes to military expedition forces, the public display of national symbols, and the protection of personal data. Nonetheless, the same caution has gifted the country with over 70 years of a stable democratic system that has kept populistic and radical right-wing parties largely at bay. Populistic agitators with racist and anti-democratic tendencies aiming for broader political influence are closely monitored by Germany's equivalent of the FBI, the *Verfassungsschutz*, ("Guardian of the Constitution"), and will be indicted the moment they commit anti-constitutional crimes such as hate-speech against minorities or inciting violence against Jews, Muslims, Christians, or any other religious and ethnical group.

To publicly display the Hitler-salute, for instance, constitutes a criminal offense in Germany and is to be punished by a substantial fine, (5,000 EUR or more), or up to three years imprisonment. (This includes, by the way, also tourists.) Differently put, what counts as "free speech" in the United States will be regarded in Germany as a clear anti-constitutional attack on the state, the population, and the

German democratic system, viz „*Principiis obsta*" – "*Wehret den Anfängen!*"

At the end of the day and regarding all the above, it seems obvious that America's *Brown Elephant in the Room* is neither as brown nor as gigantic as the terrible monster once ravaging Nazi-Germany. Yet, it is equally apparent that a lively, red-painted neo-*fascistophant* is currently sharing the same room in the china shop with the rest of U.S.-society, coincidentally resembling the heraldic animal of a certain political party. Fortunately, the United States still have the chance to nip this ugly creature thoroughly in the bud before it will become too large to fit through the exit-door. The presidential elections on November 3, 2020, will be a genuine watershed-moment in history, which will subsequently tell everlastingly whether Americans heeded the warning of *Principiis obsta* or damned history to repeat itself.

Cognitive Dissonance Avoidance

"TMI, hacks. TMI!"

○

According to current scientific knowledge, the human brain constitutes the by far most complex biological creation Mother Nature has come up with to date. Not only are there billions upon billions of neuronal connections contained in these three pounds of gray matter, but to further top this already incredible feat, every single human brain that has ever existed or will exist also represents a completely unique and individual manifestation.

This said, a surprisingly large number of mental processes in all human craniums nonetheless remain which prove universally identical. Whether such "pre-programmed" neurological reactions are in fact genetically imprinted or rather rooted in some sub-consciously entrenched common human experience is a debate for another day. Suffice it to say that nobody can claim to be immune to these scientifically substantiated, neuronal reactions that get triggered by specific outside stimulations, from the primal fear of the dark, to the fright and disgust provoked by spiders, rats, or snakes, to the gag reflex-inducing smell of fresh vomit, feces, or puss.

Certain trainings and therapies, like the infamous shock-therapy, can help to reduce such fears and repugnances by conditioning the brain to consciously recognize the negative external stimuli and react to them rationally rather than instinctively. Sufficiently trained minds are in fact considerably less likely to be helplessly overwhelmed by the brain's hardwiring when the next spider crawls across the pillow. However, the fact remains that humans fighting their own brain usually draw the short straw when push comes to shove.

In this regard, one of the most destructive defenses the mind can muster against a perceived threat to its integrity constitutes the eponymous *Cognitive Dissonance Avoidance*, executed by the brain in complete disregard to its owner's conscious will. This devil of a mind-defense caught the attention of psychologists as early as in the 1950s, when scientists first identified the mind's very disagreeable reaction to any information it identifies as contradictory to one or more of its owner's core-beliefs constituting the cornerstones of man's self-perceived identity.

To seriously attack a person's fundamental beliefs represents therefore no less than calling their very existence and *raison d'être* in question. Consequentially, to accept defeat and relinquish the core of their very being would be tantamount to the dissolution of their identity. A devastating outcome that frequently can lead to mental breakdowns, uncontrolled violence, severe depression, and even suicide. It is hardly surprising therefore, that the mind will revert to drastic measures to avoid any *Dissonance* between the *Cognition* of its own subjective worldview and objective reality.

- When Truth Truly Hurts -

"For somebody who's never run for office before, Donald Trump understands that old axiom, 'Define yourself before you're defined'." – Kellyanne Conway, former Adviser to U.S.-President Donald J. Trump

Holding certain beliefs and subjective truths as true makes up a large part of any sentient human's identity. In fact, these core-beliefs are the cornerstones of people's individual existence on which their lives are built. Of course, people base their core-identity on a huge variety of foundations, from bookworm to gun-nut, from philanthropist to xenophobe, from progressive to conservative, from socialist to capitalist, from Star Wars-fan to Star Trek-fan. Yet, while most individuals have strong feelings for their passions and convictions, merely possessing a strongly felt identity will not lead automatically to a state of *Cognitive Dissonance* whenever this identity will become seriously challenged. For the brain to enter an emergency *Cognitive Dissonance Avoidance*-mode, it needs a bit more than just being called out on loving *Star Trek: Discovery* or *The Last Jedi*.

When comparing educated minds unaffected by the *Dunning-Kruger Effect* or other self-delusions with non-self-reflexive and wilfully ignorant minds, it appears that the former group in the main resembles the strong, yet flexible stalks of the bamboo while the latter rather compares to the rigid, brittle branches of the cottonwood tree, since any information contradicting their core-beliefs will need to assert only little mental pressure on the *cottonwood-mind* to make it snap while a *bamboo-mind* will react flexible and adapt.

When an inflexible *cottonwood-mind* is confronted with new input, threatening the validity of its core-beliefs, it will begin to experience an on-setting state of *Cognitive Dissonance,* triggered by the information contradicting its subjective worldview. At this point, still before any actual realization regarding the objective falseness of its own core-beliefs will set in, the threatened mind will go to Red Alert and initiate its *Cognitive Dissonance Avoidance* (CDA) protocol, protecting itself from having its belief-system crashing down right then and there.

While the typical outward reaction of a *Cognitive Dissonance Avoider* will be well known to anyone who had the misfortune to debate an anti-vaxxer mom, zealous monotheist, flat-earther, die-hard facemask-rejecter, virus-denier, lockdown-protester, or Trumpist, the following hypothetical example of *Stephen the Stooge* will perhaps still provide some interesting insights into the processes in a *Cognitive Dissonance-Avoider's* mind while feeling subjectively under attack.

The Struggles of Stephen the Stooge

Please meet exemplary Trump-disciple Stephen, a man who wholeheartedly embraces one of Donald Trump's most classical lies, viz, *"An invasion of illegal immigrants is threatening the security of our American citizens".* Stephen, who grew up in a traditionally conservative, Christian household, has readily accepted this allegation and implemented it rather swiftly into his set of core-beliefs that form the guardrails of his life and influence almost all of his decisions and behaviors. Accordingly, Stephen initiated a 24-hour neighbourhood watch, bought several semi-automatic rifles for him, his wife, and his four kids, ("in pink for the girls"), reports eagerly every dark-skinned person to the sheriff's department, spends his holidays "hunting" at the southern border with his friends of the *Texas border militia*, and has long since severed all ties to former friends who did not take the impending flood of dangerous criminals seriously enough.

Life is good for Stephen in his neighborhood in Fort Worth's Tarrant County, Texas, where he is safely surrounded by like-minded, proper (read: white) Christians, sharing his conviction that the U.S. is only one unbuild border wall and some AR-15s away from being overrun by job-stealing and lazy, muscular and plague-ridden sub-humans with melanin-rich skin.

This is until the day Stephen switches accidentally to the wrong TV-station while looking for FOX News. Caught by the picture of a particularly dirty, illegal immigrant and the wailing toddler in her arms Stephen cannot help but hearing what the respectable-looking expert in the scene's foreground explains. Accompanied by several graphs and statistics now replacing the image of the immigrant woman and baby, the PhD-professor presents one government officials-approved fact and number after another culminating in the ironclad conclusion that although anti-immigrant groups continue to maintain that the number of illegal immigrants is constantly increasing, thoroughly research-based estimates by the *Pew*

Research Center are showing that the number of undocumented immigrants in the U.S. declined in fact from 12.2 million in 2005 to 10.5 million in 2017. Furthermore, for the first time since 1990 undocumented Mexican immigrants are representing with 4.95 million less than half of the 10.5 million undocumented people living in the U.S., equalling just 3.18 % of a total of 330 million Americans. A percentage that lies well below post-1850 highs, recorded by decennial censuses between 1860 and 1920, when immigrants made up over 13% of the U.S.-population.

Subsequently, the expert on TV cites Alex Nowrasteh, Director of Immigration Studies at the *Cato Institute's Center for Global Liberty and Prosperity*, who writes on the *Cato Institute* website, [www.cato.org/blog/illegal-immigrants-crime-assessing-evidencee], *"All immigrants have a lower criminal incarceration rate and there are lower crime rates in the neighborhoods where they live according to the near-unanimous findings of the peer-reviewed evidence."*

Stephen dumbfoundedly continues to watch as the expert closes his report by quoting from a paper published in 2019 by Director Alex Nowrasteh and Michelangelo Landgrave, doctoral student in political science at the University of California, stating, *"that illegal immigrant incarceration rates are about half those of native-born Americans in 2017"*.

The TV-screen suddenly blares music, showing the latest Gillette®-spot, *("The Best Men Can Be"*, duh), while Stephen is slumping onto his couch, his personal hero Donald J. Trump's own words from June 2015 resonating in his ears: *"When Mexico sends its people, they're not sending their best. They're not sending you. They're not sending you. They're sending people that have lots of problems, and they're bringing those problems with us. They're bringing drugs. They're bringing crime. They're rapists. And some, I assume, are good people."*

So, how is it possible that these government-approved scientists come to such a diametrically opposed conclusion, when President Trump had said many times, such as on March 1, 2016, in his Super Tuesday victory speech: *"You look at countries like Mexico, where they're killing us on the border, absolutely destroying us on the border. They're destroying us in terms of economic development"*? And if Director Nowrasteh says that, *"illegal immigrant incarceration rates are about half those of native-born Americans"*, how then can President Donald J. Trump declare in a meeting with local Californian leaders opposed to sanctuary city-policies on December 11, 2019 that, *"We have people coming into the country or trying to come in, we're stopping a lot of them, but we're taking people out of the country. You wouldn't believe how bad these people are. These aren't people. These are animals!"*?

Stephen gets up from his couch and walks over to the family-laptop. Sitting down, firing up the machine, and going on Google takes two minutes, with another minute of a quick search for an overview of Alex Nowrasteh's research. Then, Stephen reads with growing trepidation Director Nowrasteh's report from March 4, 2019, including the following lines.

"If anything, Texas is more serious about enforcing laws against illegal immigrant criminals than other states. But

even here, illegal immigrant conviction rates are about half those of native-born Americans – without any controls for age, education, ethnicity, or any other characteristic. The illegal immigrant conviction rates for homicide, larceny, and sex crimes are also below those of native-born Americans. The criminal conviction rates for legal immigrants are the lowest of all.

The Texas research is consistent with the finding that crime along the Mexican border is much lower than in the rest of the country, homicide rates in Mexican states bordering the United States are not correlated with homicide rates here, El Paso's border fence did not lower crime, Texas criminal conviction rates remain low (but not as low) when recidivism is factored in, and that police clearance rates are not lower in states with many illegal immigrants – which means that they don't escape conviction by leaving the country after committing crimes."

Stephen closes the laptop and leans back in his chair. The die-hard Trumpist finds all of this rather hard to swallow and even harder to stomach. As long-time resident in Texas' most conservative, large-sized county, Stephen has dedicated the better part of his adult life to the "good fight" against the hordes of brutal Mexican gang-members, cartel-killers, and day-laborers overrunning the southern border in droves to push their filthy drugs, rape innocent U.S.-girls, steal well-paying jobs from honest American workers, and hence destroy "real" America from the inside. And suddenly here is all this fool-proof evidence to the contrary, implying that his adamantly held core-beliefs might after all be built on no more than lies and propaganda.

Three. … Two. … One. … *KA-BOOOM!* In this instant, Stephen's mind realizes that his core-belief in the *'dangerous, evil, America-destroying Mexican immigrant'* is being seriously challenged by government-provided facts and figures, proving the exact opposite of what his spiritual guide Donald J. Trump has maintained for decades. Suddenly, two prior distinctly separate worlds are about to violently collide as objective reality threatens to crash into Stephen's subjective fantasy-reality.

Presupposing Stephen to be capable of accepting scientifically collected data as evidence for an objective reality, i.e., that his mental faculties still allow the distinction between objective right and wrong, the die-hard Trumpist will now find himself trapped in a classic Catch 22-situation, damned if he does believe the scientific facts and damned if he doesn't.

The battle raging in Stephen's mind between an objective truth recognized as such due to his ability to reason on the one side and his subjective, make-believe "reality" representing the largest part of his self-perceived identity on the other side is just about to erupt into a full-blown *Dissonance,* a state of confusion in which the metaphorical dog is going to try catching its own tail until it drops dead. In the space of micro-seconds, Stephen's brain is now speeding through every trick in the book, attempting to somehow align the two diamctrically opposed "realities". But the harder his brain is trying, the more it is realizing the unbridgeable discrepancy and with it the inherent falseness of Stephen's core-belief. Not a second has passed when Stephen's brain is coming to the conclusion that *alignment* is not an option and accordingly and instantly switches to its *Cognitive Dissonance Avoider* emergency protocol.

First point of order, determining Stephen's subjective loss-gain balance in case of accepting the veracity of the new information opposing his core-belief, while simultaneously evaluating any short- and long term-consequences coming with such an acceptance. As soon as the evaluation-results are in, Stephen's mind gets busy checking the other side of the equation, reassuring itself of the subjective value of the attacked core-belief for Stephen's overall well-being. After all, it took many years for Stephen to painstakingly create and defend this core-belief, representing not only the foundation of every important relation in his life, from his wife and children, to his friends, colleagues, acquaintances, and neighbors, but moreover also the bedrock of his self-respect and of his public reputation.

Having concluded the value-evaluation of Stephen's core-belief, followed by a quick final comparison of both evaluation-results, the Trumpist's brain is now safely inferring that the only viable course of action to protect Stephen from short-circuiting consists in squarely rejecting the new information and to uphold Stephen's present core-belief under all circumstances.

For most *cottonwood-minds,* the *Cognitive Dissonance Avoidance*-process concludes here. With the conservative bubble on Twitter, Facebook, Reddit, and other social media platforms offering a wide range of ready-made platitudes, quotes, memes, and fake news, providing the brittle-minded *Cognitive Dissonance Avoider* with enough bite-sized arguments to "debunk" any information perceived as hostile to Trumpist core-beliefs, any *Cottonwood-Trumpist* can easily replace the rejected information with a pseudo-fact, lie, or fallacious argument, to "counter" the hostile information and push the world back into balance.

Yet, some gradations of delusion exist even among the 35% of Americans remaining ensnared by Trumpublican propaganda. Assuming for the sake of the argument that Stephen is found on the less-delusional end of the scale, his mind's decision to stick with the familiar lie will not be able to spare him completely from the nagging feeling caused by the facts and figures pointing in the exact opposite direction of his beliefs. It is one thing for Stephen to deny the veracity of those unwelcome facts out loud at the next Trump-rally with his raucous buddies, but it is a completely different matter lying to himself in the silence of his bedroom. At 4:00 a.m., the grating cogs and grinding gears in Stephen's mind will most likely come to a near stand-still, attempting to deal with the ongoing inner conflict of a state of *Cognitive Dissonance*.

When facing an onslaught of unwelcome information, less experienced *Cognitive Dissonance Avoiders* frequently tend to revert to aggressive behavior, trying to banish the bearer of disagreeable information verbally or even physically. More advanced *Avoiders* on the other hand manage to literally become deaf and blind, failing to hear or see any core-belief disproving information, while another type of *Avoider* is setting up a battery of false narratives, tall tales, and "alternative facts", vehemently counter-attacking any potential threat to their core-belief.

This said, under normal circumstances zealots like Stephen's hyper-trumpist buddy Kevin, who scores high on the *cottonwood*-reaction scale and who can tune out any *"defeatist, unamerican anti-Trump propaganda"* faster than you can say *Hydroxychloroquine,* will simply not come into any situation where his mind could be subjected to the kind of information likely to induce a state of *Cognitive Dissonance*.

Any sound-minded person out on a city late-night walk, coming across a dark alley offering a short-cut home will rely on experience and instinct to conclude that it would be prudent to avoid the alleyway, since being mugged, raped, or worse, is not the most desirable experience. Differently put, it lies in our human nature to avoid uncontrollable danger.

In Kevin and his brittle-minded MAGA-comrades, this fundamental human notion can be found in their instinctive shying away from any source of potentially MAGA-contradicting information scratching at their conservative core-beliefs. Kevin knows quite well that outside of his bubble-world lots of people not only disagree with his reactionary views but will also confront him with objective facts diametrically opposed to his lopsided belief-system. Similar to members of any garden-variety religious cult, Trumpists are prone to developing their own specific safe zones. Therefore, Kevin knows precisely which of the town's waterholes will allow him to yell racist slurs with impunity after his eighth beer, which grocery store will have dropped enough, not overly subtle hints in order to keep beaners, ragheads, and n***ers out, which shooting ranges do not care if he jokes loudly about his hilarious plans for a "moving targets-event", and which fine dining-establishments to choose for taking the missus for grub without getting in touch with n***ers, Jews, and anti-American libtards with their highfaluting talk of civil rights, equality, and social justice.

Kevin and other Trumpists execute their behavioral avoidance-pattern as unconsciously as Kevin and Stephen more their thumb on the remote control, pure instinct guiding them away from ABC, CNN, or MSNBC, and accurately tuning in to FOX News every time. With their instinctive choice of social gathering-spots and information-sources, Kevin, Stephen, Karen, or Aunty Beth are displaying *pre-emptive Cognitive Dissonance Avoidance,* shunning the bright light of objective truth as members of the growing demographic of anti-vaxxers, conspiracy theorists, racists, narc-parents, far-right conservatives, die-hard Trumpists, and other denizens of the upside-down universe, who instead prefer seeking out "information"-sources reinforcing their subjective, baseless worldviews and *cottonwood*-brittle core-beliefs, further bolstering their defenses against any fact from objective reality that might trigger a state of *Cognitive Dissonance*.

A Self-Sustaining State of Stress

Incidentally, Kevin, Stephen, Karen, and their fellow Trumpists are by no means suffering from any kind of mental disorder only because they attempt to avoid *Cognitive Dissonance*. On the contrary, the intuitive desire to avoid a state of *Cognitive Dissonance* is inherent to the human mind that is striving for balance like anything else in the universe.

The theory of *Cognitive Dissonance* presupposes that every man or woman will invariably try to maintain their psychological equilibrium by balancing out subjective beliefs and external reality. In consequence, any imbalance, i.e., any discrepancy between internal belief and external reality not to be avoided must lead to a state of psychological distress. When this distress exceeds a certain level, the mind will go on Red Alert and engage in the process of *Dissonance Reduction* where the brain tasks itself with the reduction or neutralization of one of the two opposing, stress-inducing factors in order to re-establish equilibrium.

People with a healthy, critical understanding of the world and their own place in it rarely experience this emergency-process, since their critical consciousness and self-awareness allow for the necessary mind-flexibility to adopt valid, new information and to adapt existing core-beliefs accordingly. Incidentally, this human capability of adopting new information into existing theories and adapting one's point of view accordingly constitutes the foundation of all of science and mankind's complete scientific progress, from medicine to engineering, from rocket-science to genetics. Any reputable scientist will therefore also be the first to point out new information contradicting their current hypothesis, regardless of how much time, effort, or funding has already gone into its proof.

Hence, recognizing faulty conclusions represents not only a linchpin of any scientific work but also the secret to a healthy equilibrium of the mind. Since *Cognitive Dissonance Avoidance* does not constitute a mental disorder, being an inherent mechanism available to every mind that has been knocked off balance and strives to re-establish its equilibrium, this raises the question about the factual difference between a Trumpist's constant attempts to avoid exposure to dissonance-inducing input on the one side and a well-balanced person suddenly displaying signs of *Cognitive Dissonance Avoidance* on the other side.

The answer to this question lies in the word "constant". While Trumpists find themselves in a perpetual state of active denial in contrast to any sound-minded person who can become the involuntary victim of a situation in which the mind needs to protect itself from the consequences of unbearable mental stress. One drastic example for such a situation represents the horrible scenario in which parents open the door to a police officer who must inform them of the death of their child. Extraordinarily painful situations like this constitute the genuine *raison d'être* and purpose of *Cognitive Dissonance Avoidance*, when the mind is hammering down its blinds to avoid being overwhelmed by information that might lead to a collapse of sanity.

In the lives of most parents their (young) children constitute the center-point around which the largest part or their existence revolves most of the time. If this existence-defining core-belief, the role of protective, care-providing, and loving father or mother, becomes utterly shattered in one terrible moment, the mind will do a formidable job of protecting the sanity of the parent by rejecting or blanking out the terrible information contradicting in one instant the complete self-defining belief of the struck mother and father. Reactions such as the outright denial of the truth of the information, distancing oneself physically or mentally from the scene, or even physically attacking the bearer of the tragic news all are considered normal in such a situation. Moreover, reactions seen as unemotional and untypical for emergency *Cognitive Dissonance Avoidance*-behavior are frequently even regarded as disturbing, unnatural, and unhealthy.

With *Cognitive Dissonance Avoidance's* raison d'être (reason to exist) established as an important sanity protection-mechanism, guaranteeing a continuous and coherent functioning of the mind in emotionally extreme situations, this leaves the likes of Kevin, Karen, and Stephen who conclusively must find themselves in a steady self-sustaining state of mental stress. Since most Trumpists are presumably far from being clinically insane while still able to objectively distinguish good from evil and not in any imminent danger of losing their sanity due to some overwhelmingly hurtful information, the only reason left for the proverbial trumpist uncle, archconservative boss, or Evangelical neighbor to wilfully employ constant *Cognitive Dissonance Avoidance* must logically be the protection of core-beliefs serving ultimately mundane purposes.

Chief amongst these selfish purposes being the consolidation and increase of that smidgen of power the zero sum-game believers wield over other people, be it members of their congregation, company-subordinates, family-members, or any random waitress, cashier, teenager, or minority-member unfortunate enough to cross paths with such a "righteous American". Core-beliefs supporting an egocentric approach to life, like the ones preached by Donald J. Trump, will force their holders to go to great lengths in blanking out facts contradicting their *"survival of the fittest"*- and *"each one for himself"*-attitude on which these "staunch freedom-fighters" rest the legitimacy for their hunger for power.

Even on the lowest rung of the conservative ladder, any run-of-the-mill Trumpist in Hicksville, USA, concerns himself foremost with defending his tiny bit of power he assumes to be holding over those "beneath" him, like for instance the Afro-American or Latin American communities in town or his mute wife and kids at home. From a Trumpist's point of view, such "outlandish" ideas intended to increase the well-being of all members of society, like the idea of racial equality, a sales-ban for weapons of war, enforcing women's rights, or strict child protection laws, merely threaten to infringe on the Trumpist's core-belief of his "God-given" status and power as a white, Christian, male American. Nothing comes therefore more natural to Kevin and his buddies than hollering *"Hands off the Second Amendment!"*, *"Protect my freedom!"*, and, *"Don't tread on me!"* as soon as someone questions their "rights" to oppress, threaten, insult, harass, silence, violate, or attack members of other ethnicities, genders, generations, or political groups. In fact, it is this fear-driven, pre-emptive *Cognitive Dissonance Avoidance* that lies at the bottom of most of the paintball-shooting, Confed-flag waving, gun-toting, Hitler saluting, and sharp-shooting lunacy the Odd Right engaged in during the *Black Lives Matter*-protests. *"Don't tread on my right to deny you your rights!"*

The Fearful Hate -

"Jews will not replace us!"
Alt-right Tikki-torch marchers, Charlottesville, 2017 -

One of the most entertaining and simultaneously taxing games children like to play with adults is simply called *"Why?"*. The rules are easy. Whenever an adult finishes their exhaustive answer to the child's *"Why?"*-question, the kid will first nod understandingly, only to then ask innocently: *"But why?"*, thus starting the next round. Incidentally, any parent who outlasted their over-inquisitive offspring in this game of attrition deserves at the least one long and childless wellness-weekend. (But only with serious answers, of course. *"Because!"* is not a serious answer.)

Coincidentally, this same *"Why?"*-game also represents a feasible method for digging down to the emotional bedrock of average Trumpists' *Cognitive Dissonance Avoidance*, viz the basic reason for *Trumpalumpas'* wilful ignorance and apparent gullibility.

At the entrance to the bunker representing common Trumpists' minds, the first *"Why?"*-question to our hypothetical Trumpist and *Cognitive Dissonance Avoider* Stephen kicks straight into high gear: *"Stephen, why do you feel compelled to disregard objectively proven facts and to instead lie, obfuscate, and divert in order to defend your own fallacious version of reality?"*

As to be expected, the question is not yet finished when Stephen already blows up like Trump upon hearing that his personal valet had caught the virus. In an automatic response-mechanism, Stephen begins immediately to employ the tactic *"righteous indignation"*, accompanied by *"counter-insulting"* in the variation of *"ad hominem"*-attacks. While refuting the allegation of favoring lies over truth, Stephen attempts to divert the debate away from his own behavioral patterns and towards the question itself and *"lying libtards"*, in classical *What Aboutism*-manner.

In reply, the questioner calmly points out that, while the question did have the potential to anger Stephen the fact remains that Stephen did not yet provide any coherent answer to why he is convinced of his version of reality, clearly colliding with concrete and irrefutable data and facts, to be the only acceptable choice.

Exempli gratia for the considerable *fact-vs-lie*-discrepancy typically prevalent in trumpist minds:

[*Fact*]: According to WHO, Johns Hopkins University, and several further organizations, as early as April 2020, the Unites States showed the highest number of COVID-19 deaths worldwide. *"As of Sunday, April 12, 2020, Italy had reported 19,468 coronavirus deaths while the US had 20,608, according to the Johns Hopkins tally."*

[*Lie*]: *"When the fake news gets out there and they start talking about the United States is number one— but we're not number one [in death totals], China is number one."* – Donald J. Trump, April 18, 2020.

In answer to the question why Stephen prefers the lie over the facts despite all evidence, Stephen will likely reply by insinuating that the fake news are only reporting lies to weaken Donald Trump in the upcoming elections and to frighten patriotic Americans into staying at home while Democrats are robbing them of their God-given freedom. To Stephen it is crystal clear that the liberals will do literally everything to undermine America and the American Way of Life.

With the bunker-hatch of Stephen's mind now open and spewing vitriol, time to ask Stephen the 2. *"Why?"*-question. *"Why does this make you so angry, Stephen?"*

In answer, Stephen throws an incredulous look at the questioner as if he had been asked if Laura Ingraham was his supreme white goddess. *"Who wouldn't be angry"*, Stephen then elaborates, *"if the very foundations of our great country are under threat by socialists, communists, the liberals and the fake news-media?!"*

Prompting the 3. *"Why?"*-question. *"Why are these 'foundations' so important to you?"* Never missing a chance to pontificate, Stephen launches into a detailed explanation which comes down to: *"Because America is the greatest country in the world and our traditional values are the foundation of its greatness."*

The 4. *"Why?"*-question includes a short introduction. *"Okay, as a patriotic American you're obviously interested in the United States' greatness and all that. Understood. But why are these traditional values so important for you personally and individually?"* Stephen pauses for a moment to think. In case he is one of those veteran Trumpublicans who developed a sixth sense for any line of questioning that is not boding well for their cognitive equilibrium, Stephen will most likely end the conversation here abruptly with a brisk, *"None of your business!"*, or, *"If you don't know, I can't help you!"* However, Stephen has not yet reached this stadium of trumpist incrustation and hence answers: *"Well, I was raised with these values by my parents, as were all of us here in Potatoville, and it made me the man I am today! There's a natural order to things and I'll be damned if I allow some East coast-hack or West coast-puff to lay their manicured hands on my God-given rights and our traditions."*

"Why?"-question 4.1 comes as a follow-up question exemplary for the usually many follow-ups necessary with Trumpists: *"Okay, but why are these rights and traditions so important to you personally? In other words, what's in it for you personally?"* This one will let Stephen's heartrate go into Techno-beat mode. *"What's in it for me? What's in it for me?! Look here, traditions and values are the framework of any functioning community. Where would we be if anyone could just do what he wants, eh? We'd live in chaos and anarchy, that's where. Our traditional values tell you where your place is in the community and how to properly respect your betters and not to ask impertinent questions. That's in it for me, boy. To get proper respect from the likes of you!"*

Question no. 5: *"So, traditional values guarantee order and respect. Okay, got it. But can I ask why it is so crucial for you, Stephen, to be shown this 'proper respect'?"* Stephen sighs. *"Damn, you're really busting my butt here. Why is respect crucial! What a stupid question. Because if you're not respected, you're nothing. No one takes you seriously. No one listens to you!"*

In reply, question no. 6. *"Why is it important that people take you serious and listen to you?"* At the latest at this point Stephen refuses to answer any further questions, ostensibly because they are, *"nonsensical, stupid, provocative, and disrespectful"*, while the genuine reason has more to do with the questions coming a tad too close to the true motivations behind Stephen's insistence to uphold the *"tradition"* of *"showing proper respect"* to him and his white, male, native-born, Christian, trumpist friends.

If Stephen would be honest to himself and the questioner, however, his answer to the last question would be: *"It is important to me that people listen to me and take me serious because otherwise they wouldn't do what I want them to do."*

With the next hypothetical question deviating a smidgen from the *"Why?"*-format but aiming no less at the core of Stephen's admission that he simply wants people to do his bidding. *"Alright, and what do you feel when you imagine a situation where people don't dance after your pipe but instead follow their own callings, desires, and plans which might be in direct contradiction to your own traditional values?"* An honest answer to this question could be probably only had from Stephen after he has been put in a hypnotic trance and compelled to tell the truth. In which case he would answer that, *"I feel powerless. Threatened. Under attack and vulnerable. Frightened."*

With the ultimate question now being of a rather hypothetical character, predominantly serving as a conclusion to Stephen's thought-process. *"Stephen, would you say that you are terrified of becoming powerless and losing your grip on that bit of the world that you can control thanks to your traditional rules? Are you frightened that progressives, liberals, and Democratic Socialists will change the rules which always gave you the upper hand until now? Do you hate that opponents of your traditionalistic worldview might lead a more harmonious, prosperous, and fulfilled life, revealing the fallacy of your own Christian, conservative doctrine? Do you dread the day when demanding respect exclusively by intimidation, insistence on outdated traditions, and 'big bad boy'-mannerisms simply will not work anymore? Do you have nightmares about a world where you and your buddies do not any longer hold the trump card of the white, male, Christian, native-born American? Are you in fact just horribly afraid of losing your undeserved privileges along with your self-appropriated status of king of the castle, bully calling the shots, and self-proclaimed custodian of your advantageously 'God-given order of things'?"*

Now, your guess is as good as any on Stephen's reply to this final barrage. But presupposing he remains compelled to answer honestly, he presumably will sputter: *"Yes, damnit! I suffer dreadful existential fears! Happy now!?"*, hence providing the closest possible approximation to an honest answer to the original question of why trumpist *Cognitive Dissonance Avoiders* go to such extreme lengths to stave off any information presenting a potential threat to their core-beliefs.

Fear.

Fear presents the primordial catalyst responsible for nefarious lies, conspiracy theories, and baseless attacks on political opponents. For the rage-red faces hollering profanities and hate-speech. For the adamant insistence on "sacred" Christian values and the simultaneous disregard thereof. For a cult-like adoration of firearms, the wannabe-macho culture, ubiquitous sexism, rape-downplaying, and combating of legal abortion. For the exorbitantly exaggerated devotion to superannuated traditions, violent nationalism, misunderstood freedom, and a single-edged rule of law. For the hate elicited by any change, improvement, or progress proving detrimental to white Christians' wobbly position on a precariously brittle pedestal.

At the end of the tunnel inside Stephen's, Kevin's, Karen's and any other Trumpist's mind hides the same primordial catalyst responsible for the creation of the worst type of human beings, those who opted for inhumanity, violence, murder, and cold-blooded genocide in reaction to their own overwhelming fears and are hence credited for humanity's worst sufferings throughout history, either in their capacities of brutal leaders or as henchmen, enablers, supporters, or sycophants. In the immortal words of President Franklin Delano Roosevelt, *"The only thing we have to fear is fear itself."* And while the great President was referring to the crippling and petrifying aspects of fear that prevent any swift and decisive actions, his words are nonetheless equally true for the fear that lurks like a venomous spider beneath the surface of reactionary, conservative minds poisoned to perceive threats and dangers everywhere.

That Dreadful Dread

Since times immemorial, fear has been humanity's strongest motivator for turning against itself. Fear makes people hate those who threaten their possessions, beliefs, and lives, makes people callous and numb to the plight of others, and lets people come up with the most outlandish excuses for heinous acts committed in "good faith" to prevent enemies from attacking first. Fear leads to the abuse of power in order to prevent the loss of self-same power. At the bottom of this mountain of fears resting to a larger or lesser extent on everyone's shoulders then lies the most primitive and powerful fear of all. The fear of death, often followed by the existential worry for the lives of loved ones.

When mankind's cave-dwelling ancestors found themselves on the brink of starvation in a particularly harsh winter, the specter of the tribe's extinction was motivation enough to go out in the dark of night and kill all members of the rivalling tribe across the street in their sleep, with the looted Mammoth-steaks and the elimination of the hunting-competition being an acceptable justification for cold-blooded murder.

Several thousand years later, the first farmers skulled each other with the first flails in the first battles over arable land. While later wars seemingly were fought over more abstract matters like the one true religion, or the best form of government (fascism, communism, democracy), or the "superiority" of specific races, these quoted reasons go only skin-deep, barely hiding the genuine motivations, i.e. the same old fear that the own tribe and consequentially oneself will "have not enough", (land, people, oil, trade, food, power, et.al.) in order to survive and prosper. And in the 21st century, wars over fresh water-supplies from the dwindling rivers in the Middle East and Asia are already looming on the horizon.

Almost as fundamental as the fear of death by starvation, enemy-attacks, illnesses, etc. has always been also men's deep-rooted worry of being unable to procreate in order to pass on their genes and frankly also to not have enough or any sex. A lack of (fertile) women once constituted at least as much of a stimulus as juicy Mammoth-steaks for raiding next door's tribe and kidnap their girls and young women. The "loot" would then be raped repeatedly, securing the kidnappers' own progeny and weakening or destroying the neighbours' family lines. Although, in many cases the rapists' sole interest had been sex for pleasure often followed by the mutilation and murder of their victims. A "tradition" that kept its ugly head up throughout history and remains alive in certain parts of the world even today.

Of course, the United States has no common custom to wantonly attack, overwhelm, and rape defenseless women. This old tradition has actually been outlawed by Western society despite the insistence of traditionalists that the good old times had been so much better in so many ways. And still, rape lamentably remains one of the most widespread and heinous crimes permeating all levels of global society in the 21st century, with a flabbergasting number of conservative lawmakers continuing to regard the horrible crime alternatively as *"understandable"*, *"a natural occurrence"*, or *"not sooo bad after all, eh?"* [*wink*]. Frequently, rape-victims in court are still forced to describe their outfit at the time of the rape, as if their choice of clothes would justify the horrendous act of the perpetrator in any way. In such cases, the apparently *"understandable"* urge of the rapist not to miss out on an "enticing opportunity" [*wink*] for relieving the pressure in his shrivelled ball-sack appears to play at least partially a role in the decision-making process in courts where defense lawyers and judges are cast from the same "old school"-mould [*wink*].

Next to "Lust", Christianity's go-to compendium for all aspects of life lists another six deadly sins, viz Greed, Gluttony, Sloth, Wrath, Pride, and Envy, all of which can be traced back with varying degrees of direct linkage to one common denominator.

Fear.

With the dreadful dread's influence on Greed and Gluttony being rather self-explanatory, the fear at the bottom of the "sin" of Sloth, (inactivity), is fed by several sources, from social anxiety, to depression, to an overwhelming fear of failure. Wrath, on the other hand, constitutes merely an emotional expression deriving from a whole range of fears , while Pride and Envy connect most directly to the fear of losing the individual smidgen of power and influence that is the result of a life of subservience and obedience, as well as to the fear of missing out on "essential" status symbols, (prestigious job, big house, Porsche 911), and consequentially to not receive "enough" respect, i.e. affirmation of the status and power necessary for keeping oneself and one's relatives supplied with all necessities and amenities to "survive in style".

The book in which these seven "deadly sins" are listed can trace its origins back to an age and to a world-region where small tribes of goat-herding, illiterate nomads and equally uneducated peasants dwelling in clay huts had been in need of some basic, written rules for a more orderly and peaceful co-existence. These written rules made it once and for all clear that *"coveting a neighbor's house, wife, slaves, animals, or anything else"* will come with dire consequences, while any lengthy, legalese texts would certainly have been wasted on this target-group. Which is why the book's authors had come up with 10 easy to remember sentences covering those legal fields, predominantly concerning possessions, most in need of higher authority-regulations.

The perpetual progress of civilization in the millennia following the introduction of these rudimentary rules, however, added layer upon layer of job-specifications and work-diversifications, fundamental changes in society structures, new types of relationships and family-constellations, added responsibilities of the individual, and a plethora of further circumstances all together leading to the rise of ever more indistinct and elusive fears branching off from the original trunk of mankind's primal set of fundamental fears. As one example, a surprisingly large number of people profess today to the paralysing fear of making a fool of themselves in public. To be negatively judged by one's peers or even total strangers has become a crippling concern for thousands of mostly young people not only in so-called "first world" countries. An anxiety based on a more primitive fear of being shunned by one's own community, a dread that may itself be rooted in the primal fear of being ostracised by the tribe and left to fend for oneself, in a final turn leading to the animalistic fear of one's own death by freezing, thirst, starvation, illness, or being killed by hostiles or predators with nobody around to help.

A similar line of reasoning can be applied to other civilization-fears, for instance the trepidation to appear a mediocre fumbler in comparison to one's peers or colleagues, or the fear of not receiving the respect one assumes to be due, or the constant dread to be outperformed by others, as well as the worry to grow old alone respectively with a mere stopgap while others got all the good men or women, or the often wrath-inducing apprehension that one's authority is not taken seriously, or the terrifying realisation to simply be incapable of dealing with unforeseen changes and challenging, new situations.

At the bottom of these fears lies the deeper worry of partially or completely losing control over one's life and own decisions by losing the established position in the family, neighborhood, town, workplace-hierarchy, political party, the sports club popularity-list, or in the eyes of a whole nation. In consequence, such a loss of control and status will often be accompanied by a loss of available financial means, meaning less or no food on the table, no shelter for oneself and one's family, and the inability to afford treatment for usually treatable illnesses, eventually leading to preventable deaths. Unfortunately, this deep-rooted fear of a cascade of losses culminating in premature death has proven to be not considerably alleviated by huge amounts of money, as the frequently erratic behavior of billionaires and superstars shows time and again. Apparently, death is not the only great equalizer.

Please be very afraid

Ultimately, this is it then. Naked fear is constituting the primeval root of the Trumpist alacrity to blindly accept, support, and follow the Dear Leader and holler the nonsensical slogan "*Make America great again*". Goaded by these fears, Trumpists will heave a huge sigh of relief when their "Savior" denies refugees entrance to the United States, no matter whether these people are fleeing from a war-torn and bombed-out Syria, Iraq, or Afghanistan, or cartels-haunted Middle and South American countries, or poverty-stricken and hurricane-devastated Caribbean islands. Deliberately blanking out that this brutal denial is antithetical to anything that made America once genuinely great. Moreover, *"Build the Wall!"*-yellers appear to never realize how nonsensical and even harmful Trump's anti-immigrant stance really is considering that the refugees would be by all accounts and purposes the most grateful, loyal, and hard-working new American citizens imaginable. Particularly since they have already proven by their bravery, resilience, and stamina alone to be better suited for many jobs that are shunned by today's complacent Trumpists.

Alas, courtesy of Donald Trump these highly motivated people will never contribute to the growth of America's economy, pay taxes, launch new enterprises, employ American workers, develop new technologies, or assist their fellow Americans in times of need. A small price to pay, in Trumpists' eyes, for having dodged the bullet of a flood of disease-ridden musclemen, job-stealing freeloaders, tightly organized anarchists, and millions of economy-destroying minimum wage workers.

In proper *Cognitive Dissonance Avoidance* manner, the Trumpublican colleague, Evangelical aunt, or traditionally racist mother-in-law will not allow any facts to destroy their precious nightmare even when faced with indisputable statistics like these from the National Immigration Forum, (immigrationforum.org), stating that, *"refugees aged 18-45 pay an estimated $21,000 more in taxes than they receive in benefits over 20 years"*. Or that, *"in 2015, refugees possessed $56.3 billion in disposable income"*, a staggering amount boosting local economies annually. Or that, while refugees *"initially start out with a median annual household income of around $22,000 during their first five years in the U.S., their income grows significantly in subsequent years, with the annual median income reaching $37,000 after 15 years in the U.S."*.

Facts that are routinely met by the racist MIL with disbelief, rejection, negation, and fallacious counterattacks based on *Circular Reasoning, What-Aboutism, Open* and *Closed World Assumptions* fuelled by a well-established *Cognitive Dissonance Avoidance* mechanism. If almost four decades of debating rigid conservatives, Reaganomics, Tea Party-participants, BCR-claqueurs (*Bush-Cheney-Rumsfeld*), Trumpists, and Trumpublicans have proven one point beyond doubt then that facts and figures, science and research, logic and reason, have as much chance to permeate the odd right's hermetically closed fantasy-bubble as has the devout, racist granny from across the street going to heaven.

For cracking the yard-thick wall of a Trumpist's *Cognitive Dissonance Avoidance,* tools like facts and logic are not only useless but frequently add even another concrete layer to the already impenetrable wall. To get at least one ray of truth shining through this barrier demands, apart from an almost superhuman patience, foremost a more roundabout strategy. While there is certainly no guarantee for success, feeding the Trumpist with easily digestible hints pointing at the most glaring inconsistencies while forestalling any further debate at least presents a potentially feasible method. Instrumentalizing a Trumpist's own irrationality against them and overhyping their claims to extremes represents another way to pry the tightly sealed think-box a crack open, for instance: T: *"Most Mexicans are either criminals, rapists, or cartel-members!"* – Y: *"Actually, I've read that most of them also sacrifice their first-born and eat the baby afterwards. Raw."* – T: *"Really? Oh. You're making this up!"* – Y: *"Well, you started it."*

Regardless of the method used for pulling Trumpists out of their hole of *Cognitive Dissonance Avoidance,* i.e., their self-imposed ignorance, however, anyone willing to try will need to be prepared for the inevitably following disappointment, since any debate with a proponent of far-right notions represents also a struggle with one of mankind's oldest, most resilient pre-emptive defense mechanisms.

Prejudice: The Problem with Premature Evaluation

One strategy for remaining patient and stopping the frustration-valve from exploding when dealing with a Trumpist's dumbfoundingly powerful rejection of proven facts and common sense consists of reminding oneself that the Trumpist's only alternatives to his nonsensical defense of his beliefs are, a). fainting on the spot, or b). running away, hands over his ears while warbling loudly, *"Hail to the Chief"*. Although, parts of the Trump-base have proven their preferred defense against unwelcome facts, logic, or reason to be immediate verbal or physical attacks.

In any case, Trumpists doubtlessly go to great lengths in order to escape a dreaded state of *Cognitive Dissonance,* looming constantly over their heads due to all this fact-based, publicly available information contradicting their long-nourished, and -cherished prejudices that tend to make up a good part of their core-beliefs.

"Most Mexicans are involved with drug-cartels."
"Most black American men are criminals."
"Most Arabs are potential terrorists."
"Raped women are sluts who provoked it."
"Atheists are monsters with no morale."
"Democrats are anti-American communists."
"South Americans are notorious thieves."
"Chinese are heartless bats- and dogs-eaters."
"Liberals are vaccines-poisoners."
"Scientists are fearmongering virus-propagandists."
"Lockdown-proponents are deep state agents."

Any halfway complete list of ridiculous prejudices circulating inside the Trumpist social media bubble regularly boosted by Hannity, Carlson, Ingraham, and consorts, would fill several pages, as indubitably as the Trumpministration's intention behind its dissemination of such negative stereotypes, i.e., the corroboration of existing prejudices and fears of Trumpists in order to guarantee the Trump-base's continuous adherence to Donald J. Trump's marching orders.

One of the most plausible and comprehensive explanations regarding the coercive power of *Stereotyping* enthralling over one-third of the American electorate today is provided by psychologist and California State University professor, Dr Todd D. Nelson, in his book "*The Psychology of Prejudice*", (Pearson, Allyn, and Bacon, 2006), covering the phenomenon of *Stereotyping* in detail. Nelson gives an in-depth answer to the question, why many people are so easily taken in by stereotypes and why they not only embrace these stereotypes wholeheartedly but also pass them on uncritically while convinced that claims like, "*I'm not a racist, but ...*", are acceptable proof for their self-proclaimed racial or cultural "blindness". In this regard, Nelson states that, "*people facilitate their functioning in the real world by employing human categories (i.e. sex and gender, age and race, etc.) with which to manage their social interactions with other people*".

Put differently, *stereotyping* people, i.e., classifying people into crudely labelled categories, makes it much easier for the individual to deal with an oftentimes overwhelming outside world and its confusing diversity of people. Following Nelson's exposition it appears that most people harbor prejudices, i.e. generalized negative beliefs, already before they enter for the first time into social interactions with *any* given societal sub-group or individual member of same, due to prior media-consumption, online-activities, and gossip. Even before first personal contact with a societal sub-group, people will have labelled this group and categorized it by its potential threat-level to one's physical and psychological integrity as well as one's core-beliefs.

Incidentally, people who are confident to possess all relevant information necessary to make such a decisive assessment derive their self-assuredness predominantly from the constant flow of pre-chewed opinions delivered via TV, radio, magazines, newspapers, the internet, and personal opinions of authority-figures and peers.

But the stereotyping of "others" based on third-hand information and prefabricated opinion-bites constitutes only the first step in the *Prejudice Cavalcade*. Once having identified the "others" as potentially hostile to own core-beliefs the racist, misogynist, zealot, or xenophobe will switch automatically into attack-mode. Harboring long-time, distinct prejudices against specific societal groups, these people are usually well-armed with an array of verbal ammunition, tailor-made to hurt the "enemy" most effectively. The deeply penetrating rhetorical bullets are then fired off "pre-emptively" to stun and maim the "adversary" before he or she can even begin scratching on the surface of the attacker's prejudiced core-belief. Frequently, such explosive expletives have been tried and tested over generations in the attacker's family. From a variety of cutting insults directed at physical appearances and general attributes, to openly displayed disdain, denigrating comments, rude gestures, and violent discriminatory acts, to outright social ostracism, the list of readily available ammunition is longer than one of Trump's rally-speeches. Particularly compatriots who consider their own lifestyle to be the ultimate yard stick for a "proper, God-fearing life" often possess a twitchy trigger-finger ready to fire their *logorrhea*-projectiles at the slightest "provocation" from their victims, be it a *fag, dyke, raghead, slut, commie, libtard, beaner, harpy* or, of course, *n***er*.

Once the fear-button of a *"No Progress! No Changes! No Others!"*-proponent has been pushed by a perceived threat to their lopsided belief-system, their prejudice-powered mind will spit out the ever-same barrage of slurs, insults, degradations, and brain-farts on auto-fire. Sometimes it even suffices for the prejudiced attacker to encounter a person belonging to a "threat-posing" group in some situation in which the prejudice-carrier feels out of their depth, with examples on YouTube abounding, from *BBQ Becky* to *Golfcart Gail, Permit Patty*, and *Cornerstore Caroline,* among many others.

Although infamous *BBQ Becky* and her fellow *Karens* calling 911 to report "illegal behavior" of innocent black or Hispanic Americans had been acting solo at the time, the species of prejudice-drunk, fear-ridden Caucasian-Americans usually is to be found congregating in larger packs. Like all perma-terrified species, the males and females of the racist variety, as well as the male misogynist, female misandrist, or fanatic monotheist feel most comfortable inside the protective cocoon of like-minded groups. This may also explain the "bravery" of *Gail, Becky, Caro*, or *Patty* when calling the police while being out on their own in hostile territory, since *Cornerstore Caroline* and her co-snitches labor under the (often correct) assumption that the police officers they call to the "crime scene" will be by default members of their own pack. And the delusion of *BBQ Becky* and her sisters in spirit does not end here, since not only are they deeming any police officer to be as openly racist as they demonstrably are themselves, but *Permit Patty's* species is also utterly convinced that the law will be one-hundred percent on their side in these matters, inadvertently revealing a worryingly warped understanding of the law, clearly pointing at a democracy-endangering ignorance permeating at least 35% of the American population.

A final note may pertain to one specific characteristic displayed by all *Cognitive Dissonance Avoider* sub-species from far-right racists to the fanatically faithful. That is, the astounding metamorphosis from fearful coward merely daring to dart malignant glances and mumbling insults when out alone in public in one instant into bigmouthed, braggadocious bully the moment when being surrounded by likeminded foul-mouths. A phenomenon that has been equally observed with public appearances of such packs as with gatherings exclusive to their own kind.

Whether at expensive golf- or country-clubs with their "proud tradition" of keeping Jews and colored people off the precious Green, or at misandrists-meetings disguised as "feminist" community reach-out with drinks-prices scaled according to gender and sexual orientation, or at shooting-ranges displaying Confederate flags and Swastikas with patrons are greeted by the Nazi-salute – "Safe spaces" such as these are allowing prejudice-poisoned *Cognitive Dissonance Avoiders* to genuinely come into their own. Once the Rolex®-adorned WASP-Golfers, proudly verbose "feminists", and gun-toting KKK-sympathizers are at last permitted to huddle together without fear of prying eyes and ears of non-initiated outsiders they will finally let their hair down and outdo each other with creative and classic insults for the despised "enemy", with the ones most terrified of these "others" usually leading the pack in the most venomous insults. Inside these groups (online or in real life), the treasured prejudice serves as identity-defining "hobby", connecting prejudice-carriers with like-minded haters and providing a notion of belonging.

However, defining one's self not by preferences, likes, and loves, but instead by the hatred for a specific group of people will lead in most cases anywhere else, but not to a healthy, balanced, and satisfying life. Still, in many democratic countries notorious *Cognitive Dissonance Avoiders* with strong prejudices nowadays make up large enough groups for national societies to be confronted with political parties whose sole political program consists of targeting and attacking minorities for the purpose of bagging the large voter-group of prejudice-poisoned, pathetic "patriots".

Naturally, minorities chosen for vilification and persecution differ, being Kurds in one country, Uyghurs in another, and Mexicans in yet another, with many prejudice-powered governments additionally boosting the discrimination of the LGBTQ-community as well as the persecution of political dissidents, suppression of religious minorities, and disregard for women's rights. Incidentally though, not one of the political parties, governments, or authoritarian rulers whose powers are relying on irrational prejudices have ever been able to objectively prove the claimed "dangers" apparently posed by groups branded as "enemies of the people". In the end, it seems ironic that none other than prejudice-soaked conspiracy theorists and *Cognitive Dissonance Avoiders* suspecting duplicity at every turn have become in fact the most compliant tools for modern tyrants' successful power-grab and boundless self-enrichment at their cost.

- TrumpSpeak -

"There have to be news at a place called FOX News."
- Shepard Smith, former FOX News-anchor -

One important skill of *Cognitive Dissonance Avoiders* consists of arranging everyday life in such a way that the probability of experiencing *Cognitive Dissonance* becomes as slim as possible. Simultaneously, *CD-Avoiders* are constantly on the look-out for opinions and information-sources affirming their core-beliefs and will, once having found such a safe haven supporting their core-beliefs, remain extremely faithful and emotionally attached to it. In combination, these two behavioral quirks of *Avoidance* and *Selection* are known as *Selective Exposure.* And while *Selective Exposure*-novices often still need to physically remove themselves from situations which might induce *Cognitive Dissonance,* for instance by fainting, running away, or hastily changing the TV-channel, seasoned *Cognitive Dissonance-Avoiders* have the practice of *Selective Exposure* down to a T, their everyday life carefully adjusted to an optimal exposure to belief-supporting input and simultaneously to maximum-avoidance of core-belief-contradicting information.

"If you're very stupid, how can you possibly realize that you're very, very stupid? You'd have to be relatively intelligent to realize how stupid you are. This explains almost the entirety of FOX News." - John Cleese

In the Times of Trump, even a modern-day Robinson Crusoe would be able to name the by far safest media-haven for any Trumpist, conspiracy theorist, deep-state flake, anti-lockdown loon, and *QAnus*-asshat gathering each night around the virtual campfire at FOX News.

While the internal machinations leading up to the meteoric rise of the once obscure media-sinkhole to a position of Donald J. Trump's personal propaganda-station remain mostly in the dark, it was assumedly in the year 2009, during the advent of the Tea Party movement, when a group of conservatives of the same tree as political arsonist-in-chief Newt Gingrich were sitting down with Australian media-mogul and FOX-owner Rupert Murdoch fora very productive and lucrative chat. Notably, Murdoch's 1996 established FOX News already supported predominantly the Republican Party in 2009, although at the time still being a far cry from the partisan, propagandist, pseudo-journalistic farce of today.

The long-term plan hatched in 2009, right at the beginning of President Barack Obama's first term, by Murdoch and his partners from a back-then fringe group of stop-at-nothing, morale-be-damned Republicans subsequently progressed as planned, culminating finally in the election of ex-TV-show host Donald J. Trump to the Office of U.S.-president. With this first major victory under their belts, the reclusive Wizard of FOX, Murdoch, and his Democrats-loathing partners who by now had moved from the fringes into the Republican center, ordered a full-frontal attack on progressive America. A war-cry gleefully taken up by FOX's combat dogs, whose nametags read Bill O'Reilly, Tucker Carlson, Sean Hannity, Jeanine Pirro, Laura Ingraham, and *FOX & Friends'* Stooge One, Two, and Three.

As initially successful as Murdoch's and the Gingrich-gang's plan had been in launching a massive media-missile aimed at the Democratic Party and progressive movements, its basic idea nonetheless derived from one of the biggest weaknesses all far-right *Cognitive Dissonance Avoiders* possess, that is the dire need for constant protection, confirmation, and boosting of their brittle core-beliefs. The frightened wailing of millions of self-pitying right-wingers played presumably no small role in the 2009-decision to transform FOX News into a wagon fort offering shelter to all the Obama-"traumatized" racists, white supremacists, "patriots", NRA gun-nuts, Christian fundamentalists, predator-capitalists, and stone-age conservatives. In the following seven years, this wagon fort filled with oddballs of every shade of the right-wing spectrum, eager to grab a gun and shoot under cover at anything outside the conservative corral.

But then came the day of November 8, 2016, and with it the biggest right-wing miracle since the assassination of John F. Kennedy. With the electoral college-victory of New York City's con-artist Donald J. Trump in the U.S.-presidential elections, all their positions that up to this moment had been regarded widely as regressive, unsavory, anti-social, unjust, and immoral, had suddenly become America's new mainstream-philosophy. Unsurprisingly, the first news-outlet to eagerly step out from behind the curtain to openly declare itself the new state-propaganda station was FOX News. Others followed suit soon and took second tier-positions in the Trumpministration's war on truth, with the Sinclair Broadcast Group, whose numerous regional TV-stations comprise a near-parody of Nazi propaganda-minister Goebbels' *forced-into-line* media as a close runner-up to FOX.

It is All Fun and Games. Until it is All Just Fun and Games.

Next to the Trumpublican TV-coalition, the internet developed rapidly into the second clay foot on which Trump's *Selective Exposure*-propaganda rested. Some older readers will still remember the pre-web times when right-wing radicals, conspiracy nuts, and domestic terrorists had usually been found hiding in their parent's rubbish-strewn basement, dilapidated garden sheds, or in remote cabins in the woods where they typed their crude conspiracy theories and manifestos on an old *Underwood Champion* typewriter to subsequently mail them to a newspaper with demands to print their crazy drivel. Only a couple of decades after Unabomber Ted Kaczynski's arrest in a remote cabin in the woods, however, the number of conspiracy loons exploded exponentially, with Facebook, Twitter, 4chan, Reddit, and other social media platforms providing unlimited opportunities for spreading batshit-crazy ideas not just nationally but globally.

There is little doubt of the close connection between these two occurrences, with particularly Facebook serving as Petri dish for ideological viruses like *QAnus*, anti-vaxxers, flat-earthers, deep state-conspiracies, or the latest *"Obamagate"*-fantasy. Interestingly, right at the height of this online-lunacy the United States fell into the hands of a septuagenarian Twitter-addict who is wont to spend occasionally whole weekends tweeting and re-tweeting outlandish conspiracy theories, self-glorifications, aspersions, and self-made-up "facts", rivalling the wackiest tall tale-tellers among his supporters. With no access-restrictions to speak off and only a laughable excuse for genuine supervision and necessary moderation in place, Twitter, Facebook, 4Chan, Reddit, and other platforms function today as virtual hotbeds where any extremist notion can be cultivated undisturbedly in an overheated climate ideally suited for growing the most dangerous nuts.

Although, in May of 2020, Twitter began surprisingly to flag certain tweets by the President of the United States, Donald J. Trump. In one case, Twitter provided a link in Trump's tweet to background-information debunking Trump's fallacious allegations regarding the dangers of vote by mail, ("*no evidence for potential widespread voter-fraud*"), while placing a caution-comment on another Trump-tweet relating to the riots after the murder of Black Minnesotan George Floyd by four Minneapolis police officers, a tweet that Trump had ended with the sentence, "[...] *Any difficulty and we will assume control but, when the looting starts, the shooting starts. Thank you!*" Twitter commented underneath the U.S.-President's tweet: "*This Tweet violated the Twitter Rules about glorifying violence. However, Twitter has determined that it may be in the public's interest for the Tweet to remain accessible.*"

Predictably, most Trumpists confess to consulting FOX News and the local Sinclair station, plus Twitter and Facebook as their only source of information, resulting in increasing numbers of Americans retreating ever further into their echo chambers, cutting themselves deliberately off from objective reality, hence displaying classic *Selective Exposure* behavior. In this regard, particularly Facebook will have a lot to answer for, from voluntarily leaving its own field to Russia's pro-Trump trolls, to various data safety-violations. But even when leaving these screw-ups aside, Facebook remains a textbook example for all that is going wrong with the internet in its pubertal years. Leaving the answer to the question *"Quo Vadis, internet?"* exclusively to the big data-kraken and their untouchable leaders will not be the solution for the way forward in this regard.

The United States and other countries where the market is dominated by Facebook and a few other platforms will need to ask themselves whether a hyper-exclusive club of privately led shareholder-companies (*Facebook, Alphabet/Google, Amazon, Microsoft, Apple*) is genuinely representing the most trustworthy custodian of the world's entire personal data, including each and every address, number, photo, idea, image, copy, video, theory, question, opinion, solution, answer, conversation, preference, information, and thought ever shared on these platforms.

If nothing else, Russia's massive mass-manipulation- and misinformation-campaign predominantly via Facebook in the run-up to the 2016 presidential elections has proven that an online-company employing not only the most advanced algorithms but scanning also more than 105 terabytes of data every 30 minutes (sic!) possesses every necessary means to influence the American public at will and with pinpoint precision. In light of the fact that conspiracy theory-nuts and Trumpists are eagerly accepting the "ironclad" theory about Bill Gates' Plan for World Domination, i.e., hiding nanobots in fake vaccination against a fake Coronavirus to control the nanobots via 5G-transmissions to turn people into submissive zombies (sic!), there can be little doubt that the same people will also greedily suck up the next Putin-Trump propaganda-wave with gusto. In fact, leaving such feeble-minded toddler-brains alone with the internet, unsupervised and unguided, borders on criminally wilful neglect by any responsible government.

Thus, the answer to the fundamental question of *"Where're you heading, web?"*, (*Quo Vadis?*), consists not only of individuals regaining control over their personal data and intellectual property but needs also to address the introduction and effective enforcement of precise laws, rules, and regulations concerning online-platforms. Often blinded by the amazing advantages provided by the internet as an integral part of society and everyone's life, its rapid development further expedited by the Corona crisis has left many regulations in the dust that would be urgently needed for a civilized cohabitation in the new virtual realm. The ubiquitous comparison of the web with the frontiers of the Wild West hits the nail on the head here, with large regions of webspace remaining to this day lawless territories where modern equivalents of the ruthless snake-oil peddlers of old are still posing the least of all dangers waiting on the net poses for gullible Trumpists and equally intellectually challenged people, such as conspiracy theorists, anti-vaxxer moms, or MLM-scheme victims.

As if the 1,001 ways employed by web-predators to relieve clueless Midwesterners of their hard-earned salary and savings were not bad enough, the near-impossibility of getting hold of cyber-criminals is making the internet a place even more dangerous than Dodge City after the last Sheriff took to his heels. Its absolute anonymity guarantees that there is no place in the world where hardened criminals, debauchers, conmen, and demagogues can ply their trade in the same carefree and undisturbed manner as the internet with its 4.33 billion (sic) active users.

The internet, having once begun its triumphal march as an interesting quirk, technical novelty, and predominantly great new way to have fun, remains in the public mind to this day a carefree, consequences-free, and virtually unreal place. From the start, Western society took to Facebook, Instagram, YouTube, Twitter, and the hermetically closed world of Apple like a toddler to a new puppy. Everything online was and often still is considered "Fun", whether chatting, posting, shopping, watching, listening, hating, flirting, masturbating, or playing. Doing it online makes it more exciting and less consequential at the same time.

But any occasion promising *fun and games* also represents an opportunity for the professional *Bullshitter* to catch his prey with its guard down. No matter if small-time trickster or professional Russian troll, MLM-huckster or American President, today's webspace is their new Wild West where the sheer number of cyberspace-mesmerized victims actually makes it difficult not to pull the wool over the sheeples' eyes in any one of a thousand easy ways.

Although, it appears as if a silver lining at the virtual horizon is showing at last. Despite a persisting lack of assertive rules and effective law enforcement across social media platforms, the decline and fall of cyber-civilization in recent years has finally evoked some serious resistance against the people's disenfranchisement by *Big Web*. After almost two decades of blind and careless trust in the "benevolent dictatorship" behind the major social media-platforms, a new generation of genuine digital natives is finally shaking the public awake from its honeymoon slumber with Mark 1. Zuckerberg, Tim "Apple", and their cyber-CEO colleagues. Compared to a few years ago when attitudes such as, *"I don't care if Facebook has my personal data. I have nothing to hide!"* or, *"I get all the information I need from Facebook!",* had been commonplace and didn't meet serious opposition, today's netizens have a far more differentiated opinion of the data-krakens, consequentially being also more cautious with handing out personal information on the web.

Nonetheless, the multi-billionaires behind Insta, Twitter, Facebook, Alphabet, et.al. will remain untouched by the growing resistance to their prying into all aspects of users' lives, (*"Allow Calculator access to contacts?"; "Allow Flashlight to make phone calls?"*), as long as Mark 1. and his fellow data kraken-owners will be able to manipulate politicians to do their "duty" and support the "systemically relevant" cyber-giants, essentially turning a blind eye to the continuous violations of privacy laws, ongoing neglect of supervisory obligations, and notorious exploitation of their tax-avoidance power.

Election-campaigning lawmakers who demand accountability, effective supervision, and adherence to privacy laws from all-goggling Google, Mark 1.'s Data-Mining Co., and other online-fiefdoms are clearly at a disadvantage when the Tech-elite is generously lending a helping hand to those politicians who are prone to play the *Quid-pro-Quo* game. In the political climate of the Trumpministration, these mutual backscratchers enjoy the heyday of their lives, making it in turn irrelevant how often Mark 1. will be summoned in front of a congressional committee. As a result, Facebook will continue serving as an operation-base for Putin's trolls, Trumpaganda-disseminators, conspiracy-theorists, alt-right neo-fascists, and other disinformation-spreaders, providing an ideal habitat for *Cognitive Dissonance Avoiders* longing to feel protected, supported, understood, and most of all right about their core-beliefs.

In essence, any true change will need to wait until *Herr Twittler* has vacated the White House for good and the world has come back to its senses. Four years of letting Donald Trump not only run wild but also the country has allowed the likes of Mark Zuckerberg, Larry Ellison, Sergey Brin, Larry Page, and Jeff Bezos as well as non-tech CEO's like Brendan Kennedy, Stephen Schwarzman, Bob Iger, or Charles G. Koch, to expand their influence on politics and the financial rewards it provides manifold. In these four years, restricting regulations, fair taxation, independent supervision, effective consumer protection, and other annoying obstacles to maximum profit have been weakened, rescinded, or all-out abolished under Trump's tutelage. The lifelong conman has always known on which side his bread gets buttered and while being an abysmally bad businessman, Trump's instincts will never allow him any other move than sidling up to successful money-makers. In the end, Donald J. Trump needs the plebs and their votes only once every four years but craves the dough every waking second.

Facebook and Twitter are allowing Trump and the Trumpaganda-brigade unrestricted access to the minds of millions of plebeian *Cognitive Dissonance Avoiders* who long for the Great Leader's reassuring lies and baseless allegations to bolster brittle core-beliefs. And, unsurprisingly, Facebook knows of its divisive, prejudice-encouraging, and hatred-inciting role in the current political climate while having deliberately done less than nothing to alleviate this state of affairs.

As the Wall Street Journal (WSJ) reported on May 26, 2020, *"A Facebook Inc. team had a blunt message for senior executives. The company's algorithms weren't bringing people together. They were driving people apart. 'Our algorithms exploit the human brain's attraction to divisiveness', read a slide from a 2018 presentation. 'If left unchecked', it warned, Facebook would feed users 'more and more divisive content in an effort to gain user attention & increase time on the platform'."*

The WSJ quotes also another report's conclusion that Facebook's algorithms *"exploit the human brain's attraction to divisiveness"*. According to the Wall Street Journal, Mark Zuckerberg and Joel Kaplan, policy chief at Facebook, rejected any solutions to this problem presented to them, out of fear that conservatives would regard Facebook as biased when discovering the platform's potential new stance against destructive divisiveness, revealing Zuckerberg's true motives for Facebook's reluctance to ensure a level playing field on his platform.

In the meantime, non-tech corporations outside of cyberspace support the costly Trumpaganda-machine with their own direct and indirect "donations" in return for advantageous policy-decisions, government contracts, and positive propaganda directly from the White House. An arrangement that would have earned Itself at any other time in history the label "corruption" in a heartbeat. In Times of Trump, however, the average Trumpist from Indiana, Florida, Alabama, or Kentucky does not get tired praising President Trump's *outstanding business acumen* when confronted with the President's shady deals, providing a good example for the efficacy of a system that subordinates virtually everything, particularly morale and values, to the maximization of the personal wealth and power of a few oligarchs by blatantly "reinterpreting" democratic laws and regulations.

The final chance to avert an irreversible normalization and unstoppable expansion of Donald J. Trump's corrupt Banana-Republican system carries a precise expiry-date: Tuesday, November 3, 2020. On this day, the 59th quadrennial U.S.-presidential election will decide not only who will be President for the next four years but also the path of America's foreseeable future. Never since Franklin D. Roosevelt's victory over Herbert Hoover in 1932 were the stakes higher than on this day, when every American aged 18 or older will have the opportunity to either steer the country away from the looming abyss of corruption, divisiveness, racism, authoritarian capriciousness, cronyism, and the unfettered rule of a group of multi-millionaire and billionaire oligarchs over an increasingly disenfranchised and impoverished population, or to vote for letting this exact scenario become America's sinister reality.

Incidentally, refraining to vote will haunt non-voters for decades to come, only by having to explain their inaction in the most important election of their lifetime to their children, grandchildren, relatives, friends, colleagues, acquaintances, and countless strangers over the next 30-40 years. Excuses such as Joe Biden having been *"equally bad"*, *"incompetent"*, *"too old and senile"*, *"also a sexual offender"*, *"just the same establishment-pawn in blue"*, or *"Not Bernie!"*, this time around will have no bite when the future of the nation is at stake. A "sleepy" President with a team of professional, experienced, intelligent, and morally sound experts behind him remains still the better alternative to a sleepless president only listening to himself and spending his nights tweeting temper tantrums, inscrutable word-creations, *ad hominem* attacks and accusations, uncoordinated orders, slandering insults, or straight-out lies, keeping the world perpetually on edge like a triple-espresso with three spoons of Cocaine.

Four years in a continuous state of emergency with daily damage-reports from the countless transgressions of the law, to globally damaged diplomatic relations, to a record national debt, to the gigantic failure in handling a pandemic with 200,000 and rising dead Americans, present more than enough reason to end this horrendously failed "experiment" of letting a rabid fox guard the henhouse. When English playwright and Poet Laureate, John "Glorious" Dryden, wrote, *"Beware the fury of a patient man"*, he might as well have had the majority of the American electorate in 2020 in mind whose patience just ran out.

The Tallest Tales are Still Told on Television

The internet and its countless opportunities for mass-manipulation are no doubt a growing market for all authoritarian governments and neo-fascist rulers and in all probability will become the first address for propaganda-distribution soon. Yet, in 2020 the political main-battleground remains still the television screen, including any news, late night shows, candidate debates, panel discussions, interviews, and documentaries posted subsequently on YouTube and other platforms.

In the run-up to the 2020 presidential elections, the frontlines of the battle for votes clearly runs through the studios of CNN, MSNBC, ABC, CBS, PBS, Comedy Central, and FOX News, as no one knows better than Donald J. Trump whose most important assets have never been his government-departments or agencies, nor his team of "the very best people", or any of the secretaries on his revolving-door cabinet. Instead and despite recent hick-ups in their relationship, Trump's by far most cherished asset remains a private-owned TV-station in New York City which is in all but name the official press-agency of Donald J. Trump and the Trumpublican Party.

Rupert Murdoch's *FOX Broadcasting Company* provides all necessary means for a well-oiled, nation-spanning propaganda-machine, including appropriate personnel from a venom-spitting, hate-hissing ex-county judge, to a triumvirate of couch-potato sycophants spinning even the worst blunder into the Master's latest triumph, to *Pawn* Hannity and *ucker Carlson as the obligatory off-kilter, crazily blustering chief-agitators - an indispensable must-have for any sycophantic broadcasting company sucking up to the authoritarian regime de jour.

With FOX News already being an all too real "*NewSpeak*"-manifestation straight out of an Orwellian nightmare, the Trumpaganda-brigade of *on-air* airheads includes furthermore the *Sinclair Broadcast Group*, headquartered in Baltimore and a textbook-example for media-outlets making themselves complicit in undermining democracy. Currently the largest TV-station-operator in the United States, Sinclair lays claim to 59 FOX affiliates, 41 ABC affiliates, 30 CBS affiliates, 25 NBC affiliates, and nine Univision and other affiliates plus its own network (Comet), together covering over 40% of all American households. Alarming numbers for any functioning democracy and its inherently vital plurality of information, yet dire reality in a United States facing a nationwide near-monopoly of local TV-stations owned and run by an ultra-partisan, right-wing billionaire-family constantly pushing for further acquisitions.

Only someone whose TV has been stuck on *Nickelodeon* for the last two decades would be unable to answer the question whether the four sons of David Sinclair Smith (†1993) presently running the company are perhaps just a tad politically biased. But even the last cartoon-fanatic will come to a clear conclusion of this subject after watching five minutes of Sinclair-TV, particularly when seeing one of

Sinclair's so-called *"must-run"*-segments broadcasted on every Sinclair-affiliated station with the exact same text, a uniquely surreal viewer-experience that will make any democracy-defender's hair stand on end.

YouTube provides first-hand experience of these Orwellian horror-shows in dozens of videos showing anchors of various Sinclair-stations simultaneously reciting *must-run* monologues, e.g. *"Sinclair's Soldiers in Trump's War on Media"*, with new editions popping up whenever the four Smith-brothers feel a need to flex their muscles in direct support of Donald John. In such cases, a dispatch from Sinclair-HQ will go out to all stations, with the unequivocal order to all news-presenters to read out the attached proclamation precisely as it was written in as natural a tone as possible. Invariably leading to one of the most surreal and terrifying spectacles on post-WWII-television, not only in the USA but in any democratic country to date, with scores of robot-news-hosts doing their insufficient best injecting a modicum of fake emotions into the despicable act of announcing state-propaganda while pretending to voice their own opinion. A scene that inevitably forces the image of a specific historic figure to come to mind, who would have certainly enjoyed using this mass-propaganda tool for his own manipulation of umpteen millions.

Luckily, however, Hitler's propaganda minister Joseph Goebbels, while having been extremely successful in enforcing conformity across the German media, had literally gone up in flames before he could get his gnarly hands on the most influential mass-medium prior to the internet. It was therefore up to the following generations of dictators, authoritarian rulers, and propaganda-chiefs to abuse the mass-medium television for the manipulation of the people's minds, thoughts, and beliefs. The gallery of TV-abusing despots, while far too extensive to name all, includes such illustrious truth-rapists as Joseph Stalin, Leonid Brezhnev, Fidel Castro, Generalissimo Franco, Chairman Mao, Uganda's Idi Amin, former dictators Saddam H. and M. Gaddafi, and for the first time in recorded history now also a ruler of a country that likes to declare itself the *"Champion of Democracy"*.

But the final word on Sinclair's Soviet-style *must run-*segments belongs to one of America's most respected and experienced journalists and news anchors, Mr. Dan Rather: *"News anchors looking into camera and reading a script handed down by a corporate overlord, words meant to obscure the truth not elucidate it, isn't journalism. It's propaganda. It's Orwellian. A slippery slope to how despots wrest power, silence dissent, and oppress the masses."* [sic].

- The Illusory Truth Effect -

"When people learn no tools of judgment and merely follow their hopes, the seeds of political manipulation are sown."
- Stephen Jay Gould, American palaeontologist and evolutionary biologist -

In a secret location somewhere in the Russian city of Saint Petersburg, formerly Leningrad, are right now dozens of the most adept social media-manipulators on the planet sitting in front of high-performance laptops, earning their daily bread in the employ of the infamous *Internet Research Agency* (*IRA*, or Агентство интернетисследований, also known as *Glavset*). To date, no one can or will say with certainty, how crucial the *IRA's* incessant interference in the last U.S.-presidential campaign has genuinely been. Yet, all experts agree that the aptly nicknamed *Trolls from Olgino* have massively interfered in the 2016-elections and that those thousands of memes, forum-posts, fake websites, blogs, Facebook-pages, comments, and other *IRA* online-activities have played far more than a mere peripheral role in Donald J. Trump's election-victory.

Despite the Trump-campaign's proven ties to the Kremlin and its close collaboration with the right-wing media, it remains of course pure speculation whether the FOX News-propagandists and the *Putinbots* in Russia exchanged some useful tips on effective media mass-manipulation prior to the elections in 2016. In hindsight, though, such exchange seems to have been hardly necessary since both organizations have long proven their individual proficiency in the art of propaganda-dissemination. If they would be thusly inclined, both groups could actually offer advanced university-courses in political propaganda and mass-deception, making it much more likely that Kremlin-Trolls and FOX-Fabulists are relying independently on one of the most effective mass-manipulation techniques available to any large-scale propaganda enterprise, called the *Illusion of Truth Effect*,

Anyone who has seen some of the memes posted by the Russian *IRA* prior to and during the election-campaign between 2014 and the end of 2016 will have noticed that their intellectual and creative quality have been anything but gold-standard. For example, one such meme showed an obviously photoshopped picture of a Latin American woman holding a baby with one hand and in the other hand a placard with the words: *"Give Me More Free Shit"*. The headline above the doctored picture read, *"Illegals Cost U.S. Taxpayers $113 Billion A Year. While Contributing Only $12 Billion A Year."*, with the subline underneath demanding: *"Stop Rewarding. Start Deporting."*, with an add-on underneath, *"Like If You Agree."*

Any tangentially intelligent person will naturally check these suspicious numbers before forwarding or posting the meme without comment or with a *"See, I told you so!"* underneath, particularly after noticing the obviously manipulated picture. Yet, *Selective Exposure*-practitioners already harboring a prejudice against immigrants have hyped this ridiculous meme as yet another confirmation of their core-belief. Still, if the Russian branch of the Trumpaganda-machine would have been content with 100 or 200 similar memes, strategically placed for right-wingers to stumble upon, their impact presumably would have been rather negligible. Some Trumpublicans might even have become somewhat sceptical of the memes' unsubstantiated claims after a while. However, Putin's trolls and Murdoch's mouthpieces know all about the decreasing efficacy of badly crafted lies over time. Hence, both bad actors are heavily relying on the titular *Illusory Truth Effect*, also known as the *validity* or *reiteration effect*. Concretely, the *Illusory Truth Effect* refers to people's tendency to believe a false information to be true when being repeatedly exposed to the fallacy. In a nutshell, the more often you hear a lie the more you believe it to be true.

Naturally, this effect is not exclusive to Trumpists but can be experienced by anyone – with one major difference. Distinguishing the average *Trumpalumpa* and *Trumpette* from any mature, self-reflecting person is the latter's ability of independent and critical thinking paired with a healthy dose of scepticism for unreliable sources. Together with the willingness and necessary know-how for independent research to validate suspicious assertions, people taught to think critically can therefore muster far more sturdy defenses against the relentless bombardments of lies, [*"Immigrants dangerous"*, *"Economy great"*, *"China pays for tariffs"*, *"No collusion"*, *"Perfect call"*, *"Hurricane hits Alabama"*, *"Wall gets build"*, *"Read the transcript"*, *"Best tests in the world"*, *"Corona is like the flu"*, *"America is doing great"*, et.al.], once more proving comprehensive education based on scientific and humanistic principles to be the most effective vaccination against propaganda-strategies such as the *Illusory Truth Effect*.

But back to the events leading up to the 2016 presidential elections. With Trump increasingly more likely to become the 45th U.S.-president, the times when FOX News grudgingly throttled its subtext-output promoting the acceptance of white supremacism, jingoism, misogyny, bigotry, and oligarchic rule were finally over. From the day when Donald Trump floated down that golden escalator, the opinion-broadcaster sailing under the false flag of a news-station went all-in, ceaselessly barraging the nation with a handful of cardinal falsehoods constituting the bedrock of Trump's personal tower of lies.

Spearheading FOX News' commando style attack on objective reality had been the now long forgotten, choleric narcissist Bill O'Reilly. Once the sexual harasser had been outed and shortly after kicked to the curb by the chiefs at FOX, the pseudo-news station installed Sean Hannity as O'Reilly's replacement, rapidly followed by the employ of a whole squad of second- and third-tier sycophants and conspiracy-theorists all aiding and abetting the chief-propagandist by executing the same marching order: Bombard the audience of FOX News with the always same prevarications, but wrapped in varying garments. While the performance-styles of Ingraham, Pirro, Doocy, Kilmeade, or *ucker Carlson are therefore appealing to different sub-target groups, in the end they all fulfil the same role as *Illusory Truth Effect*-amplifiers, repeating relentlessly the same lies day in, day out, thus transforming lies into "truths" with no signs of letting off anytime soon.

Putin's web-warriors in the St. Petersburg *IRA*, on the other hand, chose a more gradual approach when they began their attacks on the American population in 2013-2014. The *Trolls from Olgino*, a district of Saint Petersburg, targeted initially Americans on Facebook, Twitter, and YouTube with propaganda-pieces aimed at both sides of the Great American Divide.

Not much later began the second phase, with fake accounts on Instagram and Tumblr created and supervised by individual trolls added to the mix. In 2015, Putin's E-Force further expanded its sphere of influence by establishing and promoting their own groups and forums on platforms like 4chan, 8chan, Reddit, and, of course, Facebook.

The preliminarily last phase, as far as publicly known today, had been initiated as soon as the Kremlin-Gremlins concluded that the number of their unsuspecting "followers" had reached critical mass, ready to take the intended chaos out of webspace and onto America's streets. To this end, the virtual *agents provocateurs* released a new type of memes and messages, designed to incite the *alt-right,* and to a lesser extent the *resistance,* to act out their resentments, hate, triumph, and despair on Main Street, USA. Once again, the sheer quantity of messages in hundreds of disguises had the desired *Illusion of Truth Effect*, resulting in violent clashes between protesters, counter-protesters, and police forces and in a surge of hate crimes against minorities.

A lot can be said about Putin's perfidious propaganda-people, but certainly not have been lazy in the last years. Ivan and his *IRA*-colleagues have indubitably overachieved their objectives by establishing a fully-fledged, virtual mirror-universe, versatile and highly flexible yet believable and convincing enough for Trumpists to feel right at home without becoming suspicious.

Deeming themselves invincible in the anonymity of forums like the sub-Reddit *r/The_Donald*, (now quarantined), many Donald-devotees divest themselves of their last moral inhibitions and give their hate-powered prejudices and distorted worldviews free rein, presumably to the delight of their Russian manipulators who doubtlessly take meticulously note of their "clienteles'" online-activities. Preceded by a thorough analysis of the latest hate-trends in the *CoCoCo* (Conservative Conspiracy Community), Ivan and his troll-comrades are always ready to create a new wave of finely adjusted propaganda-messages in the form of "funny" memes, fake news-reports, staged YouTube videos, and bogus articles on *National Enquirer*-level. The new batch of disinformation and inciting hate-texts will then be sent with one mouse-click directly onto the screens of millions of American "patriots". Hence, the *Illusory Truth Effect,* sent from Russia with love, also reaches Aunt Becky, proud member of the *Women for Trump* Astroturf-organisation, who will subsequently have her nieces and nephews know, thank you very much, that there is no doubt in her mind that *"Obamagate"* has always been real and that *"Hussein Obama"* has definitely committed some crime or other against *"our honest, unsuspecting President"*. After having been sufficiently bombarded with "proof", Aunt Becky will then elaborate: *"I mean, just go on the internet! They uncover new evidence every day. Obamagate is everywhere! I got a dozen new reports on Facebook alone today. You wanna tell me that this is ALL fake news? Wake up, little sheeple! It's the biggest crime against an American President in history, just as Donald Trump said, and everyone who reads the real news knows this!"*

Any further questions by her nieces or nephews regarding the nature of the alleged crime apparently committed by President Obama will be countered by Aunt Becky optionally with mutterings of *"cover-ups by the deep state"*, promptings to *"go and do your own online research!"*, ominous prophesies like, *"You will see, you will all see soon enough!"*, or angry defenses like, *"Wouldn't you like to know, you little hussy! Well, if you're so clever,* you *tell* me *how there are dozens of sources on Facebook alone all confirming Obamagate if it's not true. Eh?"*

Presumably, even the Kremlin-Gremlins themselves would admit that the feat of converting *Dunning-Kruger Effect*-afflicted Aunt Becky into a true *Bullshit*-believer constitutes not necessarily a psychological masterpiece. At the bottom-line Putin's *fifth column* follows after all merely a certain Austrian master-populist's teaching on the matter who already wrote in 1925 in his infamous "oeuvre", *Mein Kampf,* (my fight; struggle; battle): *"Make the lie big, make it simple,* keep saying it, *and eventually they will believe it."*

An essential leitmotif for any ambitious populist and propagandist, having lost nothing of its unfortunate verisimilitude, as can be observed at any given day on FOX News, Sinclair-affiliated TV-stations, or on One America News Network (OANN), the fringe-broadcaster representing the peak of ridiculous Trump-partisanship in 2020. Further multipliers include talk-radio with its notoriously unhinged hosts, led by Rush Limbaugh and Alexander "Alex" Emerick

Jones, as well as tons of alt-right conspiracy websites and online-movements, all following the underlying *Illusory of Truth Effect*-rationale once penned down by the co-inventor of modern mass-manipulation over 90 years ago.

Even Hitler and Goebbels might have been surprised, alas, how flawlessly and quickly the ilk of propaganda-spreading, lies-supporting, and hatred-inciting broadcasters and platforms has become a generally accepted normalcy in such a short time since Trump's inauguration. While the vast majority of European nations and most other English-speaking countries long since have put strict regulations and a vigilant system of checks and balances in place to scotch the emergence of radically left-, or right-winged, anti-democratic, human rights-disregarding news-outlets, broadcasters, newspapers, and other media-platforms, once again the United States decided to go in the opposite direction. Resulting in a nation where such ubiquitously used and universally known words like *"Fuck"*, *"Dick"*, *"Pussy"*, or *"Tits"*, remain social taboos routinely bleeped out on television while at the same time public Hitler-salutes and *"Heil Trump!"*-cries, the derisive mocking of a disabled journalist on TV by the American President himself, or public gatherings of white-robed ultra-racists and Swastika-flag waving Neo-Nazis fall safely under the *"Freedom of Speech"*-clause.

[According to *uscourts.gov*, the First Amendment incidentally grants *"lesser or no freedom of speech-protection"* in certain categories, including *"obscenity, fraud, child pornography, speech integral to illegal conduct, speech that incites imminent lawless action, speech that violates intellectual property law, true threats, and commercial speech such as advertising".* Not included are, for instance, grave insults like the N-word, the glorification of fascism, Stalinism, or other totalitarian systems, public recruiting for organizations aiming at replacing democracy with a totalitarian system, et.al.]

America's veneration of the First Amendment presents unquestionably a gift from heaven for Putin's Kremlin Gremlins who must be thanking the Founding Fathers every day for their work and American education for the nation's infatuation with it. Not, as one might assume, because the 1st Amendment is preventing all serious controls and regulations for an effective filtering and scotching of disinformation, hate speech, and other socially divisive and disruptive messages. Although this Amendment-inherent failure presents an additional boon, it is more than likely that the *Trolls from Olgino* would find ways around such a guardian-system, as they have already proven with a far more subtle guerrilla propaganda-campaign in Germany during and after the peak of the Syrian refugee-crisis in 2015. Nor are the *IRA*-trolls grateful for the Amendment-derived absence of legal repercussions, since these would hardly give Ivan and his troll-comrades any sleepless nights as they are safely nestling among over 5 million inhabitants in Russia's second-largest metropolis, St. Petersburg.

Instead, the actual reason why members of the *IRA* are thanking the Founding Fathers every day for the First Amendment and raise their Vodka-glasses to the American habit of glamorizing anything USA, from Constitution to

American football, lies in America's attitude in regard to the evaluation of information that has always been strongly influenced by the devotion to *"Freedom of Speech"*.

Generally, American children grow up holding the belief that *"Freedom of Speech"* is sitting up there with the loftiest of American values. The fundamental right to say what you want, when you want, and to whom you want has been deeply ingrained in the American soul. In consequence, there has never been any perceived need for a democratic consensus on certain limitations for society-dividing hate speech, violence-inciting invocations, or equally peace-disrupting utterances. In short, all speech is equal before the First Amendment. This almost communist attitude leaves every American to their own devices, without any universally agreed upon guiding principles. This task is instead taken over by the individual moral compass, intellect, and education, creating a mind that is constantly attempting to pigeonhole an endless, unfiltered avalanche of news, articles, postings, messages, programs, memes, videos, podcasts, broadcasts, teachings, gossip, hearsay, and conversations.

Most Americans are nonetheless convinced that they are more than adequately equipped for this endless effort, confidently relying on their "superior" morale, knowledge, and intelligence, to effectively separate the wheat from the chaff, lie from truth, fake news from news, opinion from fact, and genuine indignation from malicious rabble-rousing. A relatable attitude, considering that the nation's elected representatives and lawmakers have made it clear from day one that they are going to stay out of any verbal firefights, quarrels, or brawls between their citizens, similar to libertine and traditionalist parents leaving the kids to *"fight it out among themselves"*.

Evidently, though, this laissez-faire attitude also increases exponentially the importance of every American's individual "mental equipment". Alas, not a few bigmouths are daily falling victim to the *Dunning-Kruger Effect,* adding to the growing mass of Americans believing themselves much more knowledgeable and intelligent than their talk and walk proves them to be. More than a healthy number of people today tend to overestimate their ability to "see through" the skilfully crafted lies and deceptions, anger-inciting "facts", and distrust-invoking, covertly racist "personal experiences" found on Facebook, FOX News, Twitter, Instagram, Reddit, and elsewhere. Moreover, when *Circular Reasoning-* or *Closed World Assumption*-based allegations are not doing the trick on their own, the *Illusion of Truth Effect* can still sneak up on the unsuspecting owner of an archetypically American "open" mind.

The general acceptance of propaganda-stations such as FOX News as a legitimate part of the media-landscape across all political lines indubitably owes much to America's infatuation with the First Amendment. And the widely spread ignorance towards these system-corroding, bad actors proves to be nothing new, as shown by FOX News' gradual movement over two decades from the fringes into the center of American politics. Moreover, the notorious Kremlin-Gremlins began to exploit the same weak underbelly of American democracy only a few years after Murdoch's Foxes and Gingrich's weasels had begun their own attacks on the system of checks and balances and the Democratic Party under the protection of *"Freedom of Speech"*. Long before the first federal watchdogs perked their ears, both anti-democratic organizations had been laying the grounds for their current, uncontrolled exertion of influence over the American people.

Whether out in the open like FOX News or clandestine like the Russian trolls of the *IRA*, the rogue players charged like bulls on steroids onto the democratic playing field, determined to disrupt any fair, lawful, and balanced competition between their selected *Manchurian Candidate* and the loathed party of Barack Obama. Armed with an abundance of lies and misinformation and making full use of the *Illusory Truth Effect,* FOX News, its copy cats at Sinclair and OANN, as well as the Grand Master of Directed Chaos, Vladimir Putin, and his troll-army, are possessing all resources necessary for continuing their long game, well knowing that many little strokes will fell even the biggest oak.

The Bigger the Turd the Better to Swallow

Since the term *Illusory Truth Effect* first appeared in a psychology-paper in the late 1970s, the effect has been extensively studied, with multiple clinical psychology experiments backing its validity. Still, a more suitable experimental environment for the verification of the *Illusory Truth Effect* than today's hermetically sealed Trump-World is hard to imagine when being such a perfect hotbed for *Selective Exposure*-practitioners. With the bubble already established, all FOX and its friends still need to do is to fill this echo-chamber with alt-right talking points, partisan opinions, alternative facts, and sycophantic praises.

By hearing the same assertions repetitively from different sources on FOX News and other trumpist news-outlets, Trumpists experience a growing assuredness in the truth of these false claims, thus falling prey to the fallacious "conclusion" that something often said by many people must be true. Once caught in the *Illusion of Truth Effect*-trap, any objective reality facts or logic reasoning will barely play any role anymore. Far from being an arbitrary subjective observation, this typical demeanor of *Illusion of Truth Effect*-victims has been scientifically documented by German psychology-professors Dr Stefan Schulz-Hardt, Georg-August Universität in Göttingen, and Dr Peter Fischer, Universität Regensburg, in their extensive study-report, "*Selective exposure and information quantity: how different information quantities moderate decision makers' preference for consistent and inconsistent information*" (J Pers, Soc Psychol. 2008, Feb.).

Herein, the psychologists conclude that it is not the argumentative quality, (logical, fact-based, proven, etc.), of a position which most convinces people of its veracity, but first and foremost, *"the quantity (amount) of decision-relevant information that the participants were exposed to"*, which, *"had a significant effect on their levels of selective exposure"*.

Schulz-Hardt and Fischer further found that, "*in situations with a very small amount of decision-consistent as well as decision-inconsistent information, individuals become more doubtful of their initial decision due to the unavailability of resources. They begin to think that there is not enough data or evidence in this particular field in which they are told to make a decision about. Because of this, the subject becomes more critical of their initial thought process and focuses on both decision-consistent and inconsistent sources, thus decreasing his level of selective exposure.*

For the group who had plentiful pieces of information, this factor made them confident in their initial decision because they felt comfort from the fact that their decision topic was well-supported by a large number of resources. Therefore, the availability of decision-relevant and irrelevant information surrounding individuals can influence the level of selective exposure experienced during the process of decision-making."

In summary, Schulz-Hardt's and Fischer's findings have led to the conclusion that, the higher the *quantity* of homogenous claims will be, the more *credible* these claims will appear to those buying into *Closed World*-argumentation. Translated into practice, any bible-thumping granny, gun-toting stepfather, MAGA-hat parading neighbor, and confederate flag-waving cousin religiously and exclusively watching opinion-makers such as FOX News' rhetoric *PirroManiac* Jeanine, *Shame* Hannity, or **ucker* Carlson, are willingly surrendering their morale, decency, and common sense, in exchange for the warm and cosy feeling of a daily fix of fresh manure engulfing their minds.

The Not So Subtle Subversion of the Soul

Metaphorically speaking, FOX News has evolved in the last five years into the Walter White (*"Breaking Bad"*) of soul-smack dealers, with disinformation-peddlers like Laura *"HydroxychloroQueen"* Ingraham, Tomi *"Teargas"* Lahren, Lou

"*I Do the Lord's Work*" Dobbs, or Corey "*Womp Womp*" Lewandowski, all vying constantly for the runner-up position behind *Shame* Hannity in the ranking of most trusted pushers of the ever same merchandise. A toxic concoction full of *Circular Reasonings, What-Aboutisms, Closed World Assumptions,* and *Arguments from Authority,* lavishly peppered with chunks of disinformation, fake news, baseless allegations, reality-benders, and occasional retcon-retractions.

The basic recipe of this vitriolic mixture will be routinely adjusted according to current events and the President's mood of the day, providing an easy to swallow dish for FOX News' *Selective Exposure*-addicted audience. By serving this endorphins-triggering "fast food" to Trumpublicans every day of the year, just as the original Austrian creator of this perfidious recipe had intended, Murdoch's minions are making perfect use of the *Illusory Truth Effect,* getting their addicts ever more hooked on their product.

Regardless whether the trumpist junkies are selecting Ingraham's impertinent incriminations, Pirro's proof-lacking propaganda pieces, Hannity's hateful hollers, or Tucker's tall tales for their fix of the day, the business-model behind FOX News' toxic content pushing compares to that of any drug-dealer. Get the clients hooked until they beg for more. It takes little time before fresh addicts will reach a point where they cannot imagine their life without the daily boost of borrowed confidence. Soon, they sit around (virtual) dumpster-fires and share their watered-down, reheated, second-hand produce, nervously waiting for the next real fix straight from the source, in the meantime hanging on to the third-grade high provided by the exchange of brain-farts while gabbling on about how the world *"finally makes sense"* thanks to their pusher's "enlightening" concoction.

Butt the string of similarities between junky and Trumpy does not end here. Just like hard drugs-addicts, also Trumpists soon need ever higher doses of their fix to experience the same level of bliss. Quickly, the few hours spend on FOX News each *Illusion of Truth*-enhancing evening, receiving their daily dose of *Selective Exposure*-content, do not do the trick anymore. Like the H-junky, the FOX News-addict begins to show increasingly irrational and aggressive behavior, wilful ignorance, and callousness. As a reaction to Trumpists' growing desire for stronger, more radical produce, the pushers at FOX News will of course comply, cranking up their vitriol's potency several notches, scratching the addicts' worst itches for a short while until a familiar urge for even more radical doses sets in.

At this stage of their addiction to *Cognitive Dissonance*-deterring, *Selective Exposure*-allowing, and *Illusion of Truth*-enhancing toxin served by the *HydroxychloroQueen* and her FOX News-colleagues, most Trumpists will have finally become devoid of their critical faculties, [i.e.: *"the ability to make judgments about what is good or true"*], allowing the mind under normal circumstances to realize its own aberrations from objective reality and to readjust accordingly. FOX-hooked Trumpists, however, will have successfully replaced any such ability with the "alternative truth".

Irrespectively of their drug of choice, whether Cocaine, Heroin, Alcohol, or FOX News-propaganda, any attempts to logically reason with veteran junkies in the hope of igniting some spark of realization regarding their errors of judgement will almost always be doomed to fail, as will anyone experienced in this matter sadly confirm. Addicts will use routinely every trick in the *Book of Lies, Deceits, and Excuses* to explain, justify, and rationalise their behavior, including *Circular Reasoning, What-Aboutisms, CWA, OWA,* and any other fallacious argumentation-tactics. At the same time, addicts will never stop their frantic search for any quotable opinion, plausible-appearing explanation, or scrap of useful information that might support their untenable position.

Unfortunately, the lethal combination of distinct *Cognitive Dissonance Avoidance*-reflex and the *Selective Exposure*-induced, rapid shrinking of the one exit back into objective reality will drive Heroin-, Crack-, or Cocaine-addicted junkies just as much as FOX News-, Sinclair-, or Facebook-addicted Trumpists always further into the claws of their pushers and the poisonous stimulant they are hawking. Whenever Trumpists are momentarily not occupied with either fleeing from some core-beliefs-threatening information or with absorbing their daily dose of comforting fabrications, they will often be found communicating with fellow addicts, mutually confirming the effectiveness ("veracity") of their drug (propaganda-"facts") they have received from the same disinformation-cartel, further boosting the *Illusory Truth Effect* to the delight of the professional subverters of these once decent souls.

≡

Ipse Dixit

"Because!"

Ipse Dixit could well be the awkward name of an alternative jazz-band of three neckbearded high-school teachers, or the medical denotation for one of the 27 tiny bones in the human hand, or the Latin name for a particularly fluffy, flightless bird exclusively found in one small valley in New Zealand.

Of course, it is nothing as exotic as that.

But at least it is a Latin phrase, constituting an ancient Roman expression that translates to, "*He himself said it*". In English, the same meaning is frequently expressed by the popular retort, "*Because I said so. Period!*" Okay, this far these are all no world-shattering pieces of information. At this point the phrase might actually serve best as one obnoxious way to tell your (here exemplary female) partner that you are done with explaining your where-abouts of last night.

P: *"Just give me one good reason why I should believe your bullshit-story, you lying, cheating bas -"*

Y: *"Hey, easy Babe! All I'm saying is* Ipse Dixit, *okay?"*

P: *"What?! Who the hell is this Ipse? And what do you mean she 'digs it'?! What the hell! You better explain yourself quickly buddy, or ..."*

On second thought, it is maybe not such a great idea to try impressing your dearest with your newly acquired knowledge of Latin. But in a different context, the *Ipse Dixit*-defense is not quite so useless and even carries some genuine weight. Matter of fact, the seemingly quippy expression constitutes an official legal term frequently used in court-cases to this day. More specifically, *Ipse Dixit* will be declared whenever a testimony of an *expert-witness* turns out to be the sole point of solid evidence the expert-employing party manages to pull out of their hat.

Like many other grandiloquent terms in Legalese, the highbrow-sounding expression *Ipse Dixit* boils down to a basic human reaction most will be familiar with at least since kindergarten. Far from being an exception, a *Ipse Dixit*-situation neatly lines up with other jurisprudence-related situations in the adult-world which can trace their origins back to playroom-squabbles and kindergarten-disputes.

One of the best-known examples for such reoccurrences represents the nowadays instantly and ubiquitously yelled threat: "*I'll call my lawyer!*" A typical adult war-cry, resembling after being stripped of its blusterous pomp no more than the average squirt's default-threat: "*I'm going to tell my mummy!*"

Similarly, then, when a lawyer or DA accuses the other side of providing a defense based merely on *Ipse Dixit,* they are pointing out the same flaw that is also apparent in any pooper's miscreant reasoning when hard-pressed to produce one good reason why mommy should believe their abstruse version of events having led to two inches of water in the living room.

In both cases, that of the expert on the court's witness-stand merely providing their personal assessment as "proof" and that of little Calvin's *Ominous Case of the Overflowing*

Bathtub, the question why their version of events is true is squarely answered with a resounding *"Ipse Dixit!"*.

Another definition of the term, in a diction more familiar to overeager law-freshmen, boomers having attended a law course in 1976, and "legal expert"-moms with a degree in *Googleology* states the following: A case of *Ipse Dixit* occurs when a disputant commits the fallacy of defending a proposition solely by declaring verbosely that *"my assertion is correct because I am the expert on this matter. Hence, there is no need for any further corroborating evidence. Please send the check to the usual address. Good day."* While court-experienced experts will in probably avail themselves of a more elaborate manner of speech, the underlying reasoning basically remains the same.

Why *Ipse Dixit*-arguments are still working in many real life-situations and even in some courts will presumably remain one of the universe's great mysteries. After all, most people rapidly outgrow their toddler-phase when "instinct" compelled them to regard dog-poop as a perfectly fine alternative to *Play-Doo*, yet as adults they still believe that the exclamation, *"Because I say so!"*, is holding all the water necessary for deciding life-altering or even life-ending court-cases.

For obvious reasons, such a convenient and universally applicable killer-argument like the *Ipse Dixit*-claim cannot remain exclusive to the realm of jurisdiction. Most likely, you have already been at the receiving end of more than one *Ipse Dixit*-argument. Remember, for instance, that pig-headed boss, foreman, floorwalker, or senior colleague you had the misfortune to work with who pulled the *Ipse Dixit*-card each time s/he wanted to gag a hapless employee "challenging" their micro-ego? Their *Ipse Dixit* usually went like this: *"Who do you think you are, Bob? No, you're not here to think! You're here to follow my orders! Around here we do things the way I say they're done! And you know why, Bob? Because! I! Say! So!"*. In short, *"Ipse fucking Dixit, Bob!"*

§

"Just remember, what you are seeing and what you are reading is not what's happening." – Donald J. Trump, July 24, 2018, at a Veterans of Foreign Wars Convention.

Should you have been fortunate enough to have never encountered this specimen of entitled superior or colleague then there is still one other way to experience the world's leading *Ipse-Dixiter* at work. Just switch on your TV. Some channel will surely feature the tiny-handed man who elevated the *"Because I say so!"*-kindergarten tactic to a whole new level of political claptrap.

"Because!"-toddler-in-chief Donny Trump is offering countless examples for his use of the *Ipse Dixit*-argument. Take his ridiculous stories of "chance encounters" with ordinary citizens, military men, or government officials, for instance, who he likes to "quote" in his stories as talking to him with an abundance of interspersed "Sirs", letting any erstwhile Southern slaveholder appear liberal in comparison. Naturally, only his deluded acolytes believe these stories to be true,

while the other 65% can only shake their heads at the charade of a man-baby thinking of himself as a manipulative genius who dupes the world with his *"It's true because I said so!"*-shenanigans.

Another instance saw Trump's defense of the *"incredible people"* and *"patriots"* attending his rally in Greenville, N.C., on July 17, 2019. On this day, Trump egged the crowd on with several false allegations concerning U.S.-Congresswoman Ilhan Omar, until the mob began to holler the racist chant *"Send her back! Send her back!"*, with the Somali-born U.S.-American lawmaker as their unmistakable target.

When later asked why he didn't stop the openly racist chant instantly, instead having stepped back from the lectern to allow the crowd to repeat the slandering slogan a dozen times, Trump fell back on his default-tactic of brazenly lying without blushing: *"I started speaking very quickly!"*. Inconveniently for Trump, the incident had been recorded by several news stations, making it easy to count the seconds between the start of the racist chants and the moment Trump finally began to speak again over the thundering noise of the frenetic mob. The count revealed, that the mass-manipulator bathed in his base's racist hollering for a full 13 seconds and if you believe this to be a short time just count out the seconds yourself, beginning with *Twenty-one, Twenty-two, Twenty-three,* and so on ... ... until *Thirty-three.*

No matter what planet you are from, this timespan will only be regarded as *"very quickly"* by someone regularly ingesting *Adderall®* against his *Attention Deficit Hyperactivity*

Disorder (ADHD) and *narcolepsy* problem. Everyone else will have enough time to shout approximately 13 times *"Heil Hitler!"* or 12 chants of *"Send her back!"* Of course, when confronted with the indisputable evidence on tape, Trump simply relied once again on the power of his presidential *Ipse Dixit!* to miraculously turn his easily debunkable claim into another "truth", claiming bluntly that if he had said *"very quickly"*, then it must have been *"very quickly"*. Period.

The amount of unfounded and nefariously false claims made by the 45th president over his 4 years in office long since crossed the ten-thousand line, qirh most of these lies solely backed by Trump's own *Ipse Dixit* or variations of his preferred *Ipse Dixit by proxy*, such as, *"A lot of people say …"*, *"Many people say …"*, or, *"There are many stories about …"*.

After Trump's Greenville-attack on the four U.S.-Congresswomen of color known jointly as *The Squad,* (Representatives Tlaib, Ocasio-Cortez, Omar, and Pressley), when hollering: *"They're always telling us how to run* [the country]… *you know, if they don't love it, tell'em to leave it!"*, the political arsonist-in-chief doubled down on his racist rhetoric by tweeting on July 22, 2019: *"The Squad is a very Racist group of troublemakers who are young, inexperienced and not very smart."* Making it at the very latest there and then utterly impossible to refute the assessment that the President of the United States is a racist, if there had still been any doubts after Trump's election-victory had been wholeheartedly endorsed by hard-line nationalist Hungarian leader Viktor Orbán, Marine Le Pen of the far-right French

Front National party, and *The Crusader,* the official newspaper of the Ku Klux Klan.

Unfathomably, *Ipse Dixit*-junky Trump believed himself extremely "clever" when calling some of the least racist people in Congress *"a very Racist group"*, convinced that this label would stick by his *Ipse Dixit*-magic alone and moreover, that no one would notice his toddler-level attempt to divert from his many racist utterances.

Trump relentlessly demands from supporters and the world to *"Believe me! Believe you me!"*, while all "proof" for his public declarations of "loving all non-white races" is on his *Ipse Dixit* alone. Actually, by stating to the press at the White House on July 30, 2019, *"I'm the least racist person there is anywhere in the world"*, Donald Trump genuinely seemed to believe this *Ipse Dixit* to have been sufficient for shelving the question of a racist president for good.

The same president who accused Mexican immigrants wholesale of being *"rapists"* on the very first day of his campaign also told his base at a rally in October 2018 in Houston, *"You know what I am? I'm a nationalist, okay? I'm a nationalist. Nationalist! Use that word! Use that word!"*, and furthermore enacted the infamous *Muslim-Ban*, called COVID-19 the *"Kung Flu"*, insinuated that the judge in the Trump University-case ruled against him because *"He's a Mexican"*, and defended the murder of two *Black Lives Matter*-protesters. According to Trump and his Press Secretary, all this and much more still does not provide any "evidence" that the American President is a full-blown racist. After all, he has repeatedly stated that he is not a racist. *Ipse Dixit.*

"The doctrine of blind obedience and unqualified submission to any human power, whether civil or ecclesiastical, is the doctrine of despotism." – Angelina Emily Grimké

Behind the rather naïve reasoning of many presidential _Ipse Dixit_-adhering Trumpists oft lies the ingrained belief in the infallibility of higher authorities, accompanied by a reflexive subservience to such power-wielding figures. This demeanor usually has been instilled at an early age, starting with the first fire-and-brimstone sermons to the young church-goers, the first parental slaps in the face or belt to the butt, the first send-offs to bed without dinner, and the first severe verbal bashings administered by teacher, parents, priest, trainer, or any other of the many "betters" letting the impressionable young minds know where their natural place in God's ordained hierarchy has been determined to be.

Parents embracing die-hard conservatism, religious fundamentalism, strict hierarchies, and long-held traditions are more prone than most to teach their offspring from the cradle not to question, contradict, or refuse their superiors, (parents, family-members, clergy, teachers, policemen, et.al.), with this attitude becoming even further ingrained whenever these superiors find themselves at their wit's end and revert to the _Ipse Dixit_, viz _"Because I say so!"_, alternatively, _"Because that's how it's done here!"_; _"Because if you don't obey, you'll get the belt again!"_; _"Because your betters know better!"_; or _"Because it is God's will!"_

When the unquestioning acceptance of the *Ipse Dixit-*, aka *"Because I say so!"*-argument has been firmly drilled into the young mind, the doctrine will usually remain there as an unchallenged concept for the rest of life, frequently leading to adults suffering from severe *Bicycle-Rider Syndrome*, i.e. keeping one's back nicely bent to those above one's own station while kicking constantly down at those situated beneath oneself. Most *Bicycle-Riders* would love nothing more than to escape this unhealthy position rather sooner than later, naturally. Alas, the only way most bucking/kicking primates seem to come up with for getting out of the destructive situation appears to be climbing up and reaching the top of the monkey-tree. Up here on the highest branch, the incessant need to bend the back and take shit from above is presumed to cease at last all attention can then be focussed on what tree-top monkeys have done from times immemorial, that is kicking down and defecating on those below still riding the *Bicycle*.

In the damned *Bicycle*-position and with a good chance to never reach the top of the tree, the "comforting" explanation that this bleak fate is God's will and plan, and coincidentally also that of the community-leaders, will only provide true comfort if met with unquestioning belief in the "Highest Authority", as well as "His" spokespersons down hither. Again, *Ipse Dixit* saves the day, albeit not most people's hopes and dreams.

Incidentally, as a recommendation for anyone done with being "comforted" this way, some *Reddit*-subgroups including r/atheism; r/HumansBeingBros; r/Political_Revolution;

r/legaladvice; or r/*The_Mueller* will genuinely boost your hopes for a brighter future with reason and compassion prevailing over the currently ubiquitous tendencies of wilful ignorance, fear-driven hatred, and malicious attacks. The sheer amount of compassionate, supportive comments in answer to often heartrending experiences reported on *r/raisedbynarcissists* alone can provide anyone despairing of the situation in the United States and the world with a healthy dose of brotherly/sisterly love and compassion and will restore at least some trust in humanity's inherent goodness. But also in a broader perspective there have already been genuinely encouraging changes, particularly the unstoppable withering away of many so-called traditions and beliefs still desperately defended by the reactionary right, for instance:

- *"Women belong in the kitchen."*
- *"Atheists are in league with the Devil."*
- *"Children should be seen and not heard."*
- *"Homosexuality is a disease."*
- *"Guns don't kill people, people kill people."*
- *"It is man's God-given right to subdue the Earth and exploit it."*
- *"Medical removal of a pea-sized cell-lump is murder."*
- *"A raped woman usually provoked it."*
- *"Vaccines cause autism."*
- *"Social benefits are socialist inventions to end America.",*
  Etc., pp.

Although often with the velocity of a tired sloth, these obsolete beliefs are nonetheless destined to spiral down mankind's waste chute and onto history's dung-heap, joining other reactionary notions already dumped decades ago, such as banning women's suffrage, criminalizing homosexuality, the segregation of races, and government's unjust ability to deny its population affordable, universal health care, paid parental leave, and an adequate number of paid leave days.

Hang on …

Okay, slight correction. Universal health care, paid parental leave, and paid leave days, while indeed normalcies in Canada, Australia, New Zealand, China, Russia, and all European countries, are actually far from being reality in the United States under President Trump. No group in the U.S., with a possible exception of the post-2020 Democratic Party, appears able to muster enough power to overcome the shadowy forces opposing these and other citizen *rights* and preventing America from being finally on equal footing with the rest of the industrialized, democratic world.

Trumpists who have swallowed Trump's *Ipse Dixit* hook, line, and sinker, continue to believe social benefits to be a socialist attack on the American Way of Life, therefore being more than happy to stick with their *Emperor without Clothes* no matter how detrimental the deep-fried septuagenarian's policies are to their own well-being, prosperity, and the safe and healthy future of their children. Point of evidence: When the president as "the ultimate expert on all things American" opined that facemasks are unnecessary, will make him look "weak", and are potentially even harmful, it was all it took for "patriotic" Trumpists to roundly reject the vile, "unamerican" contraptions.

"Who's to say who's an expert?" – Paul Newman

This human idiosyncrasy to follow a presumedly "strong leader" all the way to and over the edge of the cliff in bright daylight despite all warning signs on the way will remain a spiky pebble in the humanity's shoe during our uphill struggle towards a future devoid of any blind obedience to populists and subjugation to autocrats and replaced by a prevailing sense of compassion, equal justice, and universal equality. Exactly how long and winding this road will be before reaching this waypoint by democratic and humanistic societies will depend a great deal on how much the team of progressive, forwards-striving thinkers will allow itself to be dragged down by reactionary, right-wing albatrosses around its necks.

As history proves, most ground-breaking societal changes come in two variations. They either happen nearly overnight with outbreaks of revolutions, wars, natural disasters, and pandemics, or they move with the speed of a glazier in winter, going through all necessary and unnecessary official channels while demanding superhuman patience and tenacity from their backers.

It remains to be seen whether Corona-Crisis and *Black Lives Matter*-protests in 2020 will fall into the first category or whether these igniters of social change will ultimately become bogged down by the public's short attention span, further accommodating a conservative establishment and its complacent servants in the bureaucracy. While some tentative optimism seems not completely out of place, only the middle- and long-term ramifications of the Great Upheaval around the globe in 2020 will provide a substantial answer to the question of those changes' ultimate success.

As is so often the case, smaller yet equally important changes will be easily overlooked in the shadow of such big stories as the "Awakening of the National Conscience" in the wake of George Floyd's murder. In actual fact, one decisive change that considerably weakens the notion of blind trust and belief in assertions of expert-authorities has come about in the American Courtroom with the severe curtailing of the *Ipse Dixit*-argument.

While probably still alive in the minds of many law-show viewers, the idea of an expert-witness deciding single-handedly a court-case from the witness stand due only to his expert status has been limited to the realm of outdated TV-fiction for some years now, with U.S.-courts nowadays being well forearmed against attempts of resting the burden of proof solely on any *Ipse Dixit*-argumentation. The origins of this substantial shift in legal courtroom-procedure can be traced back further than might be expected. As early as in the late 1990s lawyers everywhere had become considerably tired of having their cases predominantly decided on the grounds of some expertise by a sacrosanct professional expert. In the early 2000s ever more law-professionals had then begun to criticize this practice of presenting the court with luminaries in their respective fields, from forensic psychology and forensic dental comparison, (today a roundly debunked "forensic method"), to specialized experts on particular topics such as the manufacturing and sizes of leather driving-gloves.

Nobody appears to know exactly when the famous last straw finally broke the lawyers' backs nor where it happened. But at least one can speculate on how the decisive event had been unfolding in which *Ipse Dixit* – the unsubstantiated power of appointed experts to decide over the lives of countless accused –finally got reigned in.

Perhaps it was a fine winter-evening in a mahogany-adorned backroom of a private lawyers-club on Manhattan's Upper East Side where a group of influential senior lawyers, attorneys, and judges had assembled to deal once and for all with the *Ipse Dixit*-problem and the inflationary employment of expert-witnesses. Following a lengthy discussion over some fine Single Malt Whisky and Cuban cigars, a particularly venerable old judge will then have called a vote, and all but a couple of lobbyist-lawyers had agreed to strip the caste of professional expert-witnesses of their substantial sinecures, inappropriate influence, and undeserved fame. Afterwards, they had toasted each other with a 30 years old *Macallan Sherry Oak* before separately slipping out into the chilly New York night, and the rest is history. Either it happened like this, or an unsung hero had charged ahead and the whole legal profession happily followed suit. If so, cheers to this hero or heroine.

In any case, today most U.S.-judges are considering argumentations to be problematically *Ipse Dixit,* when a party presents the court with "*arguments based solely upon the authority of an individual or organization*", and are usually reacting far more sceptical to such an *Argument from Authority* than in the *good old days.*

It might therefore come as a bit of a surprise to ardent followers of courtroom-dramas like *Law & Order,* that in modern courts rarely will the doors of the courtroom fly open at the last minute to admit an elderly, slightly crackpot-looking professor who for the first time in over forty years has come down from his ivory tower to rescue a young girl from a certain death penalty. This is because the U.S.-Supreme Court recognized in 1997 the existence of the very real problem of *"opinion evidence which is connected to existing data only by the Ipse Dixit of an expert"* and the Texas Supreme Court made in the same year unambiguously clear that, *"a claim will not stand or fall on the mere Ipse Dixit of a credentialed witness."*

But as commendable as the U.S.-legal system's crack-down on the practice of allowing expert-witnesses' *Ipse Dixit* as main evidence appears, another even more pressing *Ipse Dixit*-problem remains unsolved. Just around the corner of the courthouse and safely out of sight of Lady Justice's watchful blind eyes, in the corridors and offices of local, state, and federal government-buildings the dishonest use of *Ipse Dixit* is very much alive and kicking.

Who will not remember how Germophobe-in-Chief Trump continued to rely on the power of his presidential *Ipse Dixit,* long after his increasingly incoherent assurances that the U.S. will be swatting the Coronavirus like a pesky fly had become a bad joke shared around the world. While most believed Trump to be merely clueless, however, it turned out that the narcissistic President knew all along about the deadliness of COVID-19 while publicly downplaying the threat. 125,000 dead Americans at the end of June. Almost 200,000 dead Americans in mid-September 2020. While the U.S. had become the global leader in infection-cases, Donald J. Trump continued his *Ipse Dixit* in increasingly desperate attempts to downplay ("*I still like to play it down!*") not only the dangers of the Coronavirus but also his disastrous incompetence, hubris, wilful ignorance, egotism, and idiocy accompanying him from the first day of the Corona crisis.

Donald J. Trump on January 22: "*We have it totally under control. It's one person coming in from China. It's going to be just fine.*"

On February 24: "*The Coronavirus is very much under control in the USA. Stock market starting to look very good to me.*" - [Known Corona-cases in the U.S. on this day: 53]

February 26: "*The 15 cases in the US within a couple of days is going to be down to close to zero.*"

February 27: "*One day it's like a miracle, it will disappear.*"

March 2: "*A lot of things are happening, a lot of very exciting things are happening, and they are happening very rapidly.*" - [Known Corona-cases in the U.S. that day: 100]

March 6: "*I think we're doing a very good job in this country at keeping it down. A tremendous job at keeping it down.*" - [Known Corona-cases in the U.S.: 319]

March 8: "*We have a perfectly coordinated and fine-tuned plan at the White House for our attack on Coronavirus.*" - [Known Corona-cases in U.S.: 541]

March 9: "*This blindsided the world.*" - [Known Corona-cases in U.S.: 704]

March 13: *"I don't take responsibility at all."* - [Known Corona-cases: 2,247]

April 06: *"So the media likes to say we have the most cases, but we do, but we do, by far, the most testing. If we did very little testing, we wouldn't have the most cases. So, in a way, by doing all of this testing, we make ourselves look bad."* - [Known Corona-cases: 332,308]

June 23: *"I say, 'What's the 19? Covid-19. Some people can't explain what the 19 … […] Some people call it the Chinese Flu, the China Flu, right? They call it the China … […] Wuhan - Wuhan was catching on. […] Kung Flu, yeah."* - [Known Corona-cases in U.S.: 2,328,562]

It has become the "new normal" for Americans to see the United States government justify its rambling leader's easily disprovable lies, dangerous decisions, and demented utterings time and again by distorting reality, (*"He was clearly joking."*), or by simply insisting on the "automatic validity" of the presidential *Ipse Dixit*. Occasionally, the regime's professional propagandists left it to "authorities" like VP Mike Pence (*"Mike is going to be in charge."* – Donald J. Trump), Secretary of Health and Human Services Alex Azar, or other members of Pence's "Corona Task Force" to back up Trump's *Ipse Dixits* with their own *Quia Sic Dixit,* ("Because *he* said so!"), following the lead of other mouthpieces ready to hop in front of the bus for Trump, like Sebastian Gorka, Mark Levin, Lou Dobbs, or Alan Dershowitz.

Predictably, Trump's *Ipse Dixit* and his sycophants' *Quia Sic Dixit*-strategy will continue to work well with the 35% of Americans holding U.S.-politics hostage since January of 2017.

But what once had been merely a threat looming on the horizon in January 2020 had turned into an unimaginable national catastrophe by fall of the same year. Next to the Trumpministration's undeniably management-failure in the Corona-pandemic, America owes its dismal world-record of Corona-deaths partially to the Dear Leader himself, who had assured his base in February 2020 that the Coronavirus was defeated, (*"We're going very substantially down, not up"*, Trump, February 26, 2020), and that infectious Americans should continue to go to work, (*"If we have thousands or hundreds of thousands of people that get better just by, you know, sitting around and even going to work – some of them go to work but they get better"*, Donald J. Trump, March 4, 2020), while also taking a public stance against facemasks, gathering thousands of supporters in indoor-arenas like in Tulsa, Oklahoma, and subsequent public events.

While Trump and his White House staff had been tested daily for the virus, with positive cases being immediately isolated, the autocratic populist continued to publicly downplay the infection-risks and dangers of COVID-19 in an extremely irresponsible if not criminal manner, (*"One day, it's like a miracle, it will disappear"*, Donald J. Trump, February 28, 2020), while being aware of the deadly dangers SARS-CoV-2 poses from the very beginning of the pandemic. (*"You just breathe the air and that's how it's passed. And so that's a very tricky one. That's a very delicate one. It's also more deadly than even your strenuous flus. This is deadly stuff"*, Donald J. Trump to Bob Woodward, February 7, 2020).

When Woodward's book *"Rage"*, (first published September 15, 2020, Simon & Schuster), revealed the 45th

President's irresponsible duplicity, Trump – who claimed to have read the book in one night (sic) - once again fell back on his presidential *Ipse Dixit* when asserting that he had merely wanted to prevent *"a panic"*. Simultaneously, Trump used every public opportunity for alluding to the "recovery" of the stock market, the one subject appearing to have been genuinely of interest to the conman-cum-president. (*"So, you think the virus totally supersedes the economy?"* [...] *"But the economy is doing — look, we're close to a new stock market record"*, Trump to Woodward, August 14, 2020).

While the average fourth-grader had little problems seeing through the Great Pretender's *Ipse Dixit*-supported lies during his Corona press-conferences even before Bob Woodward's stunning answer to the question, *"What did the President know and when did he know it?"*, Trumpists willingly swallowed every "downplaying" lie and "patriotic" call for perseverance by the self-professed *"Cheerleader"* (sic) for America.

Trumpists like Twitter-user Katie, who tweeted in reply to an AOC-tweet on March 14, 2020: *"I just went to a crowded Red Robin and I'm 30. It was delicious, and I took my sweet time eating my meal. Because this is America. And I'll do what I want."*

Or like the father of Mark Joseph, who shared this story on Twitter: *"My dad just reiterated that we are going to be fine because we 'got ahead of the curve' by Trump shutting travel down 'before it gets here'. I told him it's here. He said it's all a media hoax and this is all what living under socialism would be like."*

Or like Stacy, tweeting the same day of March 14, 2020, *"It doesn't matter what the President or some PSA says. The triggered libs will run to the ER because they are all freaked out. The media has done quite a number on them."*

Mark Joseph's father, Katie, Stacy, and millions of likeminded Trumpists indubitably lack the mental capacity to grasp the seriousness of the circumstances that make facemasks, social distancing, and other containment-measures vitally necessary for the survival of as many fellow Americans as humanly possible. Instead, the red-hatted "freedom fighters" continue to gleefully ridicule social distancing-advocates and mask-wearers, believing apparently that such preventative measures are meant to protect *them* from the virus, (*"No mask! As an American I have the freedom to make my own decisions. And when I die, I die. Simple as that."*), not even considering the possibility that facemasks might actually keep the virus from infecting older, chronically ill, and immune-compromised compatriots.

The sheer magnitude of the odd right's wilful ignorance, callousness, and indifference towards their fellow men finds their ideal catalyst in narcissist Donald J. Trump and his most brownnosed sycophants like FOX News' Sean Hannity, gladly providing Trump with a platform for all his *Ipse Dixit*-lies. For instance, when Trump called Hannity live on air on March 4, 2020, allowing millions of FOX News-viewers to hear Trump denying the World Health Organisation's (WHO) official Coronavirus death-rate publication and subsequently in all seriousness explaining that his assessment is exclusively based on *"a hunch"*. Further ramblings that night included Trump calling the Coronavirus *"Corona flu"*, comparing COVID-19 with *"the regular flu"*, and once more strongly suggesting that SARS-CoV-2-infected people should best go back to work.

With the power of the presidential *Ipse Dixit* behind him, Donald Trump then found also less than zero skepticism among Trumpalumpas, Trumpanzees, and Trumpettes regarding his barrage of unfounded allegations, fallacious assertions, erroneous claims, and straight lies during his televised Address to the Nation on the evening of March 11, 2020, the aftermath of which having been characterized by massive global confusion, irritations, and panic-reactions as well as a brief surge of ultimately unwarranted hopes.

During his infamous address from behind the *Resolute Desk*, President Donald J. Trump asserted, for example, that insurance companies will cover the treatment of COVID-19 free of charge, instantly lifting the heavy hearts of millions of Americans. Alas, the nationwide gasp of relief lasted just about as long as an average Trump rally-speech before government officials hurriedly retracted Trump's allegation, hastily clarifying that insurance companies had merely agreed to Coronavirus-*testing* without co-pay.

Only a few minutes after this first bombastic lie in the guise of relief had exploded in America's living rooms, the highest political authority in the land starred into the camera, right eye shut, and fired off another bombshell, triggering instantly the next surge of adrenaline shooting through the veins of millions of Americans employed in international trade. Without discernible signs of doubt, Donald Trump announced the implementation of new punitive tariffs and trade-limitations which, *"will not only apply to the tremendous amount of trade and cargo, but various other things as we get approval. Anything coming from Europe to the United States is what we are discussing."* While countless Americans and Europeans on both sides of the Atlantic were seeing themselves in the blink of an eye confronted with the dark spectre of reductions in salary, company foreclosures, job losses, and long-term unemployment, long-suffering White House officials were desperately preparing an official retraction of President Trump's nonsense-claim and had it published within the hour.

A couple of minutes later, President Trump's third strike of the night finally managed to create outright panic. Tens of thousands of Americans on holiday or business-trips all over Europe had to believe themselves suddenly stranded in their respective European host-country after the obese overlord in Washington had just told the world that, *"we will be suspending all travel from Europe to the United States for the next 30 days. The new rules will go into effect Friday at midnight. [...]. There will be exemptions for Americans who have undergone appropriate screenings."* Reason enough for countless, understandably panicking Americans in Europe to rush immediately to the closest airport, only to find themselves then tightly jammed together in large crowds, filling the enclosed spaces in unprepared airports and creating the perfect petri dish for the Coronavirus that had in March of 2020 only just begun its deadly victory parade around the globe. Just one more care- and thoughtlessly uttered false allegation that had dripped from the flabby lips of the man who would later that year defend his prolonged silence on the deadliness of SARS-CoV-2 in dead earnest with the intention to *"avoid a panic"*.

Such magnitude can the destructive power of an authority's *Ipse Dixit* reach that it will forever change the destinies, futures, and lives of millions in the blink of an eye. Variations of *"Because I say so!"* kicked off wars, toppled kings, sparked revolutions, and more often than not enabled brazen and audacious loudmouths to flop their flabby asses on the throne, only to subsequently rule by *Ipse Dixit*. Donald Trump's enlightening Freudian slip of talking about *"herd mentality"* instead of "herd immunity" at an ABC town hall-event on September 15, 2020, involuntarily prompts the question of the remaining validity of the ancient wisdom that you can fool all the people some of the time and some of the people all of the time but never all of the people all of the time.

Unquestionably, the end of the Trump-presidency will not bring about the end of the far-right and its *"herd mentality"* that has proven to be so ideally receptive to *Ipse Dixits*. All it might actually need for the then headless herd to start collectively bleating new variations of *"Lock her up!"*, or *"Make America great again, again!"* (sic), would be another appropriately brazen and insolent *Ipse Dixiter* conducting the odd right's latest chants, hate-speeches, and violent actions. In this sense, the approx. 65 million Trumpists and Trumpublicans are in actual fact constituting a tightly homogenous herd comprised of "all the people" cast in the same mold, leading ultimately to the conclusion that you can indeed "fool all the people all of the time", after all.

Arguments from Authority

"Yes, Sir!"

O

"The necessity of believing without knowledge, nay often upon very slight grounds, in this fleeting state of action and blindness we are in, should make us more busy and careful to inform ourselves than constrain others."
– John Locke, English philosopher and physician,
1632-1704

All things considered, it is hard to deny that all our firmest beliefs are ultimately based on one fundamental, life-shaping decision made early on in life. In fact, this moment of acceptance occurs so soon after birth that it involves by nature no conscious deliberation. In turn indicating that every toddler's apparently intuitive acceptance of so-called higher authorities, (initially most often represented by parents), as well as a similarly effortless sufferance of these authorities' powers have always come naturally to the species of homo sapiens.

However, this initially near universal, unresisting acceptance of higher authorities' superiority also continues to be a powerful tool in the box of conmen, populists, and authoritarians alike. Yet, all warnings such as philosopher John Locke's abovementioned cautioning, voiced in the 17th century – (paraphrased: *'Rushing blindly through our lives, we often believe something without knowing the full picture.*

Instead of making such blind belief, our reason for constraining others i.e. our lack of knowledge should instead rather prompt us become better informed.') – have borne no lasting fruits until today.

Whether authority comes naturally or by election, has been inherited, violently appropriated, wrangled, asserted, or peacefully handed over, once a person or group has obtained a position of authority there will be people bowing to it, with an increase in followers directly translating into an increase in power for the person of authority. It is this power, derived from man's natural tendency to submit to a greater power combined with the "magnetic" effect authoritative power exerts over the less powerful that constitutes the base of all *Arguments from Authority.*

::: *A Life between Freedoms and Fetters*

As soon as they brabble their first words, most squirts instinctively sense that grown-ups are not only bigger and stronger but, in most cases, also know better while usually having the toddler's best interests at heart. As teenagers, the same kids often begin to rebel against parental authority, having outgrown the childish belief in Dad's and Mom's once blindly accepted "omnipotence". Additionally, during the period of metamorphosis colloquially named *puberty*, teenagers begin to become aware of the genuinely infinite amount of knowledge and experience potentially to be gathered and to collect their own first shares. Without prior experience and a lack of comparable situations, however, many teens tend to overestimate their abilities and knowledge and consequentially consider themselves more knowledgeable and capable than they objectively are at this age. On top of it, nature has intended for human younglings to go through an important phase of rebellion against their personal "dictators" in order to test their own strengths, limitations, and capabilities and to subsequently begin their own lives, often initiated by a sudden urge to finally flee the nest and spread their own wings.

Alas, usually reality is quickly catching up with young people in their early 20s. At the latest when entering the job-market and moving into the first own apartment - accompanied by the first bills for rent, water, electricity, WLAN, Netflix®, car instalments, and expenses for groceries and other stuff that had in the past always simply "been there", like dish soap, toilet paper, napkins, candles, cutlery, washing powder, or bedsheets - the time has come when young professionals realize, sometimes the hard way, that adult-society constitutes foremost a maze of freedom-confining laws, rules, prohibitions, duties, and regulations to be disrespected at one's own peril.

The average tween is therefore doomed to spend quite some time acquainting themselves with all the different higher authorities doing apparently not much else but issuing new rules and enforcing existing ones. Luckily, this experience generally goes hand in hand with the development of a deeper understanding for the necessity of (most of) these regulations and for why they are (mostly) beneficial to the law-abiding individual as well as to a peaceful and functioning human cohabitation.

With the 30th birthday come and gone, the majority of youngish citizens has become accustomed to the intricate power-structure permeating every aspect of social life, having now internalized which rules apply when and where and how to make them work in one's favor. At this point, an estimated 95% of people has also made their peace with being subject to the wills, words, and whims of higher authorities deriving their powers from the public to guarantee society's smooth running.

During their Thirties, many citizens will have also gotten their own first taste of power as minor (or major) authority in their jobs. In a not entirely voluntary trade-off, however, the eagerness of younger years to protest and fight against power-abusing elites and for a more fair, just, and sustainable world will noticeably diminish and be replaced by growing disillusionment, forced realism, and the onset of exhaustion. Now, every waking minute will be dedicated to the perpetual chase for money, necessary for maintaining the kind of lifestyle deemed appropriate by the same elites once having been so clearly identified as the "natural enemy". Slowly it dawns on the working man and woman that they are not merely subject to the elected and installed authorities of their nation, state, county, city, district, and town, but furthermore that their lives are also constantly nudged in one direction or the other by their higher-ups at the workplace, at the tennis or book club, in the street's neighborhood, on the children's school board, and even in the wider family, including in-laws. And as if this would not already be enough pressure from all sides, however, modern society adds another layer of manipulators constantly vying for the individual's attention and money, from advertising companies, celebrities, the music-industry and Hollywood to insurance-companies, car-manufacturers, online-providers, oil-companies, and every other entity wielding a modicum of authority over the average citizen's personal freedoms.

Once having survived the turbulent Thirties, a majority of lower-, and middle-class Americans will now be more than ready to permanently "settle down". The children will be at least somewhat able to look after themselves, the job has become routine, bills are usually paid on time, and the annual summer-holiday at the same location has been booked for the next five years in advance. At this point in their Forties, most people usually will have also reached the peak of their personal authority-potential and are now either safely on the express-way "to the very top" in the next few years or have arrived at the highest possible rung of the ladder as head of department, regional manager, group-leader, executive secretary, foreman, or happily self-employed business owner. Being an integral part of the status quo makes any thoughts about protesting and fighting "the authorities" a thing reserved for mellow Sunday afternoons on the couch with a shared joint.

But being part of the establishment has indubitably also its perks, since most believed-to-be "safe" positions in the Big Clockwork come with a certain level of authority to be exerted with experience-derived confidence. The same experience now enables the authority-midget to suss out the optimal way to tap into the power of some authority-heavyweights. Consequentially, in the Forties and Fifties political parties, interest groups, charities, NGOs, and political movements suddenly become interesting once more, although in contrast to the rebellious teen- and tween-years, now the focus lies decidedly more on the personal advantages they can offer and much less on any "lofty" objectives to create a better world.

Accordingly, the car-salesman joins a party supporting lower gas-prices, the farmer campaigns for the candidate promising higher subsidies, the helicopter-mom gets involved in local politics to keep her neighborhood "family-friendly", and the business-owner donates lavishly to any anti-union senator, true to the age-old motto of all disillusioned, self-proclaimed realists, *"If you can't beat them, join them."*

But while it rarely turns out to be detrimental to one's own interests being on first-name terms with the town's sheriff, chief of police, judge, physician, pastor, priest, or head-teacher, such local dignitaries are nonetheless all lacking the ability to provide middle-aged "realists" with any direct means to get their hands on the literal jackpot, aka *"mo' money!"* . Here, politicians clearly have the upper hand and more to offer. Despite their oft-apparent lack of any valuable skills, talents, experience, or knowledge, the species of professional politicians can therefore also confidently claim to lead the list of most bribed, fawned over, admired, despised, envied, and thus most powerful professionals in society.

Realizing this fact not merely in a theoretical manner, as one is prone to do in college, but in practical and very personal terms as a long-established trooper in one's business and member of the community, will at the very latest now with 50+ years cement one's oft cynical yet resigned opinion of the general state of affairs in society and its authorities.

Incidentally, at this stage in life particularly men develop a tendency to adopt more conservative views, increasingly so the older they become. Presumably, the origins of this progressing mental ossification are to be found in the conservative's growing realization that his own power is dwindling, leading to this attempt of appropriating a higher authority's undisputed power, turning for instance to assumedly strong leaders, a law-and-order party, a radical right-wing movement, certain "respected" gangs, groups, or militias, or to a church, cult, or sect. These covert or open attempts by middle-aged and older men to "borrow" a smidgen of power from such "authorities" frequently come in tandem with a growing fetish for team sports and their "battles" on field or court, as well as with a fascination for all types of firearms and hours-long prattling about "manly" topics from guns to girls, from engines to eczemas.

Admittedly, above sketched "average course of life" has been painted with an excessively broad brush. Still, while there doubtlessly exist as many individual, unpredictable, exciting, joyful, and enjoyable lives as there are people living them, the fundamental nature of the direct and indirect influence higher authorities exert on any individual's life permeates civilized society to such an all-encompassing degree that its sheer ubiquity renders it invisible in everyday life.

The transition from initially being subject to the first authorities in one's life, such as parents, teachers, coaches, pastors, etc. to later becoming a law-abiding citizen accepting higher authorities governing one's life usually occurs seamlessly. Not least because somewhere along the line most people realize that the alternative, viz a society in which authorities are disrespected, disregarded, or dismissed would have a quite limited lifespan. The anarchic pipe dream of a world without authorities would in fact turn rapidly into a dystopian nightmare, with the law of the jungle ruling supreme. In such a world, anyone too weak, too sick, too old, too young, too small, or too decent to bow to ruthless and unscrupulously violent leaders would quickly disappear without a trace. Unquestionably, man's (willing or grudging) submission to higher authorities, perpetually inoculated by the ones who came before to guarantee the frictionless continuation of civilized society, has contributed its share to preventing an alternative reality where humanity would live, if at all, in a postapocalyptic world not unlike that of *The Walking Dead*.

::: *The Chink in the Armor*

Considering such a *Walking Dead*-alternative it seems obvious that any civilized society needs to rely on higher authorities to wield their powers over the populace to guarantee a safe, stable, and functioning community. Book closed, end of discussion. Right?

Of course not. Only reactionary die-hards will believe that anyone who feels uncomfortable with a porous checks and balances-system incapable of controlling higher authorities such as sycophantic Attorney Generals, shady Supreme Court-judges, lawless and brutal police-forces, and a racially biased justice system, automatically falls into the category of *"unpatriotic rabble-rousers, punks, anarchists, communists, and all-out destructive elements who need to be dealt with swiftly and in no uncertain ways by the proper authorities!"*.

In truth, an overwhelming majority of citizens suspicious of potential power-abuse by elected and appointed authorities stays safely away from any aggressive, politically motivated actions. At the end of the day, trust in the functionality of The System still outweighs any unease felt at yet another blatant abuse of power. In consequence, alas, the ingrained belief in the autoimmune-capabilities of the System and its authorities has led many citizens to buying into one of the biggest cases of mass-*Cognitive Dissonance* in recent history.

The predominantly blind trust in The System and unquestioning reliance on its sacrosanct rules constitutes in fact no less than one of the most dangerous chinks in any civilized society's collective armor. Unfortunately, this type of uncritical adherence contributes a large part to the suppression of emerging doubts and to successfully disregarding one's own inner moral compass, allowing people instead to hang on to the assumed infallibility of the established system of checks and balances. Conveniently forgetting that said system has been built exclusively on public trust in higher authorities, who in turn are being vetted by none other than self-same system. An only seemingly flawless circle resulting in apparently above-board elections and appointments of in other circumstances unacceptable candidates such as for instance women-molesting Supreme Court judges, pandemic-denying Commander-in-Chiefs, religiously extreme Attorney Generals, student-defrauding Secretaries of Education, or shady Secretaries of Commerce,.

In the current system, doubting the eligibility and bona fides of such officials amounts to doubting the infallibility of the system – the system that has been built on the public trust in these self-same officials. Merely scratching at the system's outer layer of flawlessness already presents the danger of ripping off the complete outer layer, revealing underneath badly infected patches and disturbingly undersupplied entrails, including traditionally neglected or wholly absent bits and pieces such as a compulsory, comprehensive, in-depth vetting-process for all presidential candidates. Probably, the Founding Fathers forgot to write this bit into the Constitution because they could simply not imagine a deeply rotten and festering wound right in the middle of the American political body such as the one torn open by the Republican Party in the years leading up to the 2016 presidential elections and continuously further infected and widened ever since.

::: *A Superseded Immune System*

For an inexplicably long time and with the exception of some young, dedicated, and frequently as "radicals" denounced Democratic congresswomen in the House, the leadership of the Democratic Party refused to speak up and demand an immediate stop to the cancerous excesses of the Trumpministration. Nor have most Democrats seriously attempted to close at least the worst legal loopholes, arguing that any draft of new and effective laws would die anyway a swift death in the Republican-led Senate.

Just like any representative in Congress, Democratic members of the House and the Senate have sworn an oath to fulfil their duty as representatives of the people and guardians of the Constitution. An oath that has been stretched to its limits during the Mueller-investigation into Trump's ties to Russia, Putin's meddling in the 2016-elections, and *Don the Con's* involvement in several cases of obstruction of justice and Congress. Despite Robert S. Mueller's 448 pages-long report containing a plethora of damning details particularly in its second part dealing with *Trumpelredskin's* obstruction of justice, Democrats have found neither the strength nor the commitment to control the narration, leaving it instead to the most inadequate Attorney General in U.S-history to hijack the story and disseminate a trumpagandistic version of the report purporting the opposite of Special Counsel Mueller's findings.

AG William Barr's open disavowal of the truth represents only one example for the Trumpministration-tactic of making the lie as big as possible and repeating it at any opportunity. The house of lies constructed by Trump's lawyers and Trumpublican Senators during the impeachment trial of Donald J. Trump ultimately proved the woeful inadequacy of the existing system of checks and balances to prevent a red-handedly caught conman from turning the United States into his personal kingdom. Throughout the Mueller-investigation and the impeachment-trial, *Sir Liesalot* followed the same plan that had once been implemented by the man who summarized it in his then-bestselling book *"Mein Kampf"*, in which Adolf Hitler explained that ideally one should use *"lies of such colossal dimensions"* that nobody would believe *"anyone could have the impudence to distort the truth so infamously"*. Accordingly, *Herr Twittler* ejaculating his *colossal lies* on all fronts. On the media-front, *Agent Orange's* all-caps tweets like, "PRESIDENTIAL HARRASSMENT!", or, "WITCHHUNT!", will be reliably supported by FOX News' former County District Attorney Jeanine Pirro whose diatribes bear an uncanny resemblance to the performances of Hitler's infamously staccato-talking and wildly screaming Nazi supreme judge Roland Freisler. On the judiciary front, devout Catholic William Barr bends over backwards in his unconstitutional attempts to fend off all scrutiny of *Trumpelthinskin's* presumably illegal wheeling and dealing, aided (counterproductively) by *"Rambling Rudy"* Giuliani.

Finally, on the legislative and oversight-front *Benedict Donald's* allies in the House diligently do their own portion of anti-democratic deeds. Noteworthy specimen of this new breed of super-sycophants without a shred of morale or decency include Representatives Matt Gaetz (R-FL), Jim *"Gym"* Jordan (R-OH), and Devin Nunes (R-CA). The latter topping the list of Trump-stooges with new records of utter brainlessness and exemplary blind activism, (i.e., doing things for the sake of doing things), regularly guaranteeing him the top-position. In fact, even a superficial glance at Devin Nunes' past masterworks of stupidity suffice to convince even GOPhers of Devin's deserved distinction. For instance that one time when Devin got caught by the media sending his personally picked investigators to the UK to find the author of the by now largely confirmed *Steele Dossier* while financing the unsuccessful kindergarten-"spy-hunt" exclusively with American taxpayer money.

In February 2018, the media caught *Devin the Dunce* in the act of funding his own alternative news site with the explicit objective to manipulate the news spread on the Trump-Russia investigation. Shortly after, Nunes had the great idea to threaten senior members of the FBI and the Department of Justice with impeachment for not letting him and his Trumpublican fellows see every scrap of information gathered by government agencies during the Trump-Russia investigation. Not content with this new height of national security threatening lunacy, Devin subsequently appeared on FOX & Friends, alleging that the Trump-campaign had been *"set up"* by none other than the Federal Bureau of Investigation itself. And who could forget Nunes' *"They're on to us"*-face following Gordon Sondland's testimony in the House impeachment-hearings. (*"Everyone was in the loop!"* - Gordon Sondland). The list goes on, but this suffices to provide a preliminary impression of the sheer incompetence and brownnosing displayed by an elected Representative of the American people. Still, the eyes of 65 million Americans glaze over as soon as their self-proclaimed high standards of morale and justice will clash violently with the laughably easy to detect, amoral and unconstitutional tampering of elected trumpublican representatives.

The currently abysmal state of affairs in U.S.-politics begs the question whether Nunes and his fellow Trumpublicans embody perhaps merely the newest version of incompetent, mega-partisan and unscrupulous political representatives in Washington, essentially cast from the same mould as generations of unprincipled and self-serving government officials before them. In other words, has America in the last fifty years been governed almost exclusively by politicians representing the worst type of public servants?

Luckily, the answer is a resounding *"No!"*. Prior to Trump, from Obama all the way back to Jimmy Carter, Members of the House and the Senate just as the Generals in the Pentagon, the intelligence community, members of cabinets, and 99,5% of government officials have faithfully followed the code of conduct established by the Founding Fathers. Political fights across the aisle, as fierce as they were at times, did not spill over into matters of national interest and security, and a moral understanding of do's and don'ts was accepted by all sides. Sneaky rabble-rousers and disrupters in the vein of Devin *"Devin"* Nunes were kicked out by men of honor like late Senator John McCain, even and particularly when sprouting from their own ranks.

So, what changed? Is it merely Donald Trump's complete disregard for morale, honor, and integrity that has infecting the system of checks and balances and turned it into a sewer where political bottom-feeders like Nunes, Jordan, Gaetz, or VP Mike Pence thrive? Clearly, the open rot on the political body that is the Trumpministration is not the root-cause but rather the latest result of a deeper reaching infestation. The virus weakening the System from within has begun its corroding work already several decades ago with the *Reaganomics,* to later jump over to members of the *Tea Party* and the party-over-country *Cheney-Rumsfeld-Gingrich-posse,* to finally bloom into a full pandemic in the shape of *Trumpism.*

With the *Tea Party's* ultimately underwhelming (see: *Palin, Sarah*) attack on the democratic system parried, the next mutation of the virus adopted a slightly less obvious guise with the most powerful Vice-President in history, Dick

Cheney, and his sidekick, the initial *Dark Side Donald*, G.W. Bush's Defense Secretary Donald Rumsfeld at the helm. Their version of the system-undermining infection, while further disintegrating the Framers' ideals, appeared to be more secretive and shunned initially the public light.

Finally, during the Obama-years, the putrefaction seemed to have been contained for the first time since 2001, and in some areas even reversed. Barack Obama, having inherited the worst metastases of previous Republican predator-policies, such as the banking-crisis, the wars in Afghanistan and Iraq, and the growing divide in American society, sprinted from one festering wound on the public body to the next, applying antidotes, bandaging deep cuts to prevent total exsanguination, and generally following a strategy of healing the American body. At the same time, the Republican virus had shed its skin once more and now appeared in its most toxic form to date, the *"Total Obstruction Disease"*.

Consequentially, *MoscowMitch* McConnell led the relentless onslaught on any Obama-attempt to close the festering wounds of poverty, war, social injustice, and growing societal imbalance. In the end, Senator McConnell could declare almost total victory, having even thwarted Obama's nomination for the Supreme Court by employing the so-called 'nuclear option'. Simultaneously, a small group of mega-rich right-wingers had been busy preparing the final blow to the annoyingly burdensome system of checks and balances by grooming several possible candidates for their pick of next US-President. In co-operation with other interested domestic and foreign parties, the decision finally came down to a certain Donald John Trump.

A malleable, weak, easily manipulatable, and greedy narcissist who would hand every conspirator involved their piece of the cake, as long as he was allowed to line his own pockets and to play president. And lo and behold, the military got its mega-budget, the Saudis got their arms-deals and American support, the big industries got many profit-restricting environmental-, and worker protection-laws watered down or revoked, millionaires and billionaires got their tax cut, and Vladimir Putin got not only the US-military off his back in Syria but the priceless gift of an untrustworthy, universally despised, and for decades to come diplomatically weakened United States of America as the cherry on top of the cream-pie.

But there is a silver-lining in even the darkest hours when democracy dies easiest. Neither David (†) and Charles Koch nor the other *Big Oil* and *Big Industry*-kingpins, neither Vladimir Putin nor the Saudis had reckoned with the actual level of destructiveness and uncontrollability of the toxic weapon they had installed in the heart of American government. *His Accidency Donald I.* had been spiralling out of control ever since being considered for the role of President, culminating first in his impeachment trial in January of 2020, directly followed by Trump's complete and utter failure in handling the largest pandemic in 100 years, making it abundantly clear to his financial and political backers in the shadows that the septuagenarian narcissist with the spray-tanned face was not quite the most *"stable genius"* after all. When even Laura Ingraham, the late-born Leni Riefenstahl-dream of a perfect white-supremacy woman, feels the need to stop Donald Trump in an interview from making an utter fool of himself, how then should Tsar Vladimir I. control his sock-puppet on the other side of the Atlantic?

But the always present danger of *Humpty-Trumpty* falling off the wall and into hot water raises not only concerns in Moscow, Istanbul, Tel Aviv, and Riyadh, but also in Republican-led U.S.-states, at FOX News-HQ in New York, and in Mitch McConnell's office in Washington, D.C. For a closer look at the reasons for their concerns, first a quick pop-quiz: What happens after a body had been infected by a virus and survived the attack? Yes, it developed anti-bodies, of course.

Now it appears as if these anti-bodies have begun to form on a large scale and in specialised versions all over the country. With *Sandy Hook* gun-law activists, mayors of sanctuary cities, pro-choice supporters, the *#MeToo*-movement, the LGBTQ-community, the millions of sensible and sane facemask-supporters, and most of all with the *Black Lives Matter*-campaign, in the fall of 2020 the American body is fighting back against the society-corroding Trumpublican virus.

A future America with a progressive Democratic President will then have to prove to the world and to America itself that the toxic virus of divisiveness, hatred, social inequality, and death of democratic values has not merely been defeated and driven off the field, but that the American immune system has come out of this fight considerably strengthened and improved beyond its status quo prior to the Trump-infection. Perhaps the Trump-virus is therefore even a necessary infection, after all. An infection that invigorates the American body and steels it against further anti-democratic, authoritarian attacks from within. Furthermore, the recovery-process might give the United States the strength for real change this time around, at least allowing it to close ranks with the rest of the Western world and their successful social security-, market regulation-, gun control-, and health care-solutions. An objective, however, that would also demand a shift in perspective regarding the roles, responsibilities, and duties of authorities determining by their actions the overall health of a system that can be, as it has by now been proven beyond doubt, all too easily abused.

::: *Authority: An Almost Unshakeable Illusion*

No one can claim honestly to be free from this certain comforting feeling deriving from the certainty that powerful higher authorities are watching over society and protect the status quo. No matter how much of a rebel you may be at heart, when push comes to shove it turns out to be still good to know that an entity with the means and authority to protect you is a mere three-digit-call away. The same comfort that also comes with knowing of the existence of a higher authority that passes universally accepted judgement on e.g. the sleazeball who tricked your husband or wife into investing your mutual savings in a Ponzi scheme, or of the existence of laws guaranteeing your landlord cannot let someone else move into your flat while you are on holiday, as well as of the battalions of judges and law-enforcement personnel applying and enforcing these laws.

You, me, and most other people accept these powers wielded by higher authorities because they have been installed to protect our legal rights, property, and life, to provide and secure the proper functioning of public life, and to guarantee the maintenance of law and order. Society trusts and relies on higher authorities without a second thought because it assumes that the powers-that-be use extremely thorough examination-processes to make damn sure that only the very best and morally unobjectionable individuals are allowed to fill such important positions of higher authority.

The fundamental crux of such a system relying on independent, unbiased arbiters to vet applicants for such powerful positions, alas, has become patently obvious with the enthronement of America's *Orange Overlord*. Exactly how far the coarsening of decorum and morale in the Republican Party (GOP), better known today as *Gang of Parasites* (GoP), has progressed in the past 15 years can be observed by the GoP's very dissimilar handling of two individual Supreme Court judge-nominations. The first of these two cases took its course throughout October of 2005, after President George W. Bush had set his mind on installing Assistant to the President and Staff Secretary Harriet Miers as Associate Justice on the Supreme Court.

The problem: Miers had never before served as a judge. Furthermore, her perceived lack of intellectual prowess as well as of any clear record on important Supreme Court issues brought not only Democrats but also notable Republicans to the scene. And the conservatives made no bones about their aversion to Bush's choice. Many professionals openly criticised Miers while several conservative groups, usually going through hell and high water for *"Doubya"*, even planned an organized opposition campaign against Miers' nomination. At the end of October, after various disastrous hearings, Miers finally asked President Bush to withdraw her nomination. Bipartisan common sense and dedication to the nation's best interest had prevailed.

The second case, though, came to an altogether different end on July 10, 2018. On this day, the man who succeeded Harriet Miers in the role of White House Staff Secretary under George W. Bush was finally pushed through by Trumpublican Senate Majority Leader Mitch *"The Russian Bitch"* McConnell and his *Gang of Phonies (GoP)*, to become Donald Trump's second appointed Associate Justice on the U.S. Supreme Court. Brett Kavanaugh's appointment followed one of the indubitably most undignified and embarrassing Senate hearing-appearances of a Supreme Court-nominee in U.S.-history. In a rambling and frequently vociferous manner, the regular lector at Washington D.C.'s Catholic church *The Shrine of the Most Blessed Sacrament* tried to defend himself against the credible accusation by Christine Blasey Ford, a psychology professor at Palo Alto University, that he had sexually assaulted her during her time in high school.

Kavanaugh's effectuations to the Senators about beer and his past and present love of same as well as about *"boofing"* (i.e. imbibing alcohol through the rectum) and other "student-shenanigans" will no doubt be forever enshrined in the annals (*sic*) of the United States Supreme Court. Yet, Brett *"The Brat"* Kavanaugh's brazenly bad behavior still pales in contrast to the overall conduct of Trumpublican Senators during the whole affair.

Right from the start of the hearings Democrats complained that a large chunk of documents concerning Kavanaugh's time at the Bush White House had not been provided. However, their moves to adjourn or suspend the hearings were ruled to be out of order by Chairman Chuck *"Shar-Pei"* Grassley (GoP). When more than 2,400 law professors signed a letter stating that the Senate should not confirm Kavanaugh because *"he did not display the impartiality and judicial temperament requisite to sit on the highest court of our land"*, the petition was dismissed by Trumpublican Senators. An investigation by the FBI into possible lies in Kavanaugh's testimony to Congress regarding his drinking habits in his youth were, according to *The Washington Post,* stopped by the White House. Republican Senators then used the so-called "nuclear option", i.e. simple majority vote, rather than the historical three-fifths supermajority to advance the nomination to a final floor vote on October 6, in which the Senate confirmed Kavanaugh to the Supreme Court with a 50–48 vote.

The comparison of Harriet Miers' and Brett Kavanaugh's appointments throws a glaring spotlight on the apparent decay of Republican morale and decency over a mere 15 years while the abhorrent behavior of the Trumpublican Senators who voted against hearing witnesses in the impeachment trial – as well as subsequently against Trump's impeachment in the face of overwhelming incriminating evidence for *Don the Con's* high crimes and misdemeanors – show unequivocally that there exists no bottom to the pit of egotism at the center of the *Gang of Pricks* (GoP).

::: All Power Rests in the People. Seriously.

- All power rests in the people. Really. After all, a 100-Dollar bill is just a piece of rather dirty paper coming out of a hole in the wall or being handed over by a stranger in return for work or goods and wares. That piece of paper does not nourish anyone when eaten. It does not even shed any useful heat when burnt. In fact, the rectangular paper's only proven usefulness as any kind of tool is still exclusively reserved for old-fashioned cocaine sniffers.

  By all intents and purposes, a 100-Dollar bill is therefore essentially one of the most useless objects around. Yet, countless humans have been killed for such a piece of paper and countless others would readily kill for it. While again others regularly exchange their irretrievable lifetime for a tiny pack of these crumpled pieces of paper. The sole reason for this objective madness: Once upon a time society agreed that the printing on this rectangle of pulp symbolizes the actual value of a certain amount of work or commodities. For example, work in high demand or unique can equal 100 Dollar for just 10 minutes of working time while less special or less important work will amount to $100 after 12 hours or more.

  Every member of society trusts in the mutual agreement to accept this arbitrary symbol for the value of time/goods that is called *money,* as well as in the universal deal that money can be exchanged everywhere for real necessities like food and drinks, warmth, protection, mobility, and of course loads and loads of utterly useless stuff as well. Astoundingly, this universal trust is based on no more than the generally accepted higher authority of the *Treasurer of the United States*. Nothing but this one person's signature "magically" transforms a piece of printed paper into legal tender, ready to be exchanged for any life-preserving and pleasure-providing services and goods. Heck, even a criminal who kills for money ultimately acts in the safe knowledge that the appropriate higher authorities guarantee the sustained value of the grimy pieces of paper with an illegibly signature.

- All power rests in the people. Seriously. After all, a pastor or priest is just a man in some overly fancy or overly drab attire who, if he would be honest, will admit that neither he nor his superiors have ever seen, heard, or talked to any omnipotent being. And yet, millions of religious believers readily accept a priest's claim to be an official intermediary between Heaven and Earth, to have the "God-given" authority to speak in the name of this invisible entity, to bring new-borns into the fold of the religious community, to act as the final authority on marriage, to praise and condemn specific lifestyles, to absolve others from their sins, and to put people properly into the ground at the end. All this without ever presenting to anyone even a shred of visible, tangible evidence or any other proof that would reasonably justify his and his church-superiors' rather extensive appropriation of worldly power.

- All power rests in the people. Honestly! After all, any judge is just an elected or appointed person with a black robe, a law-degree, and a stern facial expression. Whether s/he was put behind the judge's table in the courtroom by election or by appointment, in both cases it is fair to say that most citizens living in the judge's judicial reach do not have the faintest idea about the man's or woman's personal qualifications for such a responsible position, let alone about his or her private conduct, morale, or sense of justice.

And yet, everyone trusts that the appropriate higher authorities have thoroughly examined, tested, and vetted this black-robed person before giving him or her the power to ultimately decide over other people's lives by sentencing them to penalty payments, probation, imprisonment, or the ultimate punishment, death. Everyone accepts that this fellow human wields such immense power solely because society trusts in faceless higher authorities to have trained, tested, vetted, and confirmed the judge to the highest possible degree. Furthermore, even though absolutely nothing is known about the authorities behind this vetting process, no one denies their power to create another higher authority accepted again in good faith. Naturally, the same is true for all priests, pastors, policemen, pilots, teachers, customs-officers, soldiers, firemen, doctors, and people of any other profession whose authority is blindly accepted by society today.

The murderer, the billionaire, the housewife, the thief, the nurse, the anarchist – every human inherently craves order, certainty, and a reliable set of universally accepted rules established and defended by proper authorities. As the social animals we are, it lies in homo sapiens' nature to organize our peaceful cohabitation by assigning specific tasks to different individuals in order to increase overall productivity and regulate interactions with each other. Only this has enabled humanity to develop from pre-historic packs governed by the *"Right of the Stronger"* and long inhibited by the "natural rule" of *"Survival of the Physically Fittest"* into what we can proudly call civilized society today.

The myriad of benefits enjoyed by each individual thanks to this development are self-evident and hardly need further explanation. Yet, as logically obvious as the advantages of a society supervised, policed, and governed by higher authorities may be, the roots of mankind's natural affinity to this idea go deeper than mere rational deliberations. The man or woman has yet to be born who can truthfully claim to be able to exist and function wholly outside social boundaries and above society's written as well as unwritten rules. No anarchist, no public enemy No. 1, not even the worst domestic terrorist will neither be able nor willing to break away from society's universally agreed upon norms, rules, guidelines, and values.

Hence, a serial-killer may well be a staunch outlaw who prides himself on his utter disregard for any laws and societal conventions. Still, after he got shot in the gut and narrowly escaped from the shoot-out with the police, his first thought will be to find a doctor. In the course of his search he will rely just as much as the next man on the veracity of certain symbols and signs to identify a doctor's office and to assure him of the legitimate authority of the man in that office. Without a second thought the murderous villain will accept the societally agreed upon signs and symbols for a medical authority without ever considering asking the man in the white coat for any further proof for his assumed authority. Furthermore, the killer relies implicitly on the appropriate higher authorities tasked with issuing medical accreditations to have thoroughly vetted the chain-smoking, stubble-bearded fella who is about to fish a bullet out of his entrails. Which just goes to show that on any given day, every single member of society is relying unthinkingly on the highly theoretical assumption that they can blindly trust the appropriate authorities with their money, loved ones, freedom, safety, health, and life. Go figure.

::: *Authority begets Authority*

At the bottom line, this imperative nature of higher authorities in a civilized society coagulates in the fundamental realization that all power of higher authorities derives ultimately from one source, i.e. public trust. A fundamental truth that makes it imperative to further scrutinize particularly one exclusive group of men and women upon whom *"We, the people"* bestow the titles of highest authorities in the land, viz our politicians. No two ways about it, a whole library could be filled with books about politicians' abuse of public trust advanced by the electorate in good faith to those whose job it is to rule and regulate self-same electorate.

The democratic idea of a *"government for the people, by the people"* comes undisputedly with the inherent weakness of being dangerously open to exploitation by any wannabe-authoritarian who sets his mind on outfoxing the system of checks and balances. Books abound on populists and authoritarians who tried this, (and often succeeded), with a certain A. Hitler of Braunau, Austria, easily leading the book-count. However, different democratic systems provide various levels of protection against such usurpers built into their specific systems of checks and balances. Amongst them for instance a multi-party system with a parliamentary hurdle of 5% or 8% election-results; a strong and independently regulated government-agency tasked with the protection of the constitution; a strict and untouchable division between a politically independent judicial branch and the executive (government); an automatic, non-rescindable voting-right for every citizen aged 18 and above without further registration; a universal, direct, free, equal, and secret plurality-vote election-system; an adamant protection of the freedom of the press; strong laws against demagoguery, hate-speech, anti-constitutional, violence-inciting, and minorities-discriminating public utterances and the guaranteed enforcement of self-same laws; a strictly supervised and regulated police force held to full accountability; an ironclad separation of state and church; a 3/4-majority rule for far-reaching decisions in parliament/congress; and clear limitations on the powers of the elected government-leader. And these constitute only some safety-mechanisms for the protection of a democracy against the whims and wilful abuse by a small group of collaborators determined to undermine the system from inside.

Measures weakening the defense of a democratic system, on the other hand, include indirect voting by representative-

(*electoral college*), pure party list-, or first-past-the-post electoral systems; any type of voter-registration requirements except citizen-registration; election-district gerrymandering; a discernibly propagandist media; unrestricted "freedom" of hate-speech, violence-inciting and minorities-discriminating public utterances; an insufficiently trained, "state-in-state" police force; an uninhibited interference in politics by religious organizations; a discernible influence of the military in governmental affairs: a leader's "right" to dismiss inspector-generals tasked with supervising his government; and a leader's power to legally bypass the legislature. All contributing to the higher probability of a group of populists establishing an *oligarchy,* (i.e., *"rule of the few"*).

The common denominator of all these weaknesses consists of their ideal suitability as tools for a direct or indirect abuse of authority. An electoral college for instance, while 120 years ago a feasible solution for a country as large as the United States, today denies voters the fundamentally democratic right to a direct vote. Voter-registration allows for a dozen of ways to manipulate the voter turn-out thus influencing the right to a universally free election. And churches meddling in politics demonstrate no less than the blatant abuse of their hold over millions of believers/voters. [*According to a recent Pew Research Center survey in April of 2020, close to half of all Americans (49%) say the Bible should have at least "some" influence on U.S. laws, with nearly a quarter (23%) saying it should have "a great deal" of influence.*]

As a final and particularly worrying example for anti-democratic tendencies in a "democratic" system serves the practice of granting a government-leader exclusive powers without legislative oversight or legal interference, opening up a can of worms with such nasty surprises as the leader's power to annul any meaningful government-oversight by inspector-generals and the ability to literally turn the world upside down at the push of a button or the stroke of a pen. Such unchecked powers are a hallmark of any authoritarian potentate.

Still, no populist or authoritarian ruler would survive his first day on the throne if not at least a sufficiently large part of the population would be convinced of their ruler's "legitimate" (i.e. rightfully taken or given) authority. These convictions, when held adamantly enough by a small group of people, have the unsavory tendency to spread outwards from an inner circle of die-hard disciples of the new emperor to a larger ring of followers generally approving of the new ruler's authority and policies, and from here to a much broader circle of easily impressable citizens caught by the fallacious notion that, *"if so many others accept the authority of the new ruler it must naturally be legitimate"*. A variation of the *Illusory Truth-Effect*. Or put differently: Authority begets authority.

But such is the nature of the feeble human mind, that the initial build-up of these consecutive rings of followers will remain by no means stable should the authoritarian populist at the center of the web not take immediate and decisive action to ensnare his victims further. Man's inherent tendency to trust and follow "proper" authorities might make an extremely sticky flycatcher, but in order to reel in the prey for good there remains some work to do for the modern authoritarian leader. Any ruler deserving the epithet "authoritarian" needs therefore to add one more ingredient to the unholy brew of his oligarchic take-over. This particularly acidic slurry is prevalently simmering in a specific part of society and is easily carved and boiled soft by the ambitious populist. That is, the soft underbelly of any educated society, the tender and malleable brains that almost instantly liquify when touched by promises and slogans of any populistic strongman. And with America's dilapidated education system and exploding social inequality in the mix there appears to be no shortage of such dainty morsels called Trumpists. A delicacy for the populist spider, reeled in by shooting it with its two strongest glue-strings:

One: The promise of an ironclad *protection* of the Trumpist from all (made up) internal and external threats, (e.g. *a flu-like germ, bad hombres, muscular lepers, Rocketman, Tchaina,"*, et.al.)

Two: The promise of a definitely very soon to come, never seen before *prosperity* tremendously benefitting the "downtrodden" trumpist masses.

Relentlessly repeated promises of *protection* and *prosperity* resonate particularly well with those who live in constant fear of losing something or other, be it their traditions, their *"God-given right to bear arms"*, their "right" to force their religious opinions on others, their wilful ignorance (*see*: antivaxxers, creationists, et.al.), their worldly possessions, their smidgen of power over even weaker individuals, or simply their fenced-in world where encountering people with non-Caucasian skin-tones, traditions, music, food, religions, or non-English languages regularly incite a more rabid response than any request to wear a facemask. Such preconditioned, fearful individuals get attached to a populist predator's sticky string of false promises easier than the fly to the toad's tongue.

Yet, the gullibility does not stop at political lines. People who regard themselves as part of the well-educated, enlightened side of society are also not immune to the mesmerizing lure emitted by powerful authority. Apart from a certain *political intelligentsia*-type who can often be found in the orbit around strong leaders on the extreme left and right alike, it is the average B.A.-, M.A.-, or PhD-graduate, teacher, professor, doctor, pilot, architect, engineer, and manager who voluntarily and in good conscience submits daily to one or the other subtle or brazen *Argument from Authority*, albeit on a more benign and ordinary level than their trumpist colleagues on the morally rotten side of town.

Two professions specifically realized long since the extensive impact an *Argument from Authority* can have on the public and the individual. And neither the advertising-industry nor the political class stopped at this realization, instead having forged the realization into several distinct manipulation-weapons today. One easily recognizable example for the effective utilization of people's inherent trust in authorities being the advertisement-industry's employment of celebrities as spokespersons for commercial products. Regarding the successes regularly produced by such endorsements, surely Don Draper's spiritual heirs will not stop any time soon utilizing the asserted authority of fashion-models and actresses to praise slimming-products, lady-shavers, kitchen-knives, and facial cremes, or the "natural" authority of golfers, Formula 1-drivers, tennis-players, football- and soccer-stars, and, of course, actors to hawk anything from razorblades to car tyres, insurances, beer, or men's slips. And why should they, when pointing the near irresistible tractor-beam of an *Argument from Authority* at the consumer's wallet continues to prove a sure-fire way to drag money out of their pockets.

Politicians, on the other hand, do not have it quite that easy making the *authority-by-proxy* tactic work in their advantage. When advertisers rely predominantly on the "star-factor" of popular, famous, and universally liked and admired celebrities to create a positive connection between celebrity-authority and product, politicians are in contrast rarely seen employing sports-, fashion-, movie-, or media-celebrities to help them get their message across. The simple reason being that politics is a serious matter and no one in their right mind would trust Heidi Klum, Lewis Hamilton, Robert Pattinson, or Selena Gomez to have the appropriate background to function as credible spokesperson for agricultural subsidies, a renewal of the Strategic Arms Reduction Treaty (START), or universal health care for that matter. Hence, politicians need authority-figures who provide arguments with significantly more substance. And the only appropriate candidates for this role, next to the occasional scientific or industry-related expert, represent other politicians. Providing at least one reason for why politicians with similar basic positions tend to band together to form an official group and call it a party.

As can be observed daily on the news, such an initial support from party-colleagues on political matters has the uncanny tendency to quickly warp into personal back-scratchings, *quid pro quos*, and extreme partisanship, in the worst case culminating in something like the *Gang of Partisans* (GoP). Although even Matt *"Gasmask"* Gaetz and *"Blind Jim"* Jordan are not simple-minded enough to overlook the circumstance that merely having each other's back will not suffice for Granny Martha in Tennessee to cast her ballot in their favor. Their skin-deep or outright make-believe political "convictions" alone certainly won't have the desired *Axe-effect* on the electorate, which is why Reps. Jordan, Gaetz, Nunes, and other professional politicians (i.e. without a real job to fall back on) tend to copy their predecessors throughout the political ages by twisting the basic concept of people's inherent trust in authority. Resulting in a hyper-sycophantic *clique of claqueurs* praising an *Orange Mussolini* as infallible Authority of Authorities in the (realistic) hope of having some drops of the *Obese Orange Overlord's* power-juice trickling down into their own, gaping mouths.

When British philosopher John Locke (1632-1704), one of the first scholars on the matter, analyzed the *Arguments from Authority,* he assigned in the habit of contemporaneous philosophers the Latin denotation *"argumentum ad verecundiam"*, (contextually translating Into, *"evidence by reverence"*), to these argumentation-strategies. In as many words describing nothing else but the tactics of utilizing the opinion of an authority as proof for one's own assertion.

For politicians publicly presenting an authority who supports their assertion, such *evidence by reverence* has, apart from bolstering their point, often the pleasant side-effect of increasing the politician's own credibility merely by association alone. Quite ironic, considering Locke had noted in his personal experience that, *'references to an external authority frequently correlate* with *hidden attempts by politicians to commit deliberate fallacies'*, referring of course to bribing, intimidating, flattering, or by making use of an expert-authority with an expertise completely unrelated to the matter of debate, a strategy laid out in detail below during the following wild slide down the tip of the iceberg and into the depths of the fascinating world of the *Arguments from Authority*.

The 3-Steps Argument from Authority

"Trust me, I'm an expert."

A recent survey by pollster *Nielsen* has shown that 67% of all U.S.-consumers are more likely to consider purchasing a product when it is endorsed by an *"unbiased expert"*. At first glance a result that appears to merely prove the common sense prevalent in two-thirds of Americans. Until realizing that the term *"unbiased expert"* includes also the gray-streaked, elderly, white man in a pristinely white lab-coat who resembles to a T the popular image of a pharmacist or medical doctor. Naturally, most people are somewhat aware that the good "doctor" is an actor or at most a doctor in an unrelated medical field, since any real medical experts selling themselves to a company and believing that their reputation in the medical community will remain untouched are about as rare as Republicans with amoral compass.

It might be hard to believe but in the eyes of ca. 221 million U.S.-consumers, or 67% of 330 million citizens, the obviously paid, (i.e. far from *"unbiased"*) man in the white lab-coat represents a *real expert* whose words carry *real weight*. No matter how many Americans are regarding themselves as being *post-consumeristic,* claiming to see through the shadow puppetry of advertisers and their masters - the subconscious tendency to identify authorities by their insignia and stereotypical characteristics, (laboratory, stethoscope, white lab-coat; elegant office, expensive suit, professional haircut; impressive uniform, crew-cut, stern expression; business-dress, glasses, briefcase; black robe, white hair, gavel, etc.), and to instinctively assume the bearer's trustworthiness has lost nothing of its convincibility and is still selling annually products and services for billions of Dollars.

What is true for the private consumer-market is twice as true for the political arena. Any average consumer has at least an inkling of their products' functionality, effectiveness, and usage and little problems comparing differing product-features of competing brands. Moreover, when it comes to products related to the consumer's work, family, or hobby, their knowledge concerning every feature, problem, advantage, and upgrade-option frequently ranges at expert-levels. This goes for the computer-tinkerer just as much as for the fashionista, the French cuisine-afficionado, or the hobby-mechanic.

When confronted with the intricate, less broad brush-painted aspects of current political issues, however, the same people who spend days on end learning everything there is to know about the theory and praxis of modding a water-cooled tower-PC, creating the perfect Consommé, assembling the next ground-breaking new summer-look, or tickling a few more horsepower out of a triple SU carburetted 3.8-litre six-cylinder Jaguar XK6 engine frequently know just about as much about political details as Donald J. Trump. A status quo making it a great deal easier for the political class to pull the wool over the eyes of the consumer, (i.e. the voter) when employing one or the other variation of *Arguments from Authority*.

| An Apparent American Affection for Authorities

In defense of Joe Six-pack, Jane Jones, or John Smith, it is in fact near impossible for the recipient of one-way information to effectively scrutinize assertions by politicians and their *fakesperts*. This does not negate the fact, though, that many Americans remain gullible enough to believe an "expert" to be an expert merely because this person claims to be an expert or when the chyron at the bottom of the screen spells *"Expert"*. But on the upside, most educated Americans at least draw the line of blind *expert*-status acceptance regarding some bespectacled dude on TV when it comes to deadly serious matters impacting their own lives, work, passions, health, loved ones, or finances. Here at the latest sensible citizens demand some additional proof for the legitimacy of the alleged *expert*-status and the veracity of *Dr Talkalot's* claims.

In such a case, John Smith will get up from his Lazy Boy® Chair in front of his 59" flatscreen and amble over to the family-laptop to google political *"expert" Dr Talkalot,* while Jane Jones might visit the office of her local representative on her way to the local butcher to inquire about the doctor's credentials. Back at the kitchen-table, both will then exchange the same reassuring information that *Dr Talkalot* has indeed received his doctorate from the "renowned" *Saint Regis University*, giving the doctor in the eyes of John and Jane all necessary credentials to believe his *expert*-opinion when he states that the current virus-pandemic merely constitutes another of *Hussein Obama's* long-term plans to weaken the greatest President ever. Usually this would be the story's happy ending, with two satisfied Trumpists who have gathered at least some further information in contrast to the vast majority of Trumpists who never dream to act any further than slouching in their Lazy Boys® while shouting profane agreement at the *expert* on FOX News.

However, unbeknownst to John and Jane, the story's epilogue contains one final plot-twist. That is, the revelation that the reputable-sounding *St. Regis University* has been found to have issued its degrees solely based on so-called "*life experience*" instead of on any actual academic courses taken. Additionally, it has been ascertained that at least 135 federal employees have held bogus degrees from *Saint Regis* before the fake university was shut down by U.S.-government-authorities in 2006 in the quite spectacular *"Operation Gold Seal"*. If only John and Jane had dug a bit further, they could have exposed the professorial appearing, eloquently lecturing *Dr Talkalot* as a *fakespert* of trumpagandist caliber. Still, the couple cannot truly be blamed since most everyone today has *to some lesser or greater degree* been conditioned to accept legitimate-appearing authorities ticking all the right boxes on the list of expectations as the "real deal". And understandably so, since the alternative of doubting each authority's verisimilitude by default would make everyday life impossible. Consequentially, people give authority-claiming individuals rather the benefit of the doubt and accept the professed status at face value, thus passing on the accepted "expert's" opinion as "verified fact".

But if no one can truly escape this ingrained notion of accepting authority by default, then the *"greater or lesser degree"* by which individuals fall under this spell becomes suddenly more than a mere interpolation. Therefore dictators, authoritarian regimes, and democratic governments alike are keen to have as many tools in the box as possible for tightening the screw on their population's belief in their "legitimate" authority. Naturally, the go-to example for a regime that cranks up the control-screw to 13 represents the Kim-family dictatorship of North Korea. Over 70 years of absolute internal oppression and external isolation have created a population stripped bare of even the tiniest alternative to total obedience. A close runner-up to this uncontested leader in brutal authoritarianism presents the People's Republic of China, where a one-party system guarantees the uninterrupted rule of a tightly knit elite of communist aristocrats over an authorities-submissive population.

Further countries where forced loyalty to official authorities reaches top-marks on the 1-10 *Authoritarian Society-scale* include, amongst others, the Islamic Republic of Iran, the Islamic Republic of Pakistan, and the Kingdom of Saudi-Arabia, whose rulers rely heavily on the clergy to keep their populations in line.

Other oligarchic governments, while sympathetic to the dominant church in their respective countries, prefer a different unifying notion as tool of choice for cementing conformity and submission to the state's authorities. The Russian Federation under President Vladimir Putin and his party *United Russia* is indubitably leading this field, having established an all-encompassing Russian nationalism in the population complete with a "strong leader" at the top, an aggressive military, a party-youth organization, and a "justified" claim to expansion.

On the other end of the scale, roughly between 1 and 3, lie the Western European countries with centralistic governed

France and the United Kingdom as perhaps still the most patriotic-minded nations among them. Yet, the majority of people in France and the UK as well as in Spain, Portugal, Italy, Greece, Ireland, Germany, Belgium, the Netherlands, Iceland and other Scandinavian countries traditionally harbor a healthy scepticism in regard to any group-, party-, or individual authority trying to reel them in with overt or covert nationalistic, religious, or leader-glorifying propaganda-tactics. The same goes for the former British colonies of Canada, Australia, and New Zealand. Although they accept Queen Elizabeth II. as their pro-forma head of state, their people stay gladly far away from any exuberant nationalism disguised as patriotism, any type of governmental hierarchy with a modern pharaoh at the top, and any political reality dominated by televised scenes such as a cluster of self-proclaimed *"men and women of God"* laying their sweaty palms on the back of a government-leader bowing his head in fake humbleness.

Noticeably absent from both lists are the United States of America due to, as is so often the case, America's special status among democratic and authoritarian nations alike. From humble beginnings as a British colony, to the War of Independence and the Indian Wars, to the conquest of the Wild West, Slavery, the Civil War, the Great War, the Great Depression, World War II, the New Deal, the Cold War, and its subsequent rise to the world's only superpower - the relatively short but extremely eventful history of the United States has shaped a colorful chimera of a nation not only in regard to the melting-pot of cultures and ethnicities but also in view of America's national consciousness.

No other culturally 'Western' nation in post WWII-history has to any similar degree been involved in so many major military conflicts as the United States - from Korea to Vietnam, the Dominican Republic, Grenada, Panama, the First Gulf War, Somalia, Haiti, Bosnia and the Kosovo, to Iraq and Afghanistan. At the same time, the national character of the USA has been shaped by massive political, social, and cultural influences by several large religious groups with the Evangelicals spearheading the strategic advancement. Simultaneously, America became a haven and heaven for the arts, from the creation and perfection of numerous music-styles and Hollywood's worldwide dominance on the silver screen, to the triumphal march of the American novel and the introduction of widely diverse sub-cultures into global mainstream. Furthermore, from the 60s onwards the dam of restricting traditions, outdated moral notions, and society-permeating bigotry began to show discernible cracks and was soon unable to contain the growing liberal, progressive, free-spirited current that swept predominantly through the coastal regions of America, carrying with it all sorts of positive and negative trends, from the broadly based commercialization of pornography, to the inception and establishment of grassroot movements, NGOs, and INGOs such as Greenpeace (1971), Human Rights Watch (1978) or the Sothern Poverty Law Center (1971).

These four major developments alone make up a considerable part of present-day America's cultural roots. Simultaneously, however, two of them are clearly at odds with the other two. And it does not necessarily help resolving this growing tension, when far-righters appropriate the traditionally liberal term *"Freedom"* and stick this label on everything from the "freedom" to carry semi-automatic rifles inside Michigan's Capitol building, to the "freedom" to refuse wearing a facemask as preventive protection of elderly and vulnerable fellow Americans, or the "freedom" to break the law by disregarding restrictions on outdoor activities during a pandemic with over 200,000 dead U.S.-citizens and counting. Nor is it particularly clearing the muddy waters of the Big American Divide when one of two relevant political parties is strutting around with ginormous placards proclaiming: *"Republicans Support Morale and Integrity!"*; *"GOP: Standing Up for Honesty & Decency!"*; *"The Republican Party: For Law and Order!"*; or *"The GOP: Home of Christian Values!"*, while the very same people miss no opportunity to trample all they allegedly stand for brutally under foot. Drastic examples for immoral, dishonest, indecent, unlawful, and unchristian behaviors of Republicans abound, with the internet overflowing with shocking proof for the depravity displayed by members of the *Gang of Pretenders* (GoP). For a tangible example, the following occurrence neatly illustrates this extent of Trumpublicans' callousness and indecency. This is

| *The Story of the Pennsylvania Plague Rat*

It was Wednesday, May 27, 2020, when Rep. Brian Sims, (D-Philadelphia), could no longer contain his anger and decided to go on an epic Facebook Live rant to vent his frustration over an occurrence that must be seen as one of the most egregious and callous displays of partisanship and disregard of human decency by Republicans at least since the *Gang of Putzes* (GoP) took the miserable deaths of young children in ICE-cages at the Southern border in stride.

Visibly distraught, middle-aged, bearded Brian Sims, who had been elected to the Pennsylvania House of Representatives in 2012, aired his grievances about his colleagues on the other side of the aisle with considerable fervor. The person chiefly responsible for Sims' rightful anger: Rep. Andrew Lewis, (R-Dauphin), who had tested positive for the Coronavirus but decided to keep his infection hidden from Democratic members of the House while clandestinely notifying his Republican colleagues that he was highly infectious.

In other words, Rep. Lewis, who spearheaded the Republicans' efforts to *'re-open the state'* and send people back to work in the midst of the COVID-19 pandemic deliberately chose to keep Democrats in the dark and simply accepted the risk of having infected numerous Democrats who would then go home and, while still unaware of being virus carriers, potentially pass the deadly virus on to their wives, husbands, grandparents, and children.

"*Every single day of this crisis*", Representative Sims said in his 12-minute video, *"this State Government Committee in Pennsylvania has met so that their members could line up one after one after one and explain that it was safe to go back to work. During that time period they were testing positive. They were notifying one another. And they didn't notify us. I never ever, ever knew that the Republican leadership of this state would put so many of us at risk for partisanship to cover up a lie. And that lie is that we're all safe from COVID*".

Andrew *"Plague Rat"* Lewis issued his own Facebook Live statement mere hours after his Democratic colleague's damning assessment. However, anyone who expected an apology, let alone a credible explanation for his reckless play with other people's lives, was to be disappointed.

Lewis merely let on that his reason for informing *"as few people as possible"* about contracting the coronavirus had been *"to protect the privacy"* of those around him. Adding that he'd only been close to a small number of House colleagues anyway, hence further displaying either complete ignorance or advanced stupidity on top of ethical egoism, callous partisanship, and disregard for anyone not around him. "*I only interacted with a couple of people. I did what I needed to do to protect their privacy. They've had time to get their test and all those things*", said Republican Representative Andrew Lewis at the Capitol in Harrisburg, hammering home once and for all that to ensure his Republican colleagues' timely escape from press and public was foremost on his mind while informing the Democratic representatives was obviously neither his first nor his forty-fifth priority.

Naturally, the blame rests not on Lewis' shoulders alone. He certainly could not have maintained such a flawless record in keeping his infection secret from every Democratic House representative without the unwavering support of Pennsylvania's Republican leadership in Congress. Particularly House Speaker Mike Turazi (R - Allegheny County) and House Majority Leader Brian Cutler (R - Lancaster County) were indispensable in hiding not only Rep. Andrew Lewis' contagion from Democrats but also Rep. Russ Diamond's (R - Lebanon County) little secret who, as a leading advocate for re-opening the state, had self-quarantining for weeks without notifying the Democratic caucus.

The case of Pennsylvania's elected Republican representatives Turazi, Cutler, Diamond, and Lewis, in normal times a scandal of international proportions, (*"House Representative Hides Life-Threatening Infection! – Over 350 Potential Virus-Victims Among Democrats and their Family-Members!"*), constitutes in Times of Trump just one more gaffe of Republican party-members. Soon to be forgotten by a majority long since numb to unending trumpublican high crimes and misdemeanors yet to be long celebrated by a vociferous minority for constituting yet another 'victory' over the *"anti-American, freedom-restricting, snowflake"* Democrats.

Next to shamelessly lying and wilfully endangering the lives of colleagues and their families as well as the many other examples for immoral, dishonest, indecent, unlawful, and unchristian behaviors of Republicans, one specific attitude still manages to stick out. The openly displayed hypocrisy of conservatives and Trumpists constitutes perhaps one of the most insurmountable obstacles for any future President's attempts to close the Great American Rift.

No doubt, pertinent examples for right-wingers' systematic employment of double standards and poorly disguised hypocrisy will make up a large section on the bookshelves and servers of future university-libraries. Such a selection will encompass 'classics' like the right-wing outrage over Barack Obama's tan-colored suit or *44* forgetting to salute a Marine soldier of Marine One, (while Trump deemed it appropriate to salute a North Korean general, of all people) as well as the unequivocally hypocrisy-revealing demeanor of the political right during the COVID-19 pandemic.

Not only that Trump, VP Pence, press-secretary Kayleigh McEnany, and others in Trump's inner circle were tested daily for the Coronavirus while they continued publicly to play down the importance of testing. Not just that the Trumpministration left the 50 states out in the rain when desperately needed ventilators, protective suits and masks for doctors and medical personnel were unobtainable, (*"The federal stockpile, it's supposed to be our stockpile — it's not supposed to be state stockpiles that they then use,"* Jared Kushner, April 2, 2020), only to subsequently claim any partial victories against the deadly virus by individual states and their governors brazenly for themselves. Not only that Donald J. Trump's own government agencies insistently called on the American public to wear facemasks in public and to keep practicing social distancing while the head of self-same government, the American President, continuously refused to wear a facemask in public and repeatedly incited his followers to disregard social distancing-rules.

No, while the fish certainly rots from the head down, the duplicity and hypocrisy displayed by the Trumpministration from day one is nevertheless preceded by a moral rot already prevalent in large parts of the conservative base for a long time. 'Preaching water and drinking wine', in a broader sense meaning the ingrained habit of applying double standards to all aspects of life, has been taught to every Christian conservative since Sunday school. In fact, without the ability to separate *Closed World Assumption* from objective reality life would be constant turmoil for any true believer, as discussed earlier.

The actual extent of this habitual hypocrisy, however, has never been more obviously on display than during the time when a deadly virus consumed the lives of over 100,000 old and young Americans. The same people who attribute every good fortune coming their way to God's will while blaming any misfortune on the persons around them could suddenly be seen out on the streets demonstrating for their "right" to a haircut, in total disregard for their fellow human beings' safety, health, and lives, let alone these people's own right to the pursuit of happiness. Storming a Capitol building with assault-rifles at the ready to 'demonstrate' for the 'freedom' to endanger and potentially kill fellow Americans because they absolutely want their fertilizers, chicken-wings, perms, highlights, and new nail-polishes, their playgrounds and malls and sermons and shooting-ranges back, fits flawlessly into the right-wingers' twisted worldview with them at the center of God's attention and of the world at large.

Though, mind you, the absolute height of this coterie's hypocrisy was reached when several female members of the nationwide congregation of "Pro-Life" anti-abortionists appeared at 'Anti-facemasks'-gatherings across the country with placards reading, "*My Body. My Choice!*" …

Now, thanks to the 2016-election and subsequent polls, the total of alt-righters, Trumpists, Trumpublicans, Evangelicals, 'traditional' conservatives, predator-capitalists, nationalists, racists, misogynists, and other factions united under *President Spanky McLiarface* can be estimated to constitute roughly 35% of the U.S.-population. But it is not just the 'radiating personality' and 'boundless authority' of Donald J. Trump and his incessant pandering to them that is holding this heterogenic mass together.

You see, not for nothing is *Cadet Bone Spurs* clumsily embracing the Stars and Stripes whenever the flag cannot escape up a pole. Not just for his own narcissistic amusement did *Godzilla with Less Foreign Policy Experience* insist on a full-blown military parade with tanks rolling on Washington's streets and fighter-jets thundering overhead. And neither is the newly established Space Force merely a particularly wet brain-fart of the *Tangerine Tornado*, nor is the *Screaming Carrot Demon's* "America First"-policy founded on any remotely sound economic, military, or diplomatic plans. Instead, the weird behaviors and outlandish actions of *Orange Julius* all serve a singular purpose: To rally his 35% and a considerable percentage of Americans outside this circle behind the probably only cause a large majority of U.S.-citizens can agree upon.

American Patriotism.

Appealing to an American's acquired pride of 'God's own country' might be picking the lowest-hanging fruit of all, yet it is still a sure-fire way to turn even a liberal New Yorker into an *"USA! USA!"*-chanting patriot at the right time. Which is where the wheel comes full circle now, to finally place America firmly where it belongs on the 1-10 *Authoritarian Society-scale.*

Without spoiling too much beforehand, America's position on this scale naturally is not found even in the vicinity of countries like China, Cuba, Iran, or Syria, let alone North Korea. On the other hand, the U.S. top the Western European democracies by several notches and under Trump have come in clear viewing-distance to Russia, and not only from Sarah Palin's house in Alaska.

The primal cause for this exceptional position the USA holds among 'first world' democratic nations has much to do with the afore-mentioned American Patriotism and the inevitably intertwined with it belief in higher authorities. To put it bluntly, the average American is trained to respect and obey authorities without questioning from an early age on. From the teacher to the football-coach, school-principal, pastor or priest, judge, sheriff, local police officer and family-doctor to the mayor and other officials to local veterans, firemen, park rangers, National Guard members, all the way to chairmen of local hunting associations, dog-breeder societies, and country or golf clubs. Not to mention the authority figures in one's own family, including N-word-loving grandpa and entitled Aunt Karen because they are family and one's elders.

Young Americans are surrounded on all sides by their "elders and betters" who constantly demand respect, attention, and obedience while safely relying on traditions and a social system supporting the rightfulness of such demands, and on a public that sanctions even drastic punishments for disobedience.

(To proactively bring this assessment in an international perspective, while European societies are far from being hands-off when it comes to proper education and teachings of universal values and morale, the mindset in regard to the status of authorities and their 'automatic' superiority is nevertheless altogether far more liberal on the Old Continent, with an early teaching-focus on critical examination and healthy scepticism of authorities.)

The full impact of a lifelong, in varying degrees subliminal indoctrination with the notion of an 'unquestionable respect for authorities' becomes not only apparent by an almost universal veneration for the office of the U.S.-President and the accompanying powers that clearly exceed any level of responsibility a single individual should be allowed to wield.

No, there is in fact another profession displaying exceptionally well the long-term effect of the American variation of authority-submissiveness permeating U.S.-society. Of all things, it is the often observable demeanor of members of the Fourth Estate in America that has become a domestically much discussed and internationally much frowned upon phenomenon.

Although a small number of journalists attending Donald J. Trump's erratic 'press conferences' or the falsehood-filled 'press briefings' of 1988-born press secretary Kayleigh McEnany have begun from 2019 on to dig deeper and even support each other during question-time, nonetheless the exaggerated moral cowardice and reverence shown by nearly all U.S.-journalists facing politicians or other 'high authorities' basically remains the same until today.

Even masterful American interviewers prefer to work their way around any direct confrontation and developed a tactic to rather let interviewees dig their own graves. (*See*: Lester Hold, Donald Trump interview, May 2017, NBC). What Americans may regard as a brazen and direct approach, e.g. by George Stephanopoulos, Jake Tapper, or Chris Cuomo, still pales in comparison to any average interview with politicians in France, Great Britain, Ireland, Italy, Germany, Scandinavia, Belgium, or the Netherlands to name but a few European democracies where journalists regard it their job to go straight for the jugular of their prime minister, president, or chancellor when the situation demands it. Without being respectless in tone, style, or demeanor, European journalists are adamant in their pursuit for substantive answers and known for being veritable terriers, not letting go no matter how evasive, aggressive, or non-sensical the politician's non-answers turn out to be, as becomes apparent in

| *The Story of the Antagonizing Ambassador*

An excellent example underlining the fundamental difference between the professional mindset of U.S.-journalists compared to the work-ethics of their European colleagues provides the by now infamous YouTube-video showing the very first press conference of U.S.-Ambassador Cornelius Peter "Pete" Hoekstra, then newly appointed to the Netherlands, in January 2018 in the U.S.-embassy in The Hague.

The backstory to this historic 'clash of civilizations' begins three years earlier in 2015. At the time, Peter Hoekstra had been invited to speak at an American Conservatives event where he felt compelled to emphasize the clear distinction between the Republicans' 'success-story' of establishing Law & Order on America's streets on the one hand and the abysmal conditions in lawless, crime-ridden Europe on the other.

During his speech to a sympathetic audience, Hoekstra particularly zeroed in on the Kingdom of the Netherlands, depicting the homeland of the International Court of Justice as a place where *"there are cars being burned. There are politicians that are being burned. [...] And yes, there are no-go zones in the Netherlands."* Statements that likely went down well with his right-wing audience on that night and endeared him further to a Republican leadership that would soon take control of the State Department and its ambassadorial assignments.

Three short years later it was none other than His Excellency, Ambassador Peter Hoekstra, the U.S.-official who made the unambiguous claim that in the Netherlands *"politicians are being burned"*, who strutted in in front of the assembled Dutch press to proudly present himself to the Dutch public as the new Ambassador of the United States to the Kingdom of *"no-go zones"*.

In a representative room used for press-venues in the American embassy, His Excellency Peter "Pete" Hoekstra, born 1953 in Groningen, Netherlands, positioned himself confidently in front of a large sign with a quote from no less a figure than John Adams, America's first ambassador to the Netherlands, expressing his hope that *"only honest and wise men ever rule under this roof."*

One of the first questions put forward to Excellent Hoekstra came from Dutch journalist Roel Geeraedts who asked whether Hoekstra had read the quote behind him. The Ambassador confirmed that he had indeed. This led to Geeraedts' next question. In a neutral tone, the political reporter for Dutch television station *RTL Nieuws* asked the U.S.-Ambassador:

"If you're truly an honest and wise man, could you please take back the remark about burned politicians or name the politician that was burned in the Netherlands?"

This question was followed by an uncomfortable silence in the room. At last, Hoekstra found his voice again and answered: *"Thank you"*, immediately followed by the American Ambassador's attempt to call on another journalist for the next question. A tactic rather reminiscent of a certain U.S.-President's go-to trick whenever a *"nasty"* journalist asks a *"nasty"* question. Amazingly, this tactic works almost always with reporters assembled in the White House Rose Garden or press briefing room. Adding a couple of *"Shut up!"*, *"Sit down!"* and *"That's enough!"* usually suffices to make the reporters quickly give up on any further attempts to receive a half-way coherent or even 10% truth-containing answer; with a few exceptions to the rule mainly from CNN.

On a side note, when for once this strategy did not work and journalists banded together in the Rose Garden to press for an answer consisting not solely of self-praise and hot gases, in an incredible move the 45th American President simply turned around and shambled off into the shadows without another word.

Back at the U.S.-embassy in The Hague, all attempts of Excellency Hoekstra to elicit further questions from other reporters to get to the enjoyable part of the event turned out to be futile. Instead, Hoekstra saw himself confronted with Geeraedts again.

"Excuse me, I asked you a question," the reporter said calmly. When the newly appointed Representative of the United States to the Dutch Royal Court tried to ignore Geeraedts further, another journalist took up the baton and asked: *"Mr. Ambassador, can you mention any example of a Dutch politician who was burned in recent years?"*

Again, the question was greeted with utter silence by Hoekstra who now began to nervously glance around the room, either looking for an ally or an exit. The words of an unnamed journalist spoken next into the persistent silence then became the final nail in Hoekstra's self-built coffin and will probably one day be the most memorable legacy of Republican Ambassador Hoekstra.

"This is the Netherlands. You have to answer questions", the reporter said.

But at this time the proud Republican with an election-campaign TV-ad (*"Yellowgirl"*) in his history Asian-American groups in 2012 called *"very disturbing"* had apparently lost any interest in the venue. Clearly, this whole thing did not go at all as he'd expected. Why did this Euro-trash not behave like back home in America where journalists knew when to stop asking pesky questions?! Didn't they known that he was a highly acclaimed political authority who could make their life a living hell if they made his life slightly uncomfortable? What was going on with these impertinent journos in backwater Europe!

Since His Excellency Peter "Pete" Hoekstra, former House Representative from Michigan's 2nd District and fierce proponent of the claim that Saddam Hussein's regime possessed weapons of mass destruction, apparently had decided to execute a mental *Trump off-shamble*, embassy counsellor Sherry Keneson-Hall, on duty to guarantee the smooth running of the press conference, weighed in with the assertion that His Hoekstra certainly was answering the questions!

Apparently not convinced by Keneson-Hall's take on alternative reality, however, the Dutch media-professionals continued to ask the founding member of the House *Tea Party* Caucus in total at least five times whether he could provide any example of a Dutch politician who was burned in recent years. But Ambassador Hoekstra, who strongly opposed gun control during his tenure, earning him an A rating from the National Rifle Association, and who probably wished for a .45 Colt Double Eagle on top of his diplomatic immunity at this moment wasn't willing to mentally shamble back on stage.

In the end, the Dutch press got neither a rectification nor an explanation, let alone an apology from the Republican who in 2006 co-initiated a website with detailed information potentially helpful for the assembly of nuclear weapons.

"The silence caused by politicizing speech is deafening."
Ambassador Pete Hoekstra (sic!).

The unnamed journalist's statement, *"This is the Netherlands. You have to answer questions"*, did not need the add-on, *"unlike in the United States"*, to be understood by the embassy-staff, journalists, and millions of Europeans watching the U.S.-Ambassador's first close contact with the Dutch press.

In fact, if the United States are known for anything in Europe apart from the usual clichés, (from Size Zero-mania to raging obesity, from school-massacres to heroic first responders, from systemic police brutality to a million-march in peaceful protest, from heart-attack hamburgers to countless types of green smoothies, from the highest forms of cinematic art to the lowest forms of pornography, from Obama to Trump), then it is Americans' eerie willingness to submit to authorities.

Many of the most influential national newspapers, magazines, and TV-broadcasters in Europe and the Western world, but also in Japan, South Korea, South Africa, or South America, frequently make a convincing case for the hypothesis that Americans' unique soft spot for authorities plays a particular role in the meteoric rise to power of a former reality show-host playing an unrelenting "boss" and selling himself as a "self-made billionaire".

A hypothesis that has its merits considering the more than adequate evidence supporting it in recent years. Yet, when this soft spot exists then it also constitutes an invitingly easy to unlock gate to the American voters' mind and as such an irresistible temptation for politicians and political agents. All it needs to gain entrance here is a finely filed and flawlessly fitting key.

Now, as it so happens, one of the most versatile yet near unbreakable, most fine-tuned yet particularly hard-hitting keys guaranteeing near universal entrance to the human mind in general and to authority-prone voters in particular comes in the shape of the *3-Steps Argument from Authority*. A millennia-old treasure in the toolbox of any successful demagogue, populist, and propagandist, providing its user with the wherewithal to assert his authority and subsequently exploit the access gained to the authority-believer's trust to his own advantage.

Its reliability and its worth for the brazen conman is already proven by the fact that the basic framework of the *3-Steps Argument from Authority* has never changed substantially over the centuries. That said, the countless possibilities to disguise, camouflage, distort, hide, and veil this seemingly simple rhetorical tactic make it harder to recognize and to pin down than Donald Trump in a circus full of clowns. The chameleon among the dozens of hoodwinking strategies in the populist's playbook hence is as a rule wrapped in extensive rhetoric garnishments, long-winding decoys, misleading flatteries and endearing falsehoods garnished with convincing acting, impressive garb, fake emotions, elaborate tall tales, and suitable conversation-styles. Altogether, a fundamentally simple *3-Steps Argument from Authority* artfully obfuscated can ensure that any suspicion regarding the genuineness of the authority-persona and their 'expertise' does not even begin to manifest.

Professional political pundits are trained in camouflaging their hidden agenda by making the absolute most out of their position and titles, buttressing the initial authority gained with success-stories and credentials, a selection of high-brow, foreign words, technical terms, and *legalese* and when applicable a list of published books and texts to cement their status as a genuine authority.

Arguing from such an established position, the expert can then figuratively look down his nose on Cuomo, Tapper, Stephanopoulos Maddow, Cooper, or Ruhle, and demand respect from these seasoned journalists despite merely employing a more or less well-disguised variation of the *3 Steps Argument from Authority*. The following hypothetical example of firearms-enthusiast and 2nd Amendment-advocate Clint Howitzer illustrates the basic mechanism of this 3 Steps-strategy in a just slightly exaggerated and simplified manner.

| *The 3 Steps Argument from Authority*

A TV-studio. A news-host and a panel of experts. Among them Clint Howitzer, organizer and spokesperson of regular pro-gun demonstrations in Alabama, Texas, Kentucky, Wisconsin, and other states. The host introduces Clint as *"expert on firearms, including proper handling, possession, and gun-violence"*. Throughout the discussion Howitzer follows the – here simplified displayed – *3 Steps* to first establish his authority, subsequently base his core argument on step 1, and finally draw his desired conclusion based on step 2.

- Clint's **Step 1** [**Establishing Authority**]: "Hello Jake, thanks for having me. Yeah, as you mentioned I am an expert on firearms and gun-violence, since *I work now for 25 years for a big gun-manufacturer / I am a seasoned pro-gun lawmaker / I am one of the longest-serving NRA-officials / I own a gun-shop for over 20 years now / I collect all types of firearms since age 10 / as a hunter I personally fire guns regularly / I was the first dad in our county who gave his 4-year old boy handguns and semi-automatics to shoot with and ten years later we're still accident-free.*"

Polite applause from the studio-audience. Headshaking from the liberal, anti-American snowflakes at the table. The host nods and asks a couple of follow-up questions to further establish Clint's status as a true authority on firearms to prove that the broadcasting company invites only the best experts and offers its audience only the highest class of expertise. The audience takes note.

After introductions all round, the host asks first one of the female anti-constitutionalists at the table why she wants an assault-weapons ban, thorough background-checks, a limit of one firearm per household, comprehensive personality-checks as part of annual renewals of gun-licences, and similar hippie-pipedreams. Instead of interrupting the feminazi's diatribe, Howitzer merely sits quietly and with a tiny smirk nods nearly imperceptible, thus conveying the impression of, *"as the expert I've heard this all before and know what BS it is."* The audience is duly impressed.

When that balls-less communist finally finishes, Clint still refrains from participating in the conversation, instead letting the other panellists erupt in incomprehensible shouting-matches until the host stops the brouhaha and turns to Clint. *"Clint, you didn't say anything yet. What's your take on Alice Braithwaite Goodyshoes' position?"*

- Clint's **Step 2** [**Argument from Authority**]: "Thank you for asking, Jake. Let me first clear something up here. No one on this table has even remotely the experience with firearms I have. Miss Goodyshoes probably never even fired anything with a bigger punch than a .22, while I grew up killing 12-pointers with my old AR-15. Now, as the only real authority on firearms here, I can unequivocally assure you that guns aren't the problem here. The real problem is, *the government's inability to identify mentally crazy lunatics / a completely insufficient school-security and unarmed teachers / the epidemic of violent video games / the ubiquitous sex and violence on TV / this generation of mollycoddled, weak-minded, liberal young freeloaders / simply not enough good guys with guns."*

Parts of the studio-audience start to clap and woohoo. The host displays a serious facial expression and employs his critical-journalist personality. With an earnest timbre in his voice he asks Clint to elaborate and explain to his viewers how he comes to this conclusion.

In his following answer Clint takes care to mention his authority-status in an unobtrusive way whenever opportune. *"Sure, Jake. Look, in my long career as [expert] I have never seen a case where a family had too many guns but a lot of cases where a burglar would've been taken down sooner if the wife and kids only would've had their own handguns too." / "Jake, you wouldn't believe how many lunatics have bought guns in my shop over the last two decades. I've seen them all." / "Look Jake, I've seen my daughter play these videogames and right after go out and pop six squirrels with her Beretta 950BS Minx 22 Short. Believe me, as a father and a gun-expert I clearly see a connection here!" / "Give me or any other highly trained expert just two hours to instruct the teachers at my son's school and they'd be ready to use their piece from 30 feet to accurately blow the brains out of any of my son's schoolmates who try some funny business. Problem solved. It's really that easy, Jake."*

After the contrived hysteria of the Eurotrash-loving, socialist trollop and her comrades at the table has finally died down and the audience-members took their seats again, the host grants the other panellists their say on the matter.

Once again, Clint simply leans back and smirks knowingly. Because he actually does know two things for sure. For one, that the fraction of the audience agreeing with him on the duty of every American to defend the 2nd Amendment to the last drop of blood now regards him as a legitimate frontrunner and spearhead of "the cause". Their belief in his authority-status, while at the beginning perhaps wavering, is now firmly established. The enthusiastic applause from his supporters in the audience, the panel-host's deferential demeanor towards Clint, and his own cool yet friendly, level-headed yet relatable manner throughout created together a positive authority-image even the America-hating friends of little Miss Goodyshoes will have a hard time to argue away.

Secondly, Clint knows that his statements have clearly enraged the other side. A satisfying result, not foremost because Clint likes to watch bitches like Goodyshoes turn purple and scream, although that's certainly a nice extra, but because Clint welcomes the raw anger and rage he managed to elicit from Missy Alice and her snowflake SJWs, particularly because they legitimize him further. The only way for Goodyshoes to really hurt his mission would have been to not take him serious at all. If she instead had stayed on script and simply shot his allegations to pieces with hard facts and witty one-liners without even directly talking to him, his "authority" would have seriously suffered for sure.

Fortunately, however, Goodyshoes and her Antifa-rabble did him the favor to attack him and his position with the gravest seriousness and a holier-than-thou attitude befitting the leader of any *Women for Prohibition!* Club of the 1910s. On this base as safely established and even 'validated' authority, Clint can now confidently execute the last part of his 3 Steps-strategy.

When the panel-host returns to Clint to ask for his final statement, Clint Howitzer takes his sweet time to sit up straight, smile at Goodyshoes and then lock eyes with Jake before he smoothly delivers his conclusion.

- Clint's **Step 3** [**Desired Conclusion**]: "*Thank you, Jake. Look, of course I know all the data and figures our friend Miss Goodyshoes presented here tonight. And nobody wants an end to gun-violence more than we, believe me! But we must do it the right way, Jake. Look, guns don't kill people. People kill people, Jake, as my decades of expert-experience have clearly proven. And that's exactly why we need more guns, not less, Jake. Look, it's an easy equation, really. More good people with more guns can kill more bad people with guns. Simple.*
Our studies have in fact shown that by merely doubling the present estimated gun-ownership ratio of 120 firearms per 100 Americans we could already stop a great number of criminals from even considering committing crimes such as for instance brutally snatching your granny's purse and seriously hurt her in the process. With a handy .22 in every granny's purse such delicts would quickly die out. Believe me, Jake.
O'course the same goes for school-shootings. Not one of the 33 school-shootings between January and April 2020 would have happened if every teacher would've been trained and armed, Jake. Not one. I've seen dozens of teachers in my career who were able to hit a target from 30 feet after just one day of training. And many clearly enjoy shooting a great deal. In fact, some even

laugh out long and loud while letting it rip with the bigger semi-automatics. See, Jake, that's exactly the kind of teachers we want, and we need to protect our children effectively. Well trained, enthusiastic, jolly, and totally unhesitating when the moment comes.

And don't even start blaming mass-shootings on guns. Really! Look, you don't need to be a shrink to understand that these people are total nut cases, every single one of them. So, instead of blaming their killing-sprees on guns we rather need to pay more attention to all the shrinks and how they deliberately neglect their duty to identify and report their patients to the proper authorities. In my professional experience, if these crazies couldn't use an assault-weapon they'd simply grab a similarly dangerous weapon, like a knife. Or a machete. Ever held a machete, Jake? Sweet Jesus, that's one hell of a murder-weapon, I can tell you that.

So, when you ask me as the only real expert on firearms here today, Jake, then I have to tell you and my new friends on this table that yes, people die from bullets, sure. But people also die in car-accidents, Jake. And in plane-crashes. Do we ban cars and planes because of that? Of course not. Driving and flying are part of our civilization. Just as guns. There's some danger involved, granted, but at the bottom line we accept that because of the many advantages, right? I mean, without cars how would we get around, right? Or a world without planes. Imagine that. I mean, our way of life would be totally crippled, right? And the same goes for firearms. Yes, that's right. I wish the people on Miss Goodyshoes' side would finally accept that and move on to really important matters. Like a deep state that's taking away our freedoms and tries to lock us into our own houses and forces us to wear masks to hide our faces like these Islam women.

See, the Framers knew exactly what they did with the 2nd Amendment, Jake. When the day comes and the deep state agents reveal themselves and force us all to wear Muslimist masks as a rule and stay at home because some fake virus allegedly killed 100,000 Americans, then you'll be glad that there are real Americans out there, true patriots who will fight for the American Way of Life to the last man. While all those socialistic Europeans will be forced to obey their double-agent scientists and meekly stay 10 feet away from each other, Americans will rise and resist, Jake. And if there's one thing my long experience as an authority on firearms has taught me, Jake, then that you can't resist anything without a gun in your hand!"

Enthusiastic applause from Clint's supporters in the audience accompanied by occasional *"USA! USA!"*-chants. Silence from Alice Braithwaite Goodyshoes. Thanks from Jake to all experts at the table for their valuable and interesting input. Clint nods and smiles into the camera.

Seeing it on paper in a slightly exaggerated example, the *3 Steps Argument from Authority* can easily be mistaken for a blindingly obvious attempt of third grade rhetoric trickery. Yet, millions are taken in by this "amateurish trick" every day. From the florist at the corner who is trusted to have an artistic vein and to know exactly what flower-arrangement looks best at one's home to the FOX News correspondent reporting from the riots in Portland or Kenosha and is trusted to deliver an unbiased picture of the scene.

Clint Howitzer's hypothetical example is only easy to see through because it has been stripped from any seriously applied garnish and lacks all the usual smoke and mirrors coming with such "authorities". If Clint would, for instance, wear a Marines-, police-, or Army-uniform and talk about his 20 years in the military, to doubt any of his effectuations would amount to a near sacrilege and be seen as an insult to a 'real American hero'. But even if Clint would just tell a short story about his first hunting-trip at age 8 with his WWII-veteran granddad or merely mention his recent bestseller-book "My Hunting Adventures: Sniping Small Game with the AR-15", his credibility as a "firearms-expert" would considerably rise in the eyes of not only his natural supporters but even a more critical audience.

Furthermore, the invitation of Howitzer to a panel on ABC, MSNBC, CNN, or FOX constitutes in itself a badge of "verified authority", since the American public has come to rely entirely on the mainstream media to scrutinize, vet, and verify the 'experts' presented to them on screen. In fact, a considerable number of former and current House-representatives, Senators, and judges have made it their lucrative business to regularly appear on TV as 'experts' on almost any political issue. Having their authority on the subject at hand cast into question is clearly the last thing they fear, irrespectively of their actual knowledge or experience of the matter at hand.

Just take the universally deployable Trumpagandists Matt Gaetz (R-FL), Mark Meadows (R-NC), and Gym Jordan (R-OH), who have fortunately been recorded for posterity when they jumped in front of the cameras in early October of 2019 to defend their Master in the Ukraine-Extortion Scandal. Knowing absolutely nothing about anything, these archetypical epitomes of the, dispensable party-soldier threw themselves into the line of fire with all their 'authority' as a political "insiders", following the playbook of the *3 Steps Argument from Authority* to a T in order to save their *Orange Overlord*.

The same modus operandi could be observed only a few months after Trump's impeachment trial and in the middle of the Trumpministration's historic failure in the Corona-crisis, when the murder of Black American citizen George Floyd by white police officers sparked the biggest civil unrest in the U.S. since the 1960s. Once again, police chiefs, mayors, governors, and of course the Instigator-in-Chief himself used the authority invested in them by the people to appropriate a level of authority over self-same people that allowed the real arsonists to deflect any responsibility away from themselves and onto the demonstrators. Blaming the protesters for the riots and outbreaks of violence, the established [Step 1] authorities argued (or rather took for granted) that their positions of authority were all that was needed to justify [Step 2] wide-spread police brutality, the deployment of the Nation Guard, and the police forces' excessive use of tear-gas, flash-bang grenades, rubber-bullets, pepper-spray, and truncheons against unarmed demonstrators. Self-evidently resulting in further violence, looting, rioting, and deaths allowing these authorities to conclude [Step 3] that their decisions leading up to this outcome had obviously been correct in the first place ...

| *To <u>trump</u> [verb] : alternat./: to blatantly abuse power*

Clearly, the man who takes the cake, eats it, and demands seconds when it comes to the abuse of power is indubitably none other than America's answer to Idi Amin. From Donald Trump's October 7, 2019 tweet stating non-ironically that, "[...] *if Turkey does anything that I, in my great and unmatched wisdom, consider to be off limits, I will totally destroy and obliterate the Economy of Turkey (I've done before!) [...]*", to his repeated insistence that Article II of the U.S. Constitution *"allows me to do whatever I want"*, (it doesn't, by the way), to the perpetual mentions of his apparently limitless pardon-powers, his regularly resurfacing "jokes" about a third term or a lifelong presidential tenure or his unconstitutional refusal to cooperate with Congress to get to the bottom of the Ukraine-scandal – in each case Donald Trump appears to be revelling in his abuse of the powers granted to the President's Office by the Founding Fathers. Deliberately misconstruing the thoughts and convictions of Jefferson, Adams, Washington and their fellow Framers whenever it is advantageous, Donald Trump perverts the American Constitution by abusing the authority of the Presidential Office at will.

Of course, Article II of the Constitution does in fact grant the U.S. President extensive executive powers. However, it also states the limits of these presidential powers. According to these limitations, the president is, for instance, *not* authorized to declare war, grant letters of marque and reprisal, regulate commerce, make treaties or appointments without the advice and consent of the Senate, pardon impeachments or violations of state law, or appoint persons to official positions without prior Senate-approval.

Furthermore, Article II, Section 3 (*Responsibilities of the president*), Clause 5, imposes the duty on the president to enforce the laws of the United States, stating that the president must "*take care that the laws be faithfully executed*". Called the *Take Care Clause* or the *Faithful Execution Clause*, it ensures that a law is faithfully executed by the president – whether he disagrees with the purpose of that law *or not*.

To better understand why Donald Trump, despite above mentioned and further legal limitations, has no problem with repetitively declaring Article II allows him "*to do whatever I want*" one needs to cop a closer look at his sole, genuine target group - Trumpists.

The first thing most often coming to mind in this regard is the proverbial political ignorance displayed by most if not all Trumpists, allowing Donald Trump to allege more or less what he wants in regard to his "constitutional powers", since any noticeable opposition to his claims from his own ranks would first of all need a measurable number of Trumpists who know more about the American Constitution than the phrases, "*We the People*", "*Life, Liberty, and the pursuit of Happiness*", and, "*the right of the people to keep and bear Arms shall not be infringed*". As it stands, the convenient ignorance of Trumpists in all matters political and constitutional gives Donald Trump free rein to exploit the *3 Steps Argument from Authority* to its fullest by declaring himself the nation's indisputable highest authority in all matters political, legal, economical, and military.

In the eyes of Trumpists, the Dear Leader represents the living embodiment of *"everything that's right and good in the United States of America"*, and it is thus "only logical" that Trump would also be far more familiar with the Constitution than some obscure constitutional law professors with their bloodless theoretical knowledge. Which explains why Trumpists dismissed reports from White House insiders during the early days of the Trumpministration, according to whom the newly elected president had grudgingly listened to a legal expert's detailed effectuations on the Constitution - up to Article IV. At this point, Donald Trump allegedly rolled his eyes, pulled his lower lip down with one finger and declared the presentation finished.

If there were any doubts remaining regarding Trump's position on the Constitution, laws, and justice in general, then the George Floyd-Riots in 2020 clearly made short shrift of them. While literally hiding in his bunker beneath the unlit White House, *Herr Twittler* posted tweets demanding *"Dominance"* of the police forces over peaceful protesters like a third world-dictator during his last stand. At the same time, the internet burst with videos showing excessively brutal police officers beating, kicking, spraying, pushing, hitting, trapping, kneeling on, flash-banging, and rubber bullet-shooting demonstrators in cities across America, gravely wounding and hurting hundreds of innocent Americans some of whom lost their eyesight, their physical and mental health, and even their lives.

While Americans experienced first-hand what it means to live in a country where government abuses its authority, and while thousands of New Zealanders, Canadians, French, Germans, Dutch, and other nationalities took to the streets in solidarity with the American protesters' demands for an end to systemic racism, police brutality, and a two-tier justice for violent and murderous police officers, Trump-appointee GA William Barr ordered police to disperse peaceful protesters with teargas, rubber-bullets, and truncheons around St. John's Church near the White House to make room for a "spontaneous" photo-op of the President.

When Trump arrived in front of the church to reassure his Evangelical base that he's still in charge and will prevent the "hordes" from lynching every non-socialist this week, he began his bizarre appearance by holding a bible upside-down and front-to-back with a facial expression that seemed strangely paralyzed, either resulting from his general sociopathic emotionlessness or due to a heavy dose of some type of psychotropic drug. When asked by a reporter, "Is that your bible?", Trump starred at him for seconds before he dead-pan replied, "It's *a* bible."

Just a few minutes earlier in the White House's Rose Garden, Trump had threatened to let the U.S.-military lose on protesters, using terms like *anarchy* and *domestic terror* while promising that his forces would *"dominate the streets"*, making his disregard for his constitutional role as

President of *all* Americans and his duty to protect and serve *all* Americans once again abundantly clear.

When these examples do not suffice in demonstrating beyond any doubt that Donald Trump has only contempt for the Constitution and the system of checks and balances of the Framers, it might be worthwhile to look back at an interview Trump gave to FOX News' Martha MacCallum on April 28, 2017. In its course, Trump answered MacCallum's question, *"How would you describe your political philosophy?"*, with one of his usual lengthy, helter-skelter perorations until he arrived at the constitutional duties and the legal proceedings of Congress. Here, Trump's ill-fitting mask of a "democrat" and president who sees his powers soundly based on the Constitution and the Bill of Rights finally fell and the ugly grimace of the authoritarian strongman became visible.

"You look at the rules of the Senate, even the rules of the House -- but the rules of the Senate and some of the things you have to go through, it's -- it's really a bad thing for the country, in my opinion. They're archaic rules", Trump declared.

"And maybe at some point we're going to have to take those rules on, because, for the good of the nation, things are going to have to be different. You can't go through a process like this. It's not fair. It forces you to make bad decisions. I mean, you're really forced into doing things that you would normally not do except for these archaic rules."

With his words being on record and shared online hundreds of thousands of times, there are no two ways about it: Donald John Trump, elected 45th president of the United States, publicly admitted that he regards the Framers' 240 years old cornerstone of American democracy and the very base of the United States' existence, including its exemplary and often copied political system of checks and balances, its three independent branches of government, and the congressional oversight duties, to be a mere set of *"archaic rules"*, a political process that simply is *"not fair"* and on top of it *"a really bad thing for the country"*. The only reason any American President could have for wanting to weaken or abolish elementary democratic oversight is obvious. After all, who else but a fledging autocratic strongman would *"take those rules on because, for the good of the nation, things are going to have to be different."* ...

| *Bonus Step 4: Entrenchment*

Remember Clint Howitzer? Well, the 2nd Amendment-defender and firearms-enthusiast who established his status as an authority on anything gun-related by 'winning' the last panel-debate following the *3 Steps Argument from Authority* is not in the clear quite yet. While half of Texas, Wisconsin, and Idaho, and all of Kentucky, Alabama, and Tennessee cheered for Clint after he left the studio last time proclaiming him the new messiah of pro-gun activism, this new popularity earned him also another invitation to a further panel-discussion on the subject.

Only this time Clint will face some rather more experienced, eloquent, and professionally educated adversaries on the panel, as well as a serious, inquisitive journalist as host. For better or worse, it looks like Clint will need to defend his bogus 'conclusion' in earnest this time.

Unfortunately, though, such a setting is purely hypothetical nowadays, since the world of quality-journalism on U.S. primetime television seems by all accounts irretrievably a thing of the past. Thanks to the relentless chase of higher ratings as well as mainly tooth- and clawless news-hosts and network-journalists – with the last predator-ivories belonging to a handful of CNN-hosts and exceptionally experienced and talented investigative journalists, though otherwise exclusively to half a dozen late night-show hosts – being just two of the reasons for the decline of professional, hard-hitting interviews and panel-discussions.

Still, for the sake of the argument let's assume that the next public appearance of Howitzer takes place at a TV panel-discussion that is famous for its strict and straightforward host and that Clint's fellow panellists are quick-witted, well educated, and anything but shy professionals.

Republican pundit Clint Howitzer knows of course that his opponents know what he did last summer and that they probably will not let him get through with his *3 Steps*-strategy this time. Fortunately for any Trumpublican pundit though, the new propaganda-phalanx in the White House has come up with an almost fool-proof method to successfully deflect any attacks on their positions as well as on their self-imparted authority. A method demanding only one prerequisite all Trump-sycophants possess in abundance. A particularly thick skin.

The night of the panel-discussion. Rachel, the host, introduces Clint and his fellow panellists around the table with academic titles and a short career-overview with focus on individual career-highlights regarding gun-violence, gun-legislation, and street-experience. Clint is introduced with his job-title (*NRA-official / gun shop-proprietor / ex-Marine, or similar*), as well as long-time advocate for the 2nd Amendment, less firearms-restrictions, a "well-armed" population, armed teachers, prohibiting violent videogames, and a legal duty for psychiatrists and psychotherapists to report "suspicious" patients to the FBI.

Advocating such controversial positions marks Clint immediately as a designated target for the gun-critics at the table who came prepared with facts, statistics, personal experience-stories, historic and international comparisons, and a clear and logical line of argumentation. Clint came prepared with two double bourbons in his bloodstream, a roguish smile on his lips, and the total conviction in his mind that he will leave as the clear victor today.

Just as Clint expected, the America-destroying socialists at the table attack him right from the start. Florence Nightingale, Marie Curie, and Frida Kahlo first take his assertion apart that less guns in public circulation don't mean less deadly violence because people would simply use other 'lethal' weapons. Next, Clint's idea to arm teachers with handguns is exposed as the pipedream of a reality-detached gun nut, followed by an all-round rejection of Clint's demands for a law forcing psychiatrists to report 'suspect' patients to the authorities, soundly based on the physician-patient privilege as well as the immense potential for abuse and extensive margin of error.

Through all this Clint Howitzer sits and smiles and nods pensively. When the host finally manages to get a word in and turns to Clint, asking for his detailed reply to each of the allegations of *"wanton irresponsibility, complete reality-detachment, blatant civil rights abuse, and deliberate disregard of numerous study-results"* made by Florence, Marie, and Frida, Howitzer takes his sweet time to sit up straight before he answers Rachel in a sombre tone.

"Thank you, Rachel. Well, it looks like I'm holding the Alamo alone here today, what? But hey, that's okay. I certainly don't need a three-deep line of Amazons to prove me right, Rachel. Sorry, of Democratic Socialists, I meant. My apologies. Anyway, you know what I was thinking while I listened to my dear colleagues here, Rachel? I thought about our great Founding Fathers and what they would say if they could hear these deeply un-American sentiments here today.

I think George Washington, Thomas Jefferson, Alexander Hamilton, and John Adams could not have liberated this great country from tyranny and led it to freedom, prosperity, and greatness without an armed fight. I think that the Framers were very deliberate when they included the 2nd Amendment in our Constitution because they knew exactly that liberty without a well-armed population is a dictatorship waiting to happen. And I deeply believe that it was God's plan for us to tame the greatest country on Earth with a rifle in one hand, the Bible in the other hand, and a horse beneath our bums. Pardon my French, ladies.

In short, Rachel, America wouldn't even exist without firearms. Our right to bear arms is as American as baseball, apple pie, and the 4th of July. And I'll be damned if I will just stand by idly while certain globalist, socialist agitators attempt to destroy the American Way of Life from within. These people have clearly no sense for American history, American traditions, American values, and American greatness.

As one of the leading authorities on firearms in the United States and as a true American patriot, you know what I heard here today, Rachel? I tell you the only thing I heard here today, Rachel. I heard just one more sneaky, outright attack on everything that makes America great, Rachel. You have given my fellow panellists ample time today to spread their divisive vitriol, to weaken our American resolve, to render all Americans more vulnerable and to make our great country less safe. That's what I heard here today, Rachel. And you know, it saddens me. It truly saddens me, Rachel. America deserves so much better!

Alright, thank you. Thank you, Rachel. God bless you all. And God bless the United States of America."

Roughly 35% of the studio-audience jump straight up from their seats and applaud frenetically. Of the other 65% more than half join in good-naturedly and keep going when the applause turns into rhythmic clapping accompanied by *"USA! USA!"*-chants. Recognizing an end with a bang when she sees one, Rachel ends the discussion with some general chit-chat and a few minutes later the station cuts to commercials.

Half an hour later Clint Howitzer leaves the TV-studio in a taxi. Five minutes into the ride he receives a phone call from the Special Advisor to the President, congratulating Clint and inviting him to join the President for an unofficial dinner with some of the President's 'closest friends' next month. And perhaps there will even be some time for a few holes on the Green. Who knows.

Next day, the polls show that while most viewers were apparently not all too sure about how exactly Clint intends to implement his policies in practice, Clint nevertheless outcompeted Kahlo, Curie, Nightingale, and particularly Goodyshoes, in the overall approval ratings.

Leaving a thoroughly gobsmacked group of actual "Pro-Lifers" who are advocating for a United States where not on average 7,878 children and teens between the ages 1–17 are shot with a firearm every year, with 1,584 of them dying from gun violence, 818 murdered, and 2,788 intentionally shot by someone else, according to *The Brady Plan* (*bradyunited.org*). Yet, just as he had predicted, Clint Howitzer is the indisputable debate-winner in the eyes of the public.

So, what the hell happened?

Due to the slightly exaggerated nature of that example, it is of course obvious what happened. Or rather, first what did not happen. Clint did not address any specific point of criticism, nor one single fact, statistic, exemplary case, or study-result presented by his opponents. Clint did not turn to any of his adversaries and speak directly to them for one second. Clint did not give Rachel or any fellow panellist any chance to interrupt and contradict him during his speech. Finally, Clint did not interrupt his opponents during their speeches, instead biding his time and 'accumulating' speaking-time for himself so that it appeared 'only fair' when he talked uninterruptedly for a longer time at the end, giving him de facto control over the how and when to wrap up the debate.

What did happen, on the other hand, was a literal textbook-example for safeguarding one's bogus or weak status as an 'authority' and successfully defending one's arguments and conclusions based on said authority by entrenching both behind an impenetrable barbed-wire fence of semi-sacred and highly emotions-inciting platitudes.

Clint's deliberately lavish use of specific keywords such as *"Founding Fathers"*, *"Framers"*, *"Washington"*, *"Hamilton"*, *"Jefferson"*, *"Constitution"*, *"God"*, *"Bible"*, *"traditions"*, *"greatness"*, and of course *"America"*, instinctively triggered positive emotions and associations such as national pride, American exemplarism, and a comforting sense of belonging. In comparison, Clint used the terms *"guns"* or *"firearms"* not at all or sparingly, instead concentrating on the dire consequences his opponents' demands will indubitably have for *"this great nation"*. Bottom line, Clint knew that he would win the game hands down because he never intended to play it in the first place. Nightingale and her colleagues played chess, while Clint played UNO.

The subject might change, with guns being replaced by health care, unemployment, the economy, or a deadly pandemic with 200,000 dead Americans, however, the *3 Steps Argument from Authority* strategy remains the same. Members of the Trumpministration and the Trumpublican Party employ this strategy regularly when speaking in public, sometimes obfuscating and disguising their intentions better, such as, for instance, AG William Barr by using a heap of legalese and long-winding explanations when declaring the Mueller-report actually exonerated Mr. Trump.

Other times they stoop as low as to position their obese figure audaciously in front of St. John's Church in Washington, D.C. after forcefully "dispersing" peaceful protesters during the largest anti-racism protests in history only to hold up a copy of the bible to the camera, thus appropriating the authority of the church for his propaganda photo-op, blatantly pandering to the Evangelical demographic. Successfully, alas, considering the thousands of tweets by devout Christians subsequently praising the *Bunker King* for *"wearing God's armor"* while apparently defending all of God's creation, and Evangelicals in particular, against the barbaric hordes of peaceful protesters demonstrating against the ubiquitous racial injustice and wanton police-brutality in God's own country.

As with many things in life, also employing the *3 Steps Argument from Authority* proves to be most difficult at the beginning, with its the first step the establishing of one's authority, Incidentally, the best tip in this regard comes straight from the horse's mouth. Provided a wannabe-conman is cursed with the same impertinent, impudent, and insolent character as Donald John Trump, it should prove extremely easy to follow in Trump's footsteps and *"fake it 'til you make it"*. Once a sufficiently large number of people believe in the faker's pseudo-authority, they will in fact do all the work for him to transform the mountebank's fake authority-status into genuine authority. This goes for the confident challenger of the current cartel-boss just as much as for the wealthy conman who believes himself destined for greater things and is eaten up with envy of a Black man who has everything the rich fraudster can't buy with money. Still, as it turned out money helps a great deal in assuring a faker's victory in a general election, unfortunately providing the gravitas of the new position and thus making Step 2, arguing from this new position of authority, almost a non-brainer. With his newly acquired "authority" behind him, the conman is now not only in an ideal position to support every allegation with his own position but moreover proves to be all but immune to any legal, professional, and reputational consequences or serious and impactful critique of the office-holder's 3. Step conclusions no matter how outlandish, nefarious, and false they may be. And even if an opposing authority rises for once above these "natural" inhibitions and attacks the fake-authority, the now firmly established uber-authority only needs to employ Step 4 to conveniently entrench himself behind emotional platitudes, reliably activating the outrage reflex of gullible Trumpists.

Nonetheless, while the *3 Steps Argument from Authority* over the centuries has turned out to be extremely practical and near universally applicable due to its flexibility and its countless variations of decoys, obfuscations, garnishments, and smoke and mirrors, it still only constitutes the most basic variant in the family of *Arguments from Authority* compared to the following, sophisticated manipulation-strategies based on authority.

"The Bootleg Expert"

Advanced Arguments from Authority Variation I.

Allowing propagandists a lot of legroom for duping their target-audience and the undecided part of the public, the *Bootleg Expert* constitutes an old and trusted scheme used by conservatives and the far-right to appear reputable by pretending to play by the book. The one considerable downside being, as with all *Advanced Arguments,* the intensive preparation needed beforehand. In case of the *Bootleg Expert*, the first step on the way to convincing an unsuspecting audience of the honesty and veracity of some Trumpaganda-allegation consists of recruiting a suitable, genuine authority in a field of expertise that has an impressive sound to it.

Active and retired right-wing lawyers, judges, attorneys, legislators, and law professors for instance constitute widely applicable authorities who generally do not need to be asked twice adding their two cents to any debate, regardless of their factual expertise on the matter. In the currently hyper-partisan political climate, trumpublican representatives of these professions have let few opportunities go to waste which provide them access to a broader audience for throwing their weight behind the latest Trump-allegation, with the possible exception of Donald Trump's foul deriding of American soldiers killed in action.

As a practical example, let's assume "Kelly Conman", responsible *fakespert*-handler in the Trumpaganda-brigade, selected a suitable candidate as the party's newest *Bootleg Expert*. In the next step, this pseudo-authority then needs to be thoroughly vetted and briefed. Depending on character and level of party-allegiance, the candidate might need some prior prompting and convincing, but in most cases the White House Trumpagandists can fall back on a full index box with addresses of sympathetic conservative front-fighters ready to provide the ruler in the White House with a veneer of respectability.

When the day of the *fakespert's* public appearance approaches, handler "Conman" will want to brief them on the finer points of the hot potato in question. For the sake of the argument, the *fakespert* here will be a Republican law professor and the topic he will be interviewed on is Trump's ongoing trade war with China. Naturally, hypothetical law professor Galen Derposhitz is neither stupid nor uninformed concerning this subject. Yet, he is also no expert in any way, shape, or form on trade disputes, punitive tariffs, the Chinese economy, or the American economy for that matter. Fortunately for him, however, such knowledge is not required for the *Bootleg Expert* scheme to work.

Certainly, the Trumpaganda-department would have no big problem finding a genuine expert on the China-trade war matter who could eloquently talk about it with the desired amount of pro-Trump bias. However, this expert would lack one decisive attribute: They would not come with a similarly impressive title, let alone with a well-known household-name. Professor Derposhitz, on the other hand, rightfully considers himself to be semi-famous and Kelly Conman knows that his face and name will arrest viewers' twitchy thumb on the zapper far longer than some unknown visage.

Once Derposhitz got his briefing and Kelly Conman is satisfied that the professor will come to the "right conclusions" in his interview, the moment has come for the *Bootleg Expert* to walk in front of the cameras and shine. The TV-host's introduction of the professor with all his titles and authored books allows for a closer look at the quite banal psychology behind the *Bootleg Expert's* impressive success-rate.

Now, while the impact of Derposhitz's reputation and title is easy to recognize, there still exists the problem with the incongruence of the professor's field of expertise and the topic of the interview. After all, constitutional law has about as much to do with international trade disputes and Chinese trade-politics as Kayleigh McEnany has to do with the truth. And admittedly, the whole *Bootleg Expert* scheme could hardly work if professor Derposhitz would be challenged by a hard-hitting journalist on an independent network. In fact, Derposhitz would not be invited to speak on the topic in the first place. Alas, with FOX News, OANN, and the Sinclair-stations in the picture, ample room exists for all sorts of *Bootleg Experts* to contribute their share of propaganda to the Trumpministration's grand scheme.

Furthermore, even broadcasters usually considered professional and unbiased are not above hiring Derposhitz and his fellow *Bootleg Experts* from time to time on non-related topics, subliminally presenting them as *"established voices of the conservative side"* or similar. But even so, the question remains why audiences often accept *Bootleg Experts* as legitimate authorities on matters outside of their field of expertise. The answer lies in the actual trick behind the *Bootleg Expert*, aside from the intentionally awe-inspiring reputation of such authorities already quelling potential doubts, viz its fine-tuning. That's where the dark beauty of the *Bootleg Expert* reveals its full potential.

For an example let's return to the two subjects of *"constitutional law"* and *"international trade"*. Both contents only overlap marginally, if at all. Yet, in the minds of the average citizen both fields of expertise appear to somehow belong to the same cluster of meta-subjects, since at the bottom line, both topics comprise large academic fields with thousands of books written on the subject, with their own, specific sub-languages, and with countless people studying for years to gain access to the seclusive world of specialists on these extremely complicated matters.

Hence, it is a frequent and natural assumption by non-initiated outsiders that a person with a decades-spanning career in one academic area must also have at least a good understanding of other, "related" fields. As hard as it might be to believe for academics and the better educated, a sizable part of the population makes no fine distinctions between the various non-natural sciences and disciplines, often assigning the same label of *"useless, unprofitable arts"* to the sciences of politics, sociology, psychology, philosophy, history, history of arts, cultural science, geography, geology, or archaeology, while simultaneously being awed by students of law, finances, business, trade, and medicine and regarding degree-holders in mathematics, physics, chemistry, biology, and other natural sciences as "uber-nerds" and Hollywood-like modern wizards.

With the 'awe-inspiring' fields of law, business, trade, finances, and medicine together on one pedestal, the assumption of them being "somehow related" (with the exception of medicine) is not as far-fetched as most academics would like to believe. Moreover, although most people are theoretically aware that a plethora of different fields of law exists, from international trade law to constitutional law, to divorce law, to criminal law, etc., they tend to forget this fact as soon as they meet a lawyer at a cocktail-party and start pestering the jurisprudent with their legal problem with the neighbor and his fence encroaching on their property, giving the international contract-lawyer no time to explain his professional incompetence in the matter. The same goes, as is widely known, for any Doctor of Medicine who must listen to the story of Aunt Mildred's boil and her offering to have a "quick look at it", regardless of the good doctor being an ophthalmologist. In the end a doctor is a doctor, and a lawyer is a lawyer. A generalization, albeit an involuntary, that allows those who do such things to abuse this good-natured error in reasoning to their advantage, mainly in complicity with a professional willing to function as their *Bootleg Expert*.

Incidentally, the *Bootleg Expert* ploy is not reserved for the big stage and the professional world exclusive to politicians, public relations-manager, salespersons, business consultants, CEOs, company-spokespeople, lobbyists or, of course, lawyers. On the contrary, almost everyone has made the acquaintance of one or more *Bootleg Experts* in their lives or have even taken on the role themselves. Any father or mother, for instance, unwittingly constitutes an ultimate *Bootleg Expert* for their children. A little boy's allegation of, *"My daddy says there's a car with an astonought in it flying round the Earth!"*, becomes a valid claim in children's ears with the mentioning of daddy as the (*Bootleg*) *Expert,* as does his little friend's reply: *"My dad says notting can fly round the*

Earth cause the Earth is flat, dummy!", resulting in a classic stalemate where both debate-sides brought the strongest possible argument to the table, viz the ultimate *Bootleg Expert,* aka Daddy.

After having grown out of the age when parents seem infallible, young adults start to become their own *Bootleg Expert* and its handler in one person. Embellishing their experiences during the last holiday-trip to Thailand to the level of Leo DiCaprio in *"The Beach"* in order to be seen as a "globetrotting adventurer" by their friends is just the beginning of most people's lifelong career as their own, albeit amateurish *Bootleg Expert*, since only a relatively small number of people take the next step and begin utilizing the *Bootleg Expert* strategy for the advancement of their own, selfish aims on a professional level.

One profession, for example, in which the use of *Bootleg Experts* becomes a prerequisite to remain relevant constitutes that of a TV-talk show host. Particularly daily talk shows in the morning or early afternoon are constantly in dire need of "experts" on all kinds of topics but are more often than not struggling with hiring genuine authorities for budget-, and reputation-reasons, since no respected authority wants to be seen dead on these shows. TV-audiences of such shows consist in the main of stay-at-home moms and the elderly, unemployed, or sick, while the general population mostly ignores these programs or does not take them seriously. Unsurprisingly, any public outcry regarding the extent of misinformation, fake news, reality-distortion, and stupefaction of the people coming from these talk shows will therefore be a long time in the coming. Until then it will remain not unusual for such a talk show to invite an old, bearded codger from *Duck Dynasty* and interview the duck-whistle inventor on national health care resulting in a minutes-long jabbering consisting of loony conspiracy theories, as happened.

While the deliberate stupefaction of viewers by daytime talk shows produces more widespread problems, from a general education perspective to the conditioned acceptance of *Bootleg Experts*, than is presently acknowledged in mainstream-America, their danger pales in comparison to the professional, sophisticated employment of *Bootleg Experts* in politics today. A development that has been continuously accelerated by the increasingly rapid progress made in the fields of technology, energy, engineering, finance, trade, infrastructure, diplomacy, education, law, any natural science, or national politics itself.

For citizens who are by necessity occupied with keeping up with developments and progresses in their own fields of profession in order to keep their jobs and to keep earning money there simply remains neither the time nor the energy to keep abreast of advancements made in any highly specialized academic or scientific fields. With the amount of data created every single day having reached over 2.5 quintillion bytes/day in 2020 and with an estimated 1.7 MB of data created each second for every person on Earth, it becomes apparent how utterly futile any attempt must be to follow the example of Gottfried Wilhelm von Leibniz, the last genuine polymath and one of the Enlightenment's most influential logicians, mathematicians, and natural philosophers. In actual fact, with von Leibniz' death in the year 1716 A.D. died also the idea of the universally educated Renaissance Man.

The exponential growth of knowledge beginning with the Enlightenment made it soon impossible for scientists to follow all the developments in the old and new sciences, a fundamental change forcing scientists and scholars increasingly to become one-track specialists. Soon, different academic and scientific disciplines splintered in ever smaller and more specific sub-groups each one constituting their own little kingdom with a carefully selected population of chosen ones, own initiation rites, and own sub-language. Even today, this set of specialized vocabulary serves as a badge of membership in the relevant scientific community and as shield keeping the world of clueless laymen and scientists from other disciplines at bay.

At the beginning of the 21st century', when new disciplines and innovations sprout like algae in the overheated sea at universities, research companies, scientific organizations, and in suburban garages, an uninitiated 98% of Americans is more than ever dependent on specialists and expert-authorities for intelligible explanations about the modern world. Additionally, not just research-heavy domains such as genetics, cloning, robotics, nano-tech, or artificial intelligence (AI) today are making huge leaps in no time but also disciplines like history, law, politics, sociology, and even pseudo-sciences like 'business administration' continue relentlessly diversifying, specializing, and re-organizing, creating new models, points of issue, and vocabulary.

The choice between remaining sceptical towards new developments or accepting statements and explanations of expert-authorities at face value has already been made long ago in Western societies. To constantly remain sceptical and therefore doing one's own research to personally check every expert-statement proves not only to be impractical but outright impossible, even with Google and Wikipedia. Of course, this is not deterring a certain kind of people from conducting their own research on Google and become world-class experts on such easy to grasp night school-subjects like virology, bio-chemistry, immunology, vaccines, infectious diseases, and epidemic spread-patterns.

In view of the rising tide of self-declared vaccine-"experts" but also of flat-earthers, home-schoolers, anti-abortionists, and creationists, it is an increasingly comforting thought that one bulwark stands strong against this flood of fakesperts. The scientific and academic community has done little not to deserve every benefit of the doubt as the one bastion of truth, reliability, and positive development in a rising sea of egomania, *Dunning-Kruger Effects*, greed, and gullibility. Other than the political class and specifically the conservative side today, the natural sciences have delivered and continue to deliver comprehensible, replicable, and most of all practical results that improve the lives of billions.

One example for a scientist representing anything but a *Bootleg Expert* is the Director of the National Institute of Allergy and Infectious Diseases, Dr Anthony Fauci, who functioned as a beacon of professionalism in the darkness of the Trumpministration's pandemic-bumbling.

While Fauci's colleague, White House Coronavirus Response Coordinator Deborah Birx had been unfortunate enough to be conscripted by Donald J. Trump as an ad-hoc

Bootleg Expert for one of his more outlandish brain-farts, viz injecting disinfectant into the human body to fight the Coronavirus, Dr Fauci remained largely above the fray, even contradicting some of Trump's false allegations publicly, henceforth being side-lined by the hydroxychloroquine user-in-chief.

Although examples of scientific integrity like Dr Anthony Fauci are fortunately not rare, also scientists, and scholars are merely human and as such possess desires, hopes, wishes, and needs, making them vulnerable to manipulation, bribery, and coercion by malicious agents. Corrupting a scientist or scholar by employing them as *Bootleg Expert* is therefore no trivial offense but constitutes no less than outright fraud and needs to be prosecuted as such. Alas, political parties, lobbyists, law firms, fossil fuel companies, car manufacturers, investment banks, and hundreds of further entities trying to win the trust of the public or of specific individuals remain prone to hire a variety of organizations, agencies, and companies specializing in selecting, briefing, and providing *Bootleg Experts* for every occasion. Calling themselves PR-agencies, consulting firms, think tanks, and marketing specialists, all feeding from the same trough of the booming market for *fakesperts*.

But for a last time back to professor Derposhitz and his interview on the topic of Donald Trump's trade war with the People's Republic of China since the *Bootleg Expert* ploy has one last nasty trick up its sleeve without which the manipulation-strategy would not be complete. As is undeniably the case with the complete *Bootleg*-trick, so does also this last kick with the heel not necessarily tap out "g.e.n.i.u.s", probably therefore making it the top-scoring move of the ploy. Surprisingly enough, this last act takes place after the game when professor Derposhitz has left the studio and enjoys a Single Malt in his club toasting the new total on his bank account.

With Derposhitz sipping his *Lagavulin* and his part in the play completed, the work of his Trumpaganda-handler only now begins in earnest. Kelly Conman and his team of PR-experts now rotate on all axes to spin their *Bootleg Expert's* performance to win and retain the prerogative of interpretation in the media. With a mix of sleazy chumminess, veiled threats of access withdrawal, promises of future priority-treatment, and reminders of the existing power structure, Conman contacts every relevant journalist and news-outlet to get his intended message across and in print, on air, and online. In the end, the right-wing media adopts Conman's "suggested" headline verbatim and "informs" its audience: "*Renowned Harvard-professor Derposhitz supports punitive tariffs on China.*"

Simultaneously, Conman gets the interview cut into soundbites and placed strategically on YouTube, Twitter, Facebook, and Instagram. The more copies of Derposhitz's endorsement of the President's personal feud with 1.35 billion Chinese will be in circulation the more believable and acceptable the statement will appear, (see: *The Illusory Truth Effect*). It will then not take long for Trumpists to start sharing and spreading the video until the generated attention reaches critical mass and Derposhitz's (hypothetically uttered) sentence, "*I believe the U.S. needs to oppose China's economic expansionism with a show of force on the trade-floor*", will go viral accompanied by headlines and comments like, "*Harvard professor agrees with President Trump: We need a show of force against China!"*, or, *"Derposhitz supports President Trump's aggressive course against China"*, or, *"Prof. Derposhitz to China: Now it's War!"*

At this point Derposhitz-handler and Trumpaganda-expert Kelly Conman could lean back and proudly look upon a work well done. However, one little task needs still to be checked on Conman's list, since he would not be a professional propaganda-agent if he would not think ahead and get the most out of his new asset. Derposhitz's "career" as a trumpist *Bootleg Expert* has only just begun, after all. Hence, Conman needs to make sure that the professor's newly obtained status as an authority on international trade, Chinese politics, and America's economic power will not easily be forgotten until the next interview. From here on out, Conman will regularly prompt Derposhitz to write op-eds, appear with soundbites on TV, accept invitations to interviews and panel-discussions and generally become a well-known and trusted pro-Trump face in America.

Naturally, hypothetical law professor Derposhitz is as easily exchangeable with another *Bootleg Expert* as is the Chinese trade war with another topic regarding the *Bootleg Expert Argument from Authority*. From the Trumpministration's "exceptionally good relations" with Putin's Russia to the "absolute necessity" of a $21.6 billion Border Wall, from the "great economic benefits "for all Americans deriving from massive tax-cuts for the 1% ultra-rich to the deployment of U.S.-military forces in America's inner cities to "dominate thousands of radical left Antifa-terrorists pretending to demonstrate against police brutality and racism" – Authoritarian regimes like the Trumpministration need never fear a shortage of available

Bootleg Experts saying their regime-supporting piece into the next camera.

Also known as sycophants, hypocrites, loudmouths, brownnosers, liars, fakesperts, pretenders, mountebanks, or con artists, the political *Bootleg Expert* constitutes a standard character in any authoritarian regime's playbook. In the not so distant past, these figures were believed to be exclusive to totalitarian and authoritarian regimes in the Soviet Union, Cuba, or in African, Arabian, and South American dictatorships. However, fake experts with real titles and credentials who publicly justify their regime's destructive actions are not confined anymore to undemocratic, "third world" countries since authoritarian, anti-democratic governments with autocratic strongmen as heads of state have established themselves in the so-called "civilized world", from Brazil to Turkey and from Hungary to the United States of America.

Para-military policemen firing teargas-grenades and "*less-lethal*" rubber-bullets at groups of peaceful demonstrators are for instance a common sight in the NATO-member state Turkey, as they are of course in Russia under Trump's favorite dictator Vladimir Putin, where political dissidents are regularly incarcerated on trumped up charges or simply shot or poisoned.

Other democratically elected governments striving to abolish the democratic system that put them into power include Hungary where the Corona-crisis enabled Prime Minister Viktor Orban to establish an emergency government beyond parliamentarian control and supervision, or the government of Jair Bolsonaro in pandemic-plagued Brazil. Not to forget the United Kingdom, where Prime Minster Boris Johnson came ultimately to power by continuously misleading the British population about the positive and negative consequences of Brexit.

Whether presenting themselves as the most prominent authority on a subject, thus being their own *Bootleg Expert* – as the three right-wing populists Trump, Johnson, and Bolsonaro recently demonstrated with their "professional" assessment of the dangers of the Severe Acute Respiratory Syndrome Corona Virus 2 (SARS-CoV-2) – or whether this new type of oligarchics utilize another "authority" to speak on a subject unrelated to their area of expertise, the *Bootleg Expert* strategy experiences currently a veritable boom unnoticed by most voters.

Since neither the political parties nor the mainstream-media or social media-platforms take responsibility for the ongoing appearances of *Bootleg Experts* it appears once again up to citizens to stop the danger to the democratic system in its tracks, since it has become abundantly clear after months of U.S. and global protests against the worldwide largest uniformed gang of armed and violent thugs that living in a Democracy involves more than being allowed to vote. Millions of Americans, Britons, Brazilians, and citizens of other autocratically ruled countries become aware that the amenities of a democracy they enjoyed until now in are by no means cut in stone.

Leaving aside the seemingly universally applicable number of about 30% of any population always flocking to an authoritarian strongman and regarding democratic protest as "*rabble-rousing Antifa-anarchy*", the large majority of 70% remaining should not limit its power to determine their country's destiny to a visiting the ballot-box every two, four, or six years. Next to voting, taking to the streets demanding change in a unified voice in fact constitutes the most democratic act a citizen can participate in.

Unfortunately, mass-demonstrations are not the go-to solution for every danger threatening a democratic society. Effectively tackling subversive strategies like the *Bootleg Expert* and other *Arguments from Authority* demands a different approach, specifically the employment of this other super-power possessed by any citizen of a democratic and capitalistic society: The power to withdraw support. No question, when two dozen white supremacists or bigoted zealots upload videos on YouTube of burning their Nike-shoes or smashing their coffee-machines with a baseball bat in protest of the company's pro-LGBTQ-statements or anti-racism-policies it merely serves as a good reason for a chuckle, since they already paid for the product. (Duh.) Hence, a more effective use of a consumer's withdrawal-power represents the tactic of boycotting a company *before* buying their products, whether it is a *Chick-fil-A* sandwich, a *Hobby Lobby* model-plane, or a *My Pillow*-pillow, just for example.

A good opportunity for hitting business entities where it most hurts offers a public complaint about their racist, bigoted, misogynist, or anti-democratic policies on social media, product-ratings, or on Twitter. The more they will read about a company's attitude, the more people will begin to boycott its products and services. Since all privately owned media only exist thanks to advertising revenues, any media-outlet allowing *Bootleg Experts* to spread disinformation under the guise of an "expert"-status takes proclamations with enough signatures declaring the signatories' boycott of the TV-station rather serious. Less viewers mean lower ratings mean less ad-revenue. Of course, this strategy has been applied more than once in recent times, usually with considerable success. However, triggering these effective boycotts was predominantly a specific employee (i.e., Bill O'Reilly, *ucker Carlson, Sean Hannity, Laura Ingraham, et.al.) of the media-outlet in question. Hence, widespread protest aimed at the structurally embedded practice of offering *Bootleg Experts* a public platform would constitute a new level of fighting the spread of misinformation, propaganda, and mass-manipulation pervading the media-landscape today.

Thus, when Zuckerberg's Facebook claims not to be responsible for the content of its platform and when FOX News continuously presents *fakesperts* on air, the thus manipulated public might well turn the tables and exercise its own considerable authority on its information-sources to give *Bootleg Experts* finally the well-deserved boot.

O

"The Expert Assassin"

Advanced Arguments from Authority Variation II.

One of the most notorious people known for using the *Expert Assassin* variation of the *Arguments from Authority* on television today is FOX News opinion maker, conspiracy theorist, and far-right stooge Tucker Carlson. The ruby-cheeked, eternal frat-boy with the tense stare of a constipated toddler has the well-earned reputation of a rhetorical bungler when confronted with eloquent interview-partners unwilling to be drowned out by Tucker's rising voice.

Since Carlson's exasperation increases exponentially depending on his interviewee's political allegiance, age, gender, and race, it is particularly entertaining to watch Tucker's face turn purple when attempting to debate young, black, Democratic women. Moreover, the moments when he becomes rapidly overwhelmed by the "impudent irreverence" of his zappy, quick-witted, and unimpressed opponent usually provides the best examples for Carlson's employment of the *Expert Assassin* as his weapon of last resort.

Anyone who watched Carlson more than once knows Tuck's trick to suddenly challenge the competence, professionalism, or expertise of his "young, inexperienced, overly emotional" adversary as soon as he realizes that his skins are swimming away from him, constituting in fact the essence of the *Expert Assassin* tactic in a nutshell, i.e., to brazenly deny the adversary's legitimacy by repudiating their authority point blank. An undignified and churlish tactic? Sure. Successful? You bet. Clearly, it is one of

Carlson's sure-fire crowd-pleasers with his loyal audience who love to gleefully watch how their homeboy destroys another "commie-loving, black lesbo" live on national TV.

Not to sell Carlson short, though, the professional outrage-initiator tries hard to avoid direct *ad hominem* attacks on his interview-partners, especially when they are women, likely out of the self-congratulatory notion of being an "old-fashioned gentleman". Yet, that is just about as far as Carlson will go to avoid passing even under the lowest rung of his already gutter-touching decency-setting. In these cases, Tucker therefore falls back on attempting to belittle his rhetorically superior opponents in other ways, including repeatedly interrupting them, expressing his disbelief in their apparently radical ideas with a *"Oh, come on, now!"*-attitude, repeating his questions several times verbatim despite having been given a comprehensive answer thus conveying the impression that his interview-guest "simply does not get it", as well as by abruptly ending the interview in a *"Oh, forget it, it's useless with you!"*-manner, to name only a few indirect, highly effective *Expert Assassin* slights.

Compared to his fellow Trumpagandists, Carlson's assassination-style can be considered downright elegant despite its cringeworthy display of rudeness, immaturity, and pettiness, as becomes obvious when looking at the bareknuckle fighters of the Trumpublican party like Jim Jordan or Matt Gaetz, the designated schoolyard-bullies of the far-right in Congress who apply the *Expert Assassin* strategy in the same manner they tackle everything else in life by blindly storming heads-on towards the oncoming train.

Nonetheless, there lies a certain rationale behind the *"Mad Matt & Dim Jim Show"*, since Stephen *"Ghoul"* Miller, Kevin *"Kevin"* McCarthy, and *MoscowMitch* McConnell cover the small, influential "intellectual" part of the Trump-base consisting of covertly racist and openly predator-capitalistic Noble-Trumpists while the vast majority of Trump-followers pants for a simple and coarse propaganda-diet. Here, *Mad Matt* and *Dim Jim* come into play together with a cohort of federal and state level Trumpublicans satisfying the insatiable hunger of the trumpist mob for rudeness and crudeness.

Rep. *Gym* Jordan (R-OH) gave a good example for the kind of coarse execution of the *Expert Assassin*-tactic that has become a hallmark of Trumpublican attack-dogs during the Trump Impeachment inquiry. Acting as Trumps chief-defender at the witness-hearings of the House Intelligence Committee, the former wrestling coach did not bother with rhetorical sniper-shots at the Democrats' witness, U.S.-top diplomat William B. Taylor Jr., instead instantly aiming the *Expert Assassin*-bazooka at Taylor and blasting away.

"And you're their star witness?", Jordan yelled sneeringly at America's former highest diplomat in the Ukraine after Taylor had freely admitted that he had never met the president. *"You're their first witness! You're the guy?!"*, Jordan continued mockingly. *"I've seen church prayer chains that are easier to understand than this."*

If Jordan's goal had been to rattle the seasoned diplomat Taylor, said to resemble Walter Cronkite with his full head of gray hair and stentorian voice, then the ex-wrestler would clearly have been disappointed. But although Jordan's *Expert Assassination* attempt was directed at the diplomat, it was nonetheless not Taylor's reaction Jordan was interested in but the impression his bazooka-blasts made on the TV-audience across the country and his fellow Trumpublicans in Congress.

Any facts and eye-witness accounts provided by Taylor, despite being beyond any reasonable doubt, were instantly tainted by Jordan's ongoing attacks on Taylor's reputation, credibility, and professionality. Regardless of any subsequent attempts by Democrats to put the record straight, the damage of Jim Jordan's *Expert Assassination* had been done. The Trump-base had its conviction reinforced that Democrats and their witnesses are liars and crooks while Jordan's fellow *trumpophants* got enough new ammunition out of the character-assassination to paint Democratic witnesses as unreliable partisans.

Being most interested in the successful murder of Taylor's reputation on live television, Trumpublicans in Congress naturally also gave a rat's ass about the apt description of Rep. James *"Gym"* Daniel Jordan by Mr. Julian Epstein, former Democratic lead counsel in the Clinton impeachment, who characterized the holder of a "perfect score" by the American Conservative Union as *"a carnival barker who peddles dopamine to the base"*.

Expert Assassins are by no means confined to the political major league or even politics in general, though. As with the other *Advanced Arguments from Authority*, this strategy can easily be found in everyday life-situations of employees, workers, spouses, colleagues, service-personnel, or anyone else who offers an attack-surface for jealous, angry, frightened, bigoted, racist or otherwise hostile fellow citizens.

It lies in the nature of the *Expert Assassination*-scheme to be executed with an audience present, whether in the setting of a meeting at the conference table or a group-small talk with the boss in the company-kitchen just, at a game at the bowling alley, on a trip with the supposedly best friends, or during a double-couple dinner. In such unofficial cases, the attack on a person's reputation, whether on professional skills, athletic prowess, attractiveness, or virility, often comes out of left field. But the genuine nefariousness of the *Expert Assassin* plot lies not only in the near impossibility to anticipate the first attack but also in the inherent difficulty to remove the stain on one's previously impeccably white vest again. Just like a pesky red wine- or oil-stain only getting worse the more you are rubbing at it, so does the taint of the *Expert Assassination* spread further the harder you try to explain the *Expert Assassin's* false allegations and to set the record straight, only resulting in further spreading and deepening the stain of doubt disseminated by the assassin among your colleagues, bosses, friends, significant others, or family.

Besides a suspiciously friendly behavior and talking behind your back the only warning a potential *Expert Assassin* will give their victim before striking constitute certain phrases the assassin will use to introduce his or her attack. At this point it is usually too late to counteract with your own allegations about the attacker, but sometimes the reputation-killer will succumb to their own verbosity and drag out the attack long enough to prepare an *ad hoc*-reply. For the afore mentioned reasons it is then not advisable to explain, excuse, or justify. Instead, the best defense against an *Expert Assassin* is an equally strong or stronger counterattack on the reputation of the attacker.

Phrases indicating an imminent reputation-assassination depend on private or professional environments as well as area of expertise and audience. In the professional setting of a company- or department-meeting exemplary attack-introducing phrases include classics like:

- *"I really didn't want to say anything, Ellen, but …"*
- *"Mike, y'know what your old boss told me? You …"*
- *"Hey Jane, ever tried a time management course?"*
- *"Oh, you're always so extravagantly dressed. Love it!"*
- *"Didn't I see you coming out of that strip club last night?"*

Certainly, talented *Expert Assassins* disguise their attacks slightly more elaborately, yet, false-sounding niceties, "funny" comments and jokes at your cost, toxic compliments, and a suspicious interest in your private activities and preferences are good indicators. In the political arena, *Expert Assassin* plots by politicians and pundits share similarities with their cousins of everyday life. Since the stakes are much higher and the people involved are often experienced and trained in attack-tactics, however, the phraseology of the political *Expert Assassin* differs from the one used in company-kitchens, offices, and meeting-rooms.

Political *Expert Assassins* keep a variety of verbal sniper-bullets ready to aim at the reputation of their intended target and develop over time a preference for phrases and kill-words their experience has shown to work best. Stripped down to their essential meanings, some might even sound familiar.

- *"The man is a liar. Just look at what [media x] says about him."*
- *"The man has thousands of Twitter-users against him!"*
- *"This so-called expert can't even agree with his colleagues."*
- *"This so-called expert is known for his extreme bias."*
- *"The man is a known associate of already discredited [person x]."*
- *"The man isn't even a real [journalist]. He's a fake [news hack]!"*
- *"The man is completely discredited in professional circles."*
- *"That woman is much too young to have any relevant experience."*
- *"That woman is an enemy of the people. Sit down. Shut up!"*
- *"This so-called authority is a self-confessed stoner. A drug-addict!"*
- *"The man is a socialist."*
- *"The man has socialist friends."*
- *"The man has friends who know socialists."*
- *"This total loser couldn't even get his side to win last time!"*
- *"This total loser didn't even graduate from an Ivy League college."*
- *"This total loser wasn't even born in the United States!"*

- *"The woman is a godless atheist with no moral values."*
- *"That woman is no more than an ex-bartender. A born loser!"*
- *"That woman is a dangerous, cunning manipulator!"*
- *"The woman is a Muslim. Not even a Christian, for God's sake!"*
- *"This woman is in regular contact with other Muslims. Jesus!"*
- *"This woman is the daughter of the sister of a good friend of Hillary."*
- *"The man is a lowlife, a low IQ loser who begged for a job!"*
- *"The man is a wash-out, a lowlife, who begged for a job!"*
- *"That woman wears a facemask. Anti-American communist!"*
- *"This woman had an abortion. Baby-killing slut!"*
- *"This man is gay."*
- *"This man is gay, gay, gay."*
- *"That woman is also gay!"*

- *"They want to allow abortions until the 9th month!"*
  "Actually, that's absolutely not tr – "
  "They are baby-killers!"

- *"They want to abolish the police!"*
  "No, defunding the police doesn't mean to – "
  "They want chaos and anarchy on our streets!"

- *"They want to force socialism on us!"*

"Nobody wants to force anything and certainly not social – "
"They are Stalinists!"

- *"They want affordable health care for all Americans!"*
  "Yes, in fact, that's totally correct."
  "They hate all Americans!"

Although such verbal flash-bang grenades are usually wrapped in several layers of rhetoric cotton wool and delivered with a not-the-eyes-reaching grin, one specific political actor generally does not waste any time with polite decorum or other useless niceties, instead coming straight to the point. Never mind that the point he tries to make easily compares to that of a 5-year-old discovering that blabbering a "nasty" word elicits a funny reaction from adults.

The 45th President's penchant for assigning "funny" nicknames to his many adversaries is, of course, as much related to a proper *Expert Assassination* as his nincompoop behavior resembles genuine statesmanship. Yet, in his easy to amuse fan-base the clown-in-chief still lands one knee-slapper after another with his "creative" nickname-inventions of such polished gems like:

- *Sleepy Joe*
- *Low-Energy Jeb*
- *Crooked Hillary*
- *Lying Ted*
- *Mini Mike*

- *Liddle Bob*
- *Leaking Dianne*
- *Fat Jerry*
- *Nervous Nancy*
- *Crazy Arnold*
- *Goofy Elizabeth*
- *Sloppy Steve*
- *Wacky Glen*
- *Low IQ Mika*
- *Crazy Megyn*
- *Little George*
- *Dopey Mort*

Presumably, *Liddle Donald* intends to hurt his targets with his amazing name-creations since a narcissist regarding himself as the center of the universe naturally takes everything personal and therefore assumes others do the same. However, any actual damage done by *Dopey Donald's* little wordplays is of a different and rather less ridiculous nature.

Elizabeth *"Pocahontas"* Warren can probably live well with being assigned the name of one of America's most famous women in history and of a Disney-princess to boot. The problem that arose with this nickname, that even might have been one reason for Warren's unsuccessful bid for the Democratic presidential candidacy in 2020, therefore did not lie in *Sloppy Donald's* accusation that Warren lied about her Native American heritage but rather in the unfortunate way Warren reacted to the taunt. Attempting to prove her Native American heritage by gene-test was bound to backfire into her rather Anglo-Saxon face, and the public dispute with representatives of "her" Native American tribe also did not help. Warren made the cardinal mistake most *Expert Assassin*-victims are prone to fall prey to, i.e. trying to explain, excuse, and justify instead of getting straight back at *Fat Donald* with some razor-sharp, personal attack which could have kept the damage to Elizabeth Warren's authority to a manageable level.

Even then, though, the taint would not have been completely avoided since the perfidious effect of *Expert Assassin*-mudslinging, even from a man-baby in a bunker, materializes as soon as only a speck of slanderous dirt sticks to the previously impeccably white vest of the target. No two ways about it, the aura of authority and hence credibility will be permanently damaged with seemingly insignificant irregularities like an inappropriate-deemed emotional reaction, a stuttered hence botched reply, or a nervous mix-up of dates, names, or stats, today providing enough ammunition for *Expert Assassins* to launch a character-assassination attack on TV and online. Additionally, *Expert Assassins* share their slander-mud with their posse, spreading the harmless speck of dirt across the media-landscape while using, among other psychological manipulations, the *Illusory Truth Effect* to get the smear to stick for years.

One final trick the *Expert Assassin Argument from Authority* holds in store constitutes an ingenious *double entendre* allowing *Expert Assassins* to claim final victory even in the face of palpable defeat. Moreover, the apparent defeat by an unwitting critic makes the assassin's successful kill possible in the first place.

As an example, take hypothetical *Expert Assassin* Joseph McCarthy finding himself at a side-by-side-frames interview on a prominent news show. Although McCarthy has pulled all stops trying to undermine the authority of his political opponent Joseph Nye Welch, news host Walter Cronkite has always countered with hard facts and called McCarthy out on his false allegations. But as a well-trained character-assassin McCarthy reacts to Cronkite's attacks rather differently than the occasional slanderer. Instead of pulling back or even apologizing, Joe keeps smiling, knowing that being called out on his malicious defamations is the best thing that can happen to him or any other *Expert Assassin*. After Cronkite admonishes McCarthy to stop telling half-truths and making baseless allegations against a colleague of Joseph Nye Welch and asking McCarthy exasperatedly, *"Have you no sense of decency, sir, at long last?"*, self-proclaimed House-cleaner McCarthy, on a crusade against anyone further left-leaning than erstwhile Jefferson Davis, merely nods before pulling his final card from the sleeve.

For a moment it had seemed to McCarthy that he might have lost this debate and would need to go home without achieving his aim of discrediting the authority and expertise of Welch on national television. But Cronkite's *ad hominem* attack has given him a golden opportunity to steer the conversation in the desired direction after all. *"Yes, Walter. I do indeed have decency! At least enough to let you finish your aggressive attack on me. I believe it is only fair that you allow me to say a few words now without being interrupted by you again, don't you think?"*

As the one who genuinely possesses decency Cronkite nods, inviting McCarthy to say his piece, expecting McCarthy to return to a factual and level-headed debate after Cronkite's unusually direct reprimand. Of course, this is not what happens. As the "attacked" side, McCarthy has now obtained a certain "moral right" in the eyes of the viewers to either defend himself or to use his acknowledged time as he pleases. Fair is fair and all that. Differently put, the audience will now cut him some considerable slack with a little sympathy-advance on top. Unsurprisingly, the experienced *Expert Assassin* has come prepared for this situation, if not even having instigating it in the first place, and now utilizes the "free kick" to his fullest advantage.

However, McCarthy is not out to make nice trying to regain some personal brownie-points with Cronkite or the viewers, but instead doubles down on his victim, the absent Joseph Welch. McCarthy executes his attack by initially homing in on the subject of "fairness", gathering some general approval from the audience. *"Thanks, Walter. Appreciate it. Look, Mister Welch had all the time in the world last week to speak with you and several of your colleagues on camera, I think it's only fair to treat me equal. Not better, I would never ask that. But equally fair. Okay?"*

There is not much Cronkite can say except concurring with a murmured, *"Of course."* This additional plus-point in his pocket, McCarthy gets his daggers out and jumps straight at Welch's metaphorical throat. When McCarthy previously attacked Welch's political positions, professional career, and close associates with exaggerations, lies, and misrepresentations, it had been his nice side compared to what is about to follow.

In the ensuing diatribe, Joe McCarthy exclusively concentrates on the credibility of Welch, on Welch's legitimacy as Chief Counsel for the United States Army as well as on Welch's "dubious" decency, honesty, trustworthiness, and morale. *"So, you started it, Walter. You doubted my decency. I am well within my rights to do the same now, won't you agree? It is only prudent to take a closer look at the moral foundation of Mister Welch, who also talks a lot about decency but apparently doesn't have enough to be here tonight."*

"We didn't actually invite – ", Cronkite interjects, but McCarthy steamrolls on.

"Alright, Walter, you might not want your audience to hear this, but did you know that Mister Welch is in fact a Godless and soulless atheist with no moral guidelines, only driven by animal instincts? Yes, I'm sure that many of your viewers will find this rather interesting. I mean, come on! How can an atheist whose eternal suffering in hell is a certainty be in a position where he makes decisions that influence the sacred lives of our brave heroes in uniform! Even more, as any good Christian and proud American knows, atheism leads straight to communism. Look at the Soviet Union, a huge country filled with godless commies. Do we really want a communist like Welch in any position of authority in our great nation? I think not. Also, I have heard from reliable sources that Welch is often seen in the company of younger men and – ".

"Wait a minute, Mister McCarthy. Just one moment please", Cronkite interrupts. *"There is no tangible evidence for any of your alleg – ".*

"How do you want to provide tangible evidence for the blackness of a man's soul, Walter? Or for the absence of his

soul? Yes, by looking at his deeds, of course. And what do we see looking at Welch's deeds? We see a man who never went to church once in his lifetime and who has very obviously close friends involved in anti-American activities. That's what I see, Walter. And I pray to God that's what your audience sees too!"

Here we leave McCarthy and his hypothetical slandering of the exceptionally brave, upstanding, and multiply talented Joseph Nye Welch, (1890 – 1960), to summarize the *Expert Assassin's* final trick as dragging a debate down to a personal level allowing the *Expert Assassin* to engage in a monologue on any alleged "shortcomings" of the expert-authority in question, thus giving the reputation-robber near complete control over the debate.

Best-case scenario for the *Expert Assassin*, he can lead the audience's attention deliberately away from the initial debate-topic when the conversation does not go according to his plan and simultaneously focus on the personal "shortcomings" of his target. A win-win situation for the *Expert Assassin* that can only be interrupted by vehement and unrelenting objections from the debate-host and/or other debate-participants, i.e., literally interrupting the *Expert Assassin* forcefully and unabashed, demanding repetitively corrections and apologies from the grinning character-assassin regardless of the discussion descending to a shouting-match with the trumpist sycophant. No one said it is easy to muzzle an assassin, after all.

"The Laymen Experts"

Advanced Arguments from Authority Variation III.

The Laymen Experts variation of the *Advanced Argument from Authority* constitutes one of the oldest tricks in the book on this list as well as the most elaborate and specialized strategy, its callous premise and ruthless execution representing such a level of deviousness in winning over an electorate or audience that even hardened veterans in the political arena are regularly surprised once its full extent comes to light.

Regarding its complexity, need for prior preparations, and specific area of application, the perhaps most comprehensive, albeit rather unusual way to demonstrate the mechanism of *The Laymen Experts*-scheme constitutes a quick trip back in time to observe a well-prepared populist turning politically unskilled and unaffiliated laymen into valuable assets for his own political gains. Hence, a less convoluted time in history, when Democracy just stole its first peek over the rim of its cradle, will serve as the backdrop for a hypothetical enactment of the *Laymen Expert Argument from Authority* with the most vulnerable members of society, the working poor and unemployed, as unwitting "Experts", greatly advancing a young man's political career and personal wealth. [Disclaimer: The following story makes no pretence to historical accuracy. Just saying.]

Without further ado, welcome to ancient Athens.

From our place of arrival, it is merely a short stroll to our destination on this fine summer morning. Passing along white marble pillars offering short respites from the first warming sunrays, following groups of toga-clad Athenians across masterfully paved streets lined with majestic cypresses that sway in the fresh sea-breeze we finally arrive at the center of the ancient civilized world. Feasting our eyes on the Athenian *Agora* (square) within easy sight of Athens' first assembly place, the small, rocky hill *Pnyx* as well as the *Parthenon*, goddess Athena's magnificent temple. Surrounding the large square are some of the city-state's principal buildings, amongst them the *Bouleuterion* along the west side of the *Agora* and seat of the *Boule*, Athens' Senate.

Crossing the busy, sun-drenched square and passing through the middle of the five columns fronting the *Bouleuterion* we briskly walk past two armored Athenian guards on both sides of the open, pillared entrance to a medium-sized hall and have arrived. This is the *Boule*, the Senate forum of ancient Athens, a prosperous city-state day and night teeming with sailors, artists, traders, craftsmen, soldiers, beggars, peddlers, merchants, whores, mercenaries, and citizens from all walks of life.

In the shady hall of the Senate the 500 Senators, fifty from each of the ten tribes, have taken their seats on the five-tiers-deep benches running over the corner of two walls, facing the open floor reserved for speakers. We are right on time to listen in on the speech of a young, industrious Senator and real estate-developer who just recently had his personal *"Eureka!"*-moment while pondering a specific problem that might well decide the young Senator's professional future and one not dissimilar to the "challenges" real estate-developers face in modern, 21st century cities.

As it is, the young entrepreneur invested heavily in land situated in one of the least appealing areas of Athens dominated by dilapidated housing crammed with the working poor. His plan to tear the ugly dwellings down and replace them with white-marbled villas surrounded by lush gardens and equipped with the newest fads like hot water floor-heating and extra living-quarters for servants and cooks, however, has met with a certain resistance in the Senate.

Specifically, a broad coalition of philanthropic Senators has effectively sided with the, as the young politician and investor would say, *"human rabble living in those pigsties they call homes"*. A rather unfortunate development that made the young Senator finally sit down and think the situation thoroughly through.

"As a young and relatively new Senator", thought the young and relatively new Senator, *"I actually don't have any influential authorities on my side who would back me in front of the Senate. And I certainly don't have enough drachmae to buy support.*

No respected expert on city-development and housing will, of course, speak up in my favor without hefty bribes, since he would clearly face the outrage of the lower-class populace. An inconvenience only remedied by large stacks of cash.

So, who else is there who would make my case for me? Who would be convincing enough to turn the tide in my favor and against these dirty fried-liver-munchers so loved by the do-gooders in the Senate and by the public on every agora?"

While ruminating, the young Senator's eyes gazed out of his study's large window onto the busy square in front of his unobtrusive villa and finally settled on a hunched-over man in a dusty-brown tunic gathering empty wine-amphoras from below the benches lining the square, likely to trade them in for the five *lepta* refund he would get in the next taverna. And that's when an idea struck the young politician.

"Γειά, wait a minute", said the cunning young Senator to himself. "That's it! Eureka! Who would be better suited to make me look good and respectable to the public and those old Senator-fools than the stinking rag-togas themselves! Isn't everybody siding with the poor? Sure, none of those bloody hypocrites is actually doing anything substantial to help them, but everyone still believes that the working poor, the sick, and the have-nots are the most honest and straight-talking people in all of Athens. And why shouldn't they be, since they have no social status to care about. They are not corrupt because they are too unimportant to ever be bribed. And anyway, they care more about their precious 'community' than anything else. That's why they have great street-cred, particularly with the douchebags in the Senate. Perfect!"

But back to the day when the fate of the young Senator's proposal is finally decided in the Senate. The entrepreneurial first-term Senator confidently steps into the center of the floor, half-way surrounded by his Senatorial colleagues. He greets them with a smile and the appropriate phrases and quickly repeats the cornerstones of his proposal. Only to then, in an unusual deviation from normal proceedings, wordlessly turn towards the large marble pillars forming the open entrance to the Senate and gesture with his hand a practiced "come closer"-signal to a small group of dishevelled, dirt-covered men and women who suddenly appeared at the entrance and now stand cowedly a couple of steps inside the hall, warily eyed by the armor-clad guards accompanying them.

The assembled Senators look surprised and whisper among themselves while the previously carefully by the young Senator selected three men and two women whose whole attire screams "working poor" shuffle along the marble plates until standing in front of the benevolently smiling Senator in the middle of the *Boule's* floor. Only then begins the energetic entrepreneur with his well-prepared speech.

"Honored fellow Senators, beloved citizens of Athens", he proclaims, *"you all know me, and you know how much I love our city and its citizens. And as anyone here can testify, since my appointment to the Senate I have worked incessantly to improve the lives of all those who contribute to the greatness of our shining city on the hill.*

And as you also know, I have brought before this assembly a proposal to make our jewel of a city an even more sparkling gem under the sun by eradicating one of its few remaining blemishes. I speak, of course, of Gitonia, the district on the eastern beaches where our best and hardest working brothers and sisters still live in lamentably dire conditions.

That is why I have brought before you today several representatives of this salt of the earth and backbone of our society, to explain to you in their own words how much they desire to improve their lot and to finally transform Gitonia, this rat-infested, disease-ridden trap, and horrendous eyesore for all Athenians into a shining example for the bright future of all of Athens!"

The young Senator takes a step back and with a flourish indicates to the tallest man in the group of poor laborers to come forward. "*Please, Elias, come and speak to us.*"

Hesitantly, the large, bearded man shambles forward some feet and looks at the rows of Senators who are silently watching him in return. Elias' dirty hands grab the hem of his torn, feculent toga while he clears his throat. Finally, Elias begins to speak in a hoarse, slightly quivering voice. "*Venerated Senators, I thank you and the mighty Kairos for this opportunity to be allowed to speak to you today. May Kratos look forever favorably upon you and your children and your children's children and ... uhm, yes.*" Elias harrumphs again. "*Ah, I ... I am here to report to you today that the young Senator here speaks the truth is what I would like to say, venerable Senators. The conditions in Gitonia are truly wretched indeed. And it's become even worse since most of us lost our livelihood when almost all of the smelting-εταιρίας took their business to Antioch where the laborers, so we've heard, get paid only half of what's been our own meagre wages.*

Uhm, also, well, like the Senator said, most of our houses are infested with rats and all kinds of vermin and many of our children have grown sick and once they are most die of the sickness. The rain flows through the roofs and mould grows on every wall and the heaps of waste in the alleys make even Dionysus' sulphurous wine-farts smell like almond blossom in comparison. What we dearly need, revered Senators, is some decent housing, with roofs and dry walls for the sake of our childr –".

"*Thank you. Thank you very much, Elias!*", the young Senator quickly interrupts and takes over seamlessly.

"*You've heard it yourselves, my fellow Senators, and all you wonderful citizens who came here today*", the energetic politician declares while smiling at the Senators sitting on the stony benches and the groups of citizens who observe the proceedings from the peanut-gallery. "*You've heard Elias, an honorable smelter and inhabitant of Gitonia, say it loud and clear: Gitonia is a disgraceful relic of a less civilized past. Gitonia needs a new beginning. Let's make Gitonia great again!*"

Here the young Senator makes a dramatic pause to allow his words to reverberate in the ears of the other Senators. After a sufficiently long silence, our ambitious entrepreneur launches into his last stretch on the road to victory.

"*My fellow Senators, my friends, Athenians! This is my proposal to this assembly: A new, a modern, and bright*

Gitonia. A Gitonia all Athenians can be proud of! This is what Athens needs, and this is what the inhabitants of Gitonia themselves want! The only obstacle still casting its dark shadow on the bright future of Gitonia is this tiny group of backwards-minded Senators over there", and he points at a cluster of Senators who are ominously silent while watching him grim-faced, *"who would rather waste additional funds taken from our already precariously light-weighted municipal purse for repairs, for alley-cleaners, for rat-catchers, and even, if you can believe it, for new houses build in the same style as the existing ones but with more spacious diamérismas!*

Delusional ideas that will cost Athens a plethora of drachmae and keep the city tethered to the past, to the terrible times when nearly all citizens had to live in such 'communal' living quarters! My proposal, on the other hand, will not only fill the city's purse but, on top of it, will transfer a whole city-quarter into a shining symbol for Athens' progress. But don't take my word for it. Take that of Elias here and his friends and the whole populace of Gitonia who stand behind Elias and me like one man, ready and willing to finally make Athens great again!"

Most Senators rise from their seats and their thunderous applause follows the young investor's victory-stroll to his place. Time to leave, since the subsequent debate and the ultimate vote on the young Senator's project are now mere formalities. Elias and his rag-tag group of impoverished laborers are politely but unequivocally ushered out of the Senate Hall even before the final debate begins. A last glance at the young victor reveals a broadly grinning Senator, already imagining himself celebrating his overwhelming victory later tonight in one of Athens' most expensive and most enjoyable houses of pleasure.

Yet, this is not the end of the story. In the aftermath of the young Senator's impressive performance and the subsequent approval of his plan by the Senate there still followed some smaller demonstrations, several official complaints, and the usual bureaucratic hurdles. Naturally, the young Senator took every obstacle in stride until one particularly cold day in the following winter, the last of Gitonia's original inhabitants were finally evicted and forcefully removed from the only homes they could afford and one hour later the young Senator's demolition-teams began their work.

Three summers later, the happy families of wealthy wine-merchants, marble-quarry owners, higher-echelon politicians, and government officials, as well as some famous sculptors, architects, actors, stud farm-owners, and hairstylists, and one very wealthy, young real estate developer, moved into their new white-marbled villas with lush gardens, floor-heating, and toilets connected to a central canalization. Gitonia was finally "great again".

At this point, some nit-picky critics might pose the question why the group of philanthropic Senators who positioned themselves so verbosely on the working poor's side demanding a refurbishing of the existing houses and an affordable rent for Elias and his fellow workers, in the end gave up without any mentionable fight. Moreover, the same critics might ask what happened to the public once in favor of the working poor and strongly concerned about the impoverished laborers' plight? Where was the public outcry, the large-scale protests, or the people's pressure on their Senators to provide affordable housing for the poorest part of society? Well, there had been one guy who strapped himself to a half-wrecked dwelling's supporting beam in a last-ditch attempt to stop the demolition-crews. However, according to the guards' subsequent report the crew must have overlooked him when they brought the block down in a controlled collapse. Apart from this unfortunate episode, alas, no more discernible support for Elias and his fellow laborers had been recorded.

The reason is simply. For one, any argument-filled trial balloon the *pro*-poor Senators in the *Boule* were ready to let fly in favor of Elias and his comrades had been instantly busted by Elias' speech in support of the young Senator's proposal, regardless of the rather obvious fact that the young Senator had twisted and misinterpreted Elias' words.

Furthermore, with the other Senators as well as the city-gossips and representatives of the public (the "press") in attendance on that ill-fated day, the *pro*-poor Senators had all the witnesses needed for justifying their subsequent inactions, since, except for a tiny fraction of representatives who cared genuinely about the fate of the working poor, most *pro*-poor Senators were anyway not wholeheartedly invested. In the beginning, their fine-tuned political instincts had told them what their lower-class constituents expected, and they had delivered. Now, though, in the aftermath of the devastating declaration of support for the young Senator by the very same people they had tried to save, the sheer load of upcoming work necessary to undo this damage and come out on top clearly exceeded any potential effort most *pro*-poor Senators were willing or able to invest.

Fortunately for them, hence, the Senators could now point out that the working poor of Gitonia themselves were clearly supporting the "remodelling" of their quarter. And did Elias himself not mention the rat-infested and disease-ridden reality in the quarter posing an imminent danger to the whole city? See?! Therefore, it must obviously be in the best interest of all of Athens to transform Gitonia into a far more healthy, enjoyable, and beautiful place, they reasoned.

The largest obstacle to the *pro*-poor Senators' willing capitulation, a possible outcry from social-minded constituents and a subsequent loss of their political support, had been irreversibly removed by Elias' speech. According to unwitting *Laymen Expert* Elias, representative of the working poor of Gitonia, the best any *pro*-poor Senator could still do now was either to abstain or to vote for the young Senator's plan.

While the Senate-opposition had been elegantly taken care of, the young Senator's work was still not quite done yet. Of course, news about his victory in the Senate had spread through Athens like Greek Fire and doused a lot of the formerly vocal opposition to his million *Drachmas*-project. Nonetheless, the following weeks in the young Senator's calendar were filled to the last chalk-line with what would one day be called *Public Relations*. After all, Elias and the working poor of Gitonia did not vanish simply into thin air. In fact, many

Gitonians, upon hearing of the Senate's decision, had begun to stage public protests on the *Agora* and other squares all over Athens, loudly demonstrating against their coming eviction. Not surprisingly, since in a time *when Housing and Urban Development Departments* (HUD) were a thing of the far future, the fate of thousands of Gitonians was looking seriously dire.

Luckily, at least for the young Senator, opinion makers in the relevant social circles of Athens were graciously open to humble gifts for their poor wives and daughters always in desperate need of new jewellery, clothes, perfume, or sweet delicacies. In return for these selfless donations to the struggling families of such influential traders, artists, actors, officers, and city officials, they felt obliged to take the young Senator's side in any conversation coincidentally involving the subject of Gitonia.

A few weeks later, most Athenians had moved on and did not care much anymore about the small groups of lice-infested, rag-wearing Gitonians on the squares demanding *"justice"* and to *"not be left to die on the streets"*, while any dissatisfaction still glimmering in Athens' population regarding the all-out destruction and rebuilding of Gitonia was personally addressed by the young Senator in several public speeches on the larger *agoras* of the city.

Eloquently, yet genially voicing his disappointment and "rightful" indignation evoked by the apparent ungratefulness of the Gitonians he personally had liberated from a life in squalor, Athens' latest *"Hot Bachelor of the Month"*, (according to *Helena – The Monthly Parchment for the Beautiful Athenian*), thoroughly managed to discredit Elias and his fellow "scrounging thieves", portraying them as ungrateful rabble-rousers, socialistic Spartans, and enemies of the Athenian people. After this, even the most persistent critics fell silent and decided to pick more promising fights and the cunning real estate-developer and opportunistic young Senator was able to finally savor the whole, twisted beauty of the *Laymen Expert Argument from Authority* scheme to its fullest.

In summary: The young Senator utilizes a tiny percentage (*Elias and his friends*) of a societal group (*working poor*) the public associates with certain positive attributes (*honest, hard-working, incorrupt*) to make a convincing argument for him ("*Gitonia is a lost cause!*") that would not have been nearly as convincing if it had come from himself.

The first trick of the Senator: Getting Elias to speak for him. He secures Elias' cooperation by promising him the opportunity to present his case directly to the decision makers, ("*Gitona needs help*"), by assuring Elias that he is on the side of Gitonia, showing him his plans of new houses and infrastructure for the quarter.

The second trick of the Senator: Briefing Elias prior to his public appearance on the phrases working best with the Senators. He feeds Elias with catchphrases ambivalent enough to be subsequently re- and misinterpreted by him and interrupts Elias, taking him out of the game, the moment Elias veers off-script.

The third trick of the Senator: Selling Elias to the Senators as the embodiment of all Gitonians, the voice of the whole societal group of working poor. Choosing a "typical" specimen of this group whose behavior, way of speaking, and attire matches the assembled Senators' expectations but who nonetheless possesses a certain aura of authority, (in Elias' case deriving from physical appearance and his given role), but is vain enough to be convinced of his success, yet uneducated and ignorant enough to misunderstand his role and purpose in the overall scheme provides the young Senator with the perfect *Laymen Expert* for the job.

The fourth trick of the Senator: Twisting and reinterpreting Elias' words to his own advantage. While our hypothetical example above cannot display the full artistry and cunning necessary for this feat to be guaranteed successful, it does not need a rhetorical wizard to reinterpret, deny, and twist third-party statements efficiently enough to be taken as gospel by undecided voters, let alone sympathetic followers, even if there exist dozens of YouTube-videos proving the exact opposite of the manipulator's allegations. Without such recordings, most Senators naturally remembered the words of Elias only partially at best. Yet, even with recordings available today, most people memorize only the parts they choose to remember. When these parts are then additionally reaffirmed by an "interpreter" like the young Senator, they are bound to receive the "Truth"-stamp in the observers' minds.

The fifth trick of the Senator: Selling the newly spun tale as proven truth. Selectively utilizing the parts of Elias' speech supporting his ambitions, interweaving them with his own narrative, and presenting the result as the *Laymen Expert*-approved truth constitutes the heart of this scheme. Once the initial audience, (*Senate*), has swallowed the gilded turd whole, this acceptance will then be presented as additional "proof" of the veracity of the claim to a broader audience, (*Athenians*).

The sixth trick of the Senator: Employing multiplicators to boost and spread his claim, (*"Gitonia must be torn down and rebuild"*). Winning influential opinion makers and leaders over to his side with bribes, (in many material and nonmaterial forms), allows the young Senator to further disseminate his own narrative and boost his reputation as a benevolent and fair businessman and politician.

The seventh trick of the young Senator: Anticipating the attacks from the utilized *Laymen Experts* and being prepared to counter them. Naturally, it had been only a matter of time until Elias and his people got wise to the young Senator's double-dealing. With his reputation as a fair player well in place, however, the young Senator confidently acts "hurt and disappointed" by the "vicious attacks" of the "ungrateful" working poor. By publicly declaring his "sadness and rightful indignation", the Senator adopts the role of the victim and paints the Gitonians as the villains of the play. Since the public sides preferably with a victim and consequentially allows the "unfairly attacked" party some leeway in his reaction to the "attack", at this point the *Laymen Experts*-executer is as good as through with his scheme while getting off scot-free.

The eighth and final trick of the young Senator: Slandering his former *Laymen Experts* while simultaneously preserving their value as believable witnesses for his cause. By calling Elias and his gang *"thieves"*, the young Senator reaffirms merely the idea many Athenians already have of the working poor, hence being nothing new and not demanding closer consideration. Only a "new" defamation would pique the interest of the public and in the worst case stir up new doubts about the overall narration of the young Senator. But since the slander fits right into the public's idea of the working poor, the young Senator can simultaneously degrade his opponents *and* maintain the general image of the working poor as honest (*thieves*), hard-working (*ingrates*), and incorrupt (*rabble-rousers*).

Predictably, the tricks of the ancient Greek schemer work just as well more than two millennia later. With gullible volunteers from *"Blacks for Trump"*-Afro-Americans, to piss-poor hillbillies swearing to fight universal healthcare to the last tooth, (i.e., not for long), to trumpist veterans blind to Trump's open distain for the men and women in uniform, to the members of the Trumpublican Party there is no shortage of willing and unwitting *Laymen Experts* for the Trumpaganda-machine to choose from. Whether they genuinely believe to be furthering their own cause by allowing themselves becoming mouthpieces for a demonstrably autocratic government or whether there are other reasons for their complicity, at the bottom line it never ends well for the *Laymen Experts*.

Apropos. Back in ancient Athens, summer had come and gone and the owners of the new villas spreading across *Néos Gitonia* had enjoyed the sunny days in their mosaic-adorned pools. Now, the harvest on Athens' fields was well underway while the former inhabitants of Gitonia were scattered in all four directions of the wind. Many had ended up in one of the numerous camps of lean-to huts that had recently sprung up along the outer side of Athens' city walls, presenting a nuisance to Athens' upper crust who regarded these slums as a blemish on the face of their beautiful city. Still, the rich did not care much to expel the rabble since winter saw usually to a drastic dwindling of its numbers, thus sparing the city the unsavory business of chasing the riff-raff off before torching their driftwood huts.

The last anyone ever saw of Elias, erstwhile spokesman of the working poor, had been on a rainy winter-morning when leaving his soggy driftwood-hut he had told his neighbor in a hoarse whisper that he'd be taking a little stroll up to the cliffs.

Today, at the beginning of the third decade of the 21st century with the internet and hundreds of TV-channels available at a fingertip, the *Laymen Experts*-ploy still has lost nothing of its efficacy. Instead of an unprecedented number of information-sources leading to a well-informed, critical population, millions of Americans continue to choose their info-sources selectively and with great prejudice, trusting rather a former reality TV-show-host and his *Laymen Experts* than the scientific community, intelligence community, free press, medical experts, seasoned diplomats, former government officials, and dozens of other objectively reporting and reasoning authorities.

Donald Trump knows of the appeal of "the average Joe" as his spokesperson, having made the *Laymen Expert* a recurring part of his ongoing propaganda-campaign. One example for the Trumpaganda-department's utilization of carefully selected, socially disadvantaged individuals as living and breathing proof for the Trumpministration's alleged *"support of minorities"* was displayed during Trump's State of the Union-speech on 02/04/2020, which resembled an *Oprah* "Give-Away Show" for some carefully chosen minority-representatives.

Where Presidents Barack Obama, George W. Bush, Bill Clinton, George H.W. Bush, and their predecessors conducted themselves and the event with appropriate decorum and in some cases even with grace and gravitas, former failed casino-owner and faux university-fraudster Donald Trump turned the time-honored venue into the only type of event the man appears to be capable of producing, i.e., a cheap and garish spectacle. Hence, at one point during his circus-program Trump pointed out Amy in the audience, a young military spouse who was in for a "tremendous" surprise since Trump had plucked her husband right out of the combat zone, commanded to leave his unit behind and fly back to the U.S. only to reveal him to his speechless wife during Trump's State of the Union address like a third-grade talk show-host surprising his guest with a long-lost relative. A "heart-warming" reunion made exclusively possible by the confounder-in-chief to win him the hearts of every member of the U.S.-military.

In his next show-act during the same event, Trump pointed out Janiya, a young, Black fourth grader from Philadelphia who had been invited by Trump's team and positioned strategically in the audience. With the fake gusto of a televangelist Trump announced to the assembly and TV-audience at home that he had arranged for Janiya to receive a scholarship at a school of her choice and accepted the ensuing applause from his side of the aisle similar to a slumlord bathing in the gratitude of his tenants after fixing some broken windows in the middle of winter.

The genuine gratitude visible on the two young women's faces who understandably couldn't care less about the greater implications tailing the "magnanimity" of the obese circus director at the pulpit, naturally had been caught in close-up by cameras for the whole world to see, making Amy and Janiya unwittingly Trump's newest *Laymen Experts* providing irrefutable proof for the draft-dodging President's "undying love" for the military and the black community.

In contrast to ill-fated Elias in ancient Athens both women fulfilled their role perfectly without saying a word, their overjoyed faces on TV being more than enough testimony for Trump's base to convince them once more of their President's immaculate character, selfless generosity, and pristine morale. The Pied Piper piped, the *Laymen Experts* sang, and half the nation danced to the tune.

"The Appeal to Poverty"

Advanced Arguments from Authority Variation IV.

Its very name already hints at the distinctly seedy nature of the *Appeal to Poverty* behind which lurks the malicious plot of hijacking a complete segment of the population to function as clueless stooges for the populist. Making use of their naivety in political matters the populist brazenly appropriates the voices of educationally alienated, lower class- and working poor citizens in order to substantially inflate his own political base. In certain ways reminiscent to purchasing a large contingent of fake Facebook "friends", the *Appeal to Poverty* plot nevertheless has not one dime to spend on the appropriated contingent of destitute citizens and their misguided support.

On the contrary, the enthralled group will instead willingly hand its hard-earned dollars to the political kidnapper by donating to his campaigns, fundraisers, and rallies where they can observe first-hand how the human flytrap will deliver his routine on stage as *"Man of the people"*. While hearing exactly what they have paid for, *Appeal to Poverty*-victims remain unaware of the performer's minions quietly divesting them of their last remaining literal and metaphorical possessions by handing the keys to the victims' very existence to the robber-barons in the loan departments, health insurance companies, mortgage agencies, and executive floors of Big Pharma, Big Energy, and General Big Company.

But before diving head-first into the intricacies of the *Appeal to Poverty Argument from Authority*, let's make a quick detour to its exact opposite for a closer look at the fundamental idea of *political appeals*, i.e., the malicious utilization of a societal group to boost a politician's power. This mirror-image of our titular strategy has been appropriately called

The Appeal to Wealth

For a descriptive demonstration of the *Appeal to Wealth's* inner mechanism, a short hypothetical story appears expedient. In our story, the president of a nameless country decided to appoint a specific person as his new Secretary of the Treasury. For reasons that might or might not be apparent, the president was fixated on this man who had previously been employed by a large, influential financial institution maintaining friendly ties to the president for decades, (despite the president's verbal attacks on this financial institution during his presidential candidacy).

However, the miget-handed president faced one particularly annoying obstacle to his planned appointment of the new Treasury Secretary. See, during his election-campaign the future president had promised his supporters that he would rigorously drain the corrupt swamp unanimously believed by his followers to exist throughout the government. Now to hire one of the universally despised *"Golden Men"* from the aforementioned investment company who were undeniably at the core of numerous corruption-, insider dealing-, and other financial crimes, actually might send a rather mixed signal to the president's base. Fortunately, most of the president's supporters were ... well, not among the sharpest knives in the drawer and the little president knew all about the ignorance and doltishness of his voters. Together with his most trusted propaganda-witches he concocted therefore a particularly barefaced *Appeal to Wealth*-strategy that would, as the tiny-fisted president was certain, work like a charm with his bumpkin electorate.

Thus it came to pass during one of his countless rallies across the nation, let's randomly say on June 21 of 2017 in one of the most rural stretches of his land that the portly president behind the podium raised his tiny hands confidently and spoke with aplomb thusly to his followers: *"Look, I love all people, rich or poor. But in those particular positions I just don't want a poor person. Does that make sense? Does that make sense? If you insist, I'll do it. But I like it better this way, right?"*

And lo and behold, the straw-bewigged president's loyal bumpkins rejoiced frenetically and applauded him with Coke-bucket holding, mayonnaise-smeared paws for many a minute. All prior misgivings regarding corruption-reeking bankers, bog-digging lobbyists, and other political swamp-creatures now forgotten thanks to their ingenious president's promise to hire only *"the best people, the very best people"*. And who could blame the good simpletons, when everyone and their neighbor's pig knows that only the seriously rich have that certain *'je ne sais quoi'*, this one-in-a-million talent to reliably and trustworthily handle the really big money collected from the humble taxpayer.

And as if the wee-handed president's choice of a *Golden Man* as his head of Treasury was not enough reason already to rejoice, his loyal and potbellied disciples were once and for all over the moon as soon as they realized that their Lilliputian-handed Dear Leader had hired in fact not only one but several *Golden Men* to serve in his government. No doubt, these outstanding examples of unblemished candor and impeccable morale would henceforth invest all their precious time, energy, and knowledge in their work for the common good to selflessly increase the wealth of the nation and its taxpaying citizens. Thus, the similarly potbellied president's peasantry saw that their Great Leader had bequeathed the country with a team of winner-gene possessing giants and were certain to reap their personal benefits from the soon to be forthcoming, tremendous winnings.

On the other tiny hand, the little mushroom penis-adorned president saw that his blatantly obvious *Appeal to Wealth* had worked even better than expected and was hence tremendously content with the outcome, even giving his propaganda-witches a good-natured pat on the back with one of his miniscule hands. In the meantime, the *Golden Men* in their new positions of political power were rubbing their eyes in total disbelief of this unexpected, tremendous windfall that had blown them into the very center of the same bastion their lobbyists had arduously hammered at for years. But do not fear, the *Golden Men's* astonishment quickly made way to frantic industriousness, spurred on by the certitude that nothing last forever and certainly not one of the biggest insider-heists in recorded history. And while one or the other of the *Golden Men*, as well as their close confidants and other fellow raiders occasionally fell out of grace due to stupid scandals, the Golden Looters' foothold inside the one institution potentially able to successfully stop their self-enrichment never faltered genuinely.

Some leaders of the raiding party put some extra work into establishing a more permanent base inside the occupied fort by installing their loyal minions in non-election depending and lifelong positions of power prudentially for the rainy days certain coming sometime in the future. See, the raiders had sworn themselves never to go back to times when they had been utterly at the mercy of the so-called representatives of the electorate. From here on out, they had decided, they would have their own deep-rooted base inside the castle, accessible via secret back passages even the most suspicious hacks would be unable to sniff out.

While the Golden Freebooters inside the governmental palace had been ceaselessly working to strip the populace of their meagre possessions, the red-hatted peasant army outside the walls did not tire cheering their tottering and stuttering symbol of virility, the petite-fisted septuagenarian in turn never missed an opportunity to show himself on the castle-walls to his adoring peasantry below. Waving benevolently down at the hysteric mob, the champion-cheater of wives, business partners, customers, and clients alike rested safe in the knowledge that his busy companions deep down in the castle's treasury were putting his considerable slice of the cake reliably aside to wait for him the day he would leave his dominion behind, chuckling at the thought of some cretinous do-gooder trying to salvage what had been left by him and his Golden Boys and the look at the idiot's face upon opening the looted coffers. And thusly the mushroom-penised president, his golden gang of looters, and the red-capped mob of morons all saw that it was good and lived happily ever after.

The End.

Well, not really, of course. Neither was it good nor was it the end, at least not for the milling crowd of red-hatted simpletons screaming themselves hoarse in their ecstatic praise for the little fumbling and stumbling president who raided their silver. To get an idea of the true extent of ignorance displayed by the pixy-dicked president's followers, imagine that a battalion of blue-clad horsemen had at one time come along intending to explain what was happening to their livelihood right under their noses. When the make-up-daubed president on his wall became aware of this, he pointed his teeny finger at the blue riders and screamed: *"Look! There! Socialists! Communists! Enemies of the people!"*, only for the red-faced, red-capped, and red-seeing mob to instantly take up the cries of *"Socialists!"* and *"Communists!"*, despite lacking any understanding of the terms' genuine meanings. The furious, feeble-minded fanatics hurled their feces enthusiastically at the men and women in the Blue Battalion and chased them off their barren acres while the little, paltry-palmed president saw that all was good and farted contently.

Some winters later, after the nightmare's dark hours had made way for the dawn of a new, bright morning and the rage -red masses had finally gone home, put their pitchforks and torches back into their pitchfork- and torch-stands, they suddenly noticed that not only was all their precious silverware gone but also their medicines, lights, schoolbooks, clean water, and healthy foods, their hearths and horses, their summer hay and winter wood and the walls, floors, and roofs of their houses. Sitting in the middle of the vast nothing left behind by their tiny-pricked, obese president, they remembered his words: *"Look, I love all people, rich or poor. But in those particular positions I just don't want a poor person. Does that make sense? Does that make sense? If you insist, I'll do it. But I like it better this way, right?"* And for the first time they began to doubt that the words of the little, bone-spurred president had made truly sense. Alas, by then it was too late by far and so they lived miserably ever after.

Their End.

The Appeal to Poverty

The little president's extremely straightforward *Appeal to Wealth* could not be clearer in terms of the idea behind the strategy, viz providing an argument in favor of the rich that will be easily swallowed by the gullible poor and proceed accordingly. Under normal circumstances, however, such an argument would need some more substance than a simple, *"In those particular positions I just don't want a poor person."* But sometimes reality turns out stranger than the weirdest fiction and hence these few lines have indeed been all that was needed to convince *"Drain the swamp!"*-Trumpists to accept investment bank-millionaires at the helm of the U.S.-Treasury and in further, high government positions.

Now, in contrast to the *Appeal to Wealth* that aims at convincing gullible voters of the "guaranteed societal benefits" accompanying a disproportional wealth-increase for the flush 1%, the *Appeal to Poverty* ploy instrumentalizes the hard-working masses to serve as "living proof" for a government's claim to have implemented "countless policies that greatly benefit workers, veterans, the working poor and the unemployed, as well as chronically ill, disabled, and elderly citizens".

Some may argue that this appears to constitute more or the less the same ploy as the *Laymen Experts*, as there exist indeed similarities. In fact, the two schemes particularly coincide in the aspect of allowing populists to use specifically "the poor/uneducated" to their advantage without providing anything in return. At their core both strategies possess a well-crafted construct of smoke and mirrors leading the populist's supporters to believe their hopes for the future to play a role in the populist schemer's plan while in fact merely a coldly calculating wizard is hiding behind elaborate smokescreens, keeping his gullible followers entertained while converting their support into his political power.

It would appear that the most powerful defense against being duped by a populist's empty promises constitutes the electorate's vote on election day. And although this is ultimately true, there exist several other, highly effective methods to manipulate an election-outcome besides relying on one's base. As has been aptly demonstrated in the run-up to the 2020 presidential elections by Republican officials closing large numbers of polling places in states like Arizona, Louisiana, and Texas, reducing the number of voting places from several thousands to a few hundreds. Already in August of 2018, Indiana Secretary of State Connie Lawson, (R), closed no less than 170 voting stations in Lake County, home of Indiana's largest Latino and second-largest Black community. Such actions alone will decrease the number of votes cast in these communities considerably and are further diminished by forcing members of minority groups to make their way to polling places in overwhelmingly white, conservative neighborhoods, thus guaranteeing an even larger percentage of non-voters from Black, Hispanic, and other minority-communities.

Additionally, the nefarious practice of voter-district gerrymandering, i.e. restructuring of a district to guarantee a majority of white, conservative inhabitants voting Republican, finally reduces the once sacred democratic rule of *"one person, one vote"* to little more than a quaint historic titbit. But Trumpublican nefariousness still does not end here, with the deliberate disruption and dismantling of the USPS (United States Postal Service) only the latest and most obvious example for the authoritarian mindset of a party hellbent on procuring a second term for the autocrat in the White House.

With this wide choice of election-manipulation tactics available to Trumpublicans, guaranteeing already half the battle for the Trumpublican Party, a major focus for Donald Trump lies therefore on keeping his minority-base of roughly 35% in line and fiercely loyal, and even more importantly on artificially boosting their voices, numbers, and apparent importance in the eyes of the nation and the world. For as long as Trump remains shackled by democratic norms and regulations, he needs his gullible *MAGAritas* to make as much noise as possible to provide the thin veneer of President of *all* Americans. Leaders with a powerbase of merely one-third of the population stand on shaky ground. Yet, if these 35% scream, stamp, holler, swear, and rant ferociously enough to make them appear to be a much larger mob, then the Dear Leader can even get away with tweets like this:

THE SILENT MAJORITY IS STRONGER THAN EVER!!!
— *Donald J. Trump (@realDonaldTrump) June 14, 2020*

Regardless of the fact that neither the vociferous nor the silent majority is in fact on his side and that the genuine majority opposing his rule has been far from silent for a long time. In June of 2020, at a time when Trump's polling-numbers hit a new rock bottom, his above tweet constituted nothing else but an obvious *Appeal to Poverty*, where *"poverty"* is synonymous to the educationally, intellectually, and economically challenged Trump-base. During the summer of 2020 Trump, who had lost the popular vote in 2016 by 3 million votes, had become increasingly aware of his precariously thin layer of support in a nation of almost 330 million citizens. No surprise therefore, that Trump's only reaction to the cries of hundreds of thousands of relatives of deceased COVID-19 victims, millions of workers unemployed due to the catastrophic Trumpministration-management of the Corona-induced economic crisis, and further millions enraged about systemic racism and ubiquitous police-brutality against minorities, consisted of rallying his troops of blue-uniformed and red-hatted regime-loyalists.

Despite the numbers of Coronavirus infections rising from one spike to the next, Trump had decided to hold a large rally-event in Tulsa, Oklahoma on June 20, 2020, although not without having every ticketholder sign a waiver declaring not to sue Trump or the presidential campaign in case of becoming infected with the deadly virus during the show.

Together with Trump's earlier stunt that month when he had ordered AG William Barr to use "*less-lethal*" force to disperse peaceful demonstrators in front of St. John's Church across the White House, only to then stand in front of its entrance and hold a bible up for a photo-op targeting his evangelical base, the irresponsible Tulsa-rally event as well as his "*silent majority*"-tweet all constitute examples for a populist's practiced use of the *Appeal to Poverty*.

And while any sane and rational individual is gobsmacked by the sheer audacity and ridiculous obviousness of Trump's trick it still remains one of the most notable crudities in Times of Trump that his hypnotized hicks kept their oath of fealty to Trump, a man who knows less about the bible than the average atheist, is unable to close an umbrella, mocks the physically handicapped, publicly appears with toilet paper on his shoe, admits his love to a mass-murdering dictator, can't lift a glass of water to his lips, falsifies a national weather-chart with a sharpie, suggests injecting disinfectants against a virus, congratulates another dictator to his use of concentration camps, threatens peaceful protesters with violence in crass violation of the 1st Amendment, speaks of himself in the 3rd person, and is by all accounts involved in potential cases of treason, obstruction of justice, electoral fraud, and even child trafficking and sexual intercourse with underage girls.

The reasons for this ironclad fealty are naturally manifold, with the most prominent ones found in the pages of this book, a good number of them also playing a role in the success of any *Appeal to Poverty*, the populistic glorification of the poor combined with paying lip service to their needs and demands.

Such an *Appeal* can anchor its claws only securely in the type of brain already preconditioned by other mind-manipulating methods and occurrences. Here, the *Dunning-Kruger Effect* can come into play, as well as *Cognitive Dissonance Avoidance* and *Selective Exposure,* but also the malevolent influence of a premium-class *Bullshitter* or the lifelong conditioning by fallacious *Open World Assumptions*. Easily impressable minds, frequently synonymous with less educated and more indoctrinated brains, therefore are the perfect prey for the *Appeal to Poverty*-employing authoritarian who triumphantly rallies the masses of often self-proclaimed disenfranchised, forgotten, unfairly treated, relatively poor but exceptionally proud "patriots" behind him.

> *Socialism - The Red Rag for Trumpists*

Apart from the one apparent similarity to the *Laymen Experts* discussed above, the *Appeal to Poverty* beats the *Laymen Experts* hands down on sheer deviousness alone. After all, the *Laymen Experts*-scheme gives the instrumentalized poor at least the opportunity to say their piece during their moment in the spotlight. (Although this opportunity was denied to Elias of Athens by being rather rudely interrupted). The *Appeal to Poverty* on the other hand focuses single-mindedly on the complete assimilation of the demographic group of the poor, allowing the populist to claim this complete voting block for his base. And the loquacious praise and grandiose declarations of spiritual kinship regularly ejaculated at rallies and on television by the populist endear his clueless base only further to the *Appealer to Poverty*.

One of the most spine-chilling examples of an overwhelmingly successful *Appeal* to a large group of struggling, confidence-lacking, and guidance-craving people constitutes the early Nazis' utterly on-the-nose naming of their newly founded political party.

By calling it the *National**sozialistische** Deutsche **Arbeiter**partei* (*NSDAP*), Hitler, Himmler, Hess, Goebbels, Goering, and their fellow fascist monsters ingeniously embraced the huge demographic of post-World War One destitute Germans – from the working poor and the now impoverished former middle-class to the long-time unemployed and countless disabled and deranged WWI-veterans literally crowding the streets of all bigger cities – in a more decisive, direct, and "downright" manner than any other German political party of the time. With the words *sozialistisch* and *Arbeiter,* (worker), right there in the party's denotation there could "clearly" be no doubt for whom these self-proclaimed "patriots" were fighting.

In reality, however, the *Nationalsozialisten* (national-socialists, abbrev: *Nazis*), had just about as much interest in bettering the lives of impoverished German workers, poor, and veterans than Dear Leader Kim Jong Un of the "*Democratic* People's Republic of Korea" has in introducing democracy to North Korea. Even more perfidiously ingenious, the two other keywords in the Nazi-party's name, ***National**sozialistische **Deutsche** Arbeiterpartei*, appealed to the exact opposite side of the social spectrum, to the nationalistic, conservative, upper-class Germans many of whom were happy to support Hitler financially throughout the 12 years of the "Thousand-Year Reich".

It is a long tradition of extremists on the left and right to appropriate positively loaded political labels and to claim them for themselves, (see the many uses of the term *'Democratic'* in party- and nation-names of decidedly undemocratic regimes). On the other side of the same coin exists the deliberate misinterpretation, twisting, and demonizing of labels owned by or attributed to political opponents, as becomes particularly apparent in Trumpublicans' and Trumpists' obsession with the terms *"socialism"* and *"socialist"*.

Using the demonstrable ignorance of most Americans regarding actual meaning, background, and history of the political philosophy of *socialism* and its practical effects, the far-right GOPhers are hellbent to demonize the progressive fraction in the Democratic Party, who call themselves Democratic Socialists, with a handful of the usual suspects in the Trumpublican party not finding it beneath them to point at the word *"sozialistisch"* in the name of Hitler's NSDAP and allege that Democrats such as Alexandria Ocasio-Cortez (AOC), Ilhan Omar, Ayanna Pressley, or Rashida Tlaib share the same roots with German National-Socialists, i.e., with the original Nazis.

In another mind-splitting twist, several Trump-sycophants have kept not only blabbering that *"the Nazis were socialists"* but have also been deluded enough to equate the notion of Democratic Socialism represented by

Bernie Sander, AOC, and other Democrats with the inhuman, dictatorial communism under Stalin with its own, goose bumps-inducing denomination of *Stalinism.*

Whether calling the advocates for a more just and fair society *Democratic Socialists* or *Social Democrats,* - like for instance Germany's SPD, (Social Democratic Party), the coalition-partner of Angela Merkel's CDU, (Christian Democratic Union), - nothing could be further from the truth than the allegation of any kind of relation to Hitler's National Socialists. In fact, thousands of members of the oldest German political party SPD have been persecuted by the Nazis and incarcerated in concentration camps were most starved, died from diseases, or were murdered. Therefore, many seasoned party-members of the SPD as well as traditional SPD-families who lost close relatives to the Nazis continue to this day to regard any comparison to National Socialism as an inexcusably grave insult to their lost loved ones.

As little as *Democratic Socialism* has to do with Hitler's *National Socialism,* viz absolutely nothing, as little is the political philosophy also related to Stalinism or communism, as five minutes on Wikipedia and Google will unambiguously prove.

Furthermore, the frequent allegation that *Social Democrats* are guilty of using the same *Appeal to Poverty-*strategy they are blaming conservative, autocratic populists for neither holds a drop of water. The decisive difference between policies of *Democratic Socialists* (or *Social Democrats)* aimed at empowering the working population as well as disadvantaged members of society to have an strong say in the distribution of public wealth on the one hand, and reactionary conservatives targeting the new class of poor with *Appeals to Poverty* on the other hand, consists of *Democratic Socialists* having concrete, comprehensive, and detailed policies on how to improve living conditions and advance possibilities for the disadvantaged part of the population while conservative Republicans are determined to protect the status quo and further the interests of the wealthy minority.

Democratic representatives like Alexandria Ocasio-Cortez, Bernie Sanders, and Elizabeth Warren do not demean themselves by hurling *ad hominem*-attacks at their political opponents nor are they known for whipping up fear, hatred, and disdain among their supporters to pit them against "the other side". While the *Appeal to Poverty*-strategy provides the disgruntled group of (intellectually, educationally, and morally) "poor" with a false sense of appreciation and value, simultaneously stirring up latent aggression as a political weapon, *Democratic Socialists'* political programs are based on proven facts, extensive studies, and triple-checked scientific analyses to bring about a new perspectives, hopefully followed by concrete improvements in the lives of the average American.

Incidentally, this average American citizen is not the white, suburban, 3 bedroom-house owner with two college kids, two SUV's in the drive-way, a $100,000 job in the city, and a spouse with a $40,000 half-day job. Rather, it is the struggling family-father or single mother living from paycheque to paycheque unable to afford missing a single day in their bone-breaking $25,000 job lest they find themselves out in the rain the coming month without a single dose of vital insulin for their youngest. In consequence, the notion of

Democratic Socialism derives from the understanding that such a reality has little to nothing to do with a democratic society once founded on the idea of mutual respect, acceptance and support to the benefit of all, with universal rights, equal justice, and equal opportunities for all. A notion the Founding Fathers would indubitably sign up for again in a whiffy today, since the Constitution begins with *"We, the People ..."*, not with, *"We, the Rich ..."*.

And yet, the 1980s Reaganomics as well as the Tea Party, the Gingrich-Cheney-Bush gang, the Trumpublican party, and the Trumpministration all worked ceaselessly to instil a grossly distorted view of the term *"social"* in the uneducated and emotionally unstable part of America to scare the living Bejesus out of them. While in truth the twisted understanding that being *"social-minded (socialist)* is synonymous to being *"unamerican"* represents in fact a fundamentally unamerican mindset as U.S.-history itself easily proves, from the first settlers practicing lived solidarity, aka socialism, in their settlements, to Lincoln's liberation of a considerably large percentage of Americans from being enslaved by another considerably large percentage of Americans, to FDR's "socialist" New Deal providing heretofore unknown levels of prosperity and progress for every American household in the 1950s.

However, just as everything coin has two sides there exists no doubt also a downside to *Social Democracy* or *Democratic Socialism*. One societal group in particular regards itself as the greatest loser in any predominantly social-orientated society. Clearly, the demographic of the extremely wealthy, rich, and super-rich would "suffer" most in a political climate of solidarity, mutual appreciation, equal justice, and fair opportunities for all. In short, there is one *-ism* that does not at all play well with *Democratic Socialism* and that is *Zero-Sum Capitalism.*

Once a purely economic term, capitalism has risen from the 1980s onwards to the status of a political philosophy and quasi national religion in the present-day United States that instantly triggers metaphorical cries of *"Heresy!"* as soon as a higher taxation of the Lamborghini-driving class is suggested, let alone stronger worker rights, environmental protection rules, regulations for investment banking and stock market, and consumer protection laws. A similarly anguished outcry arises from the 1%, their lobbyists, and lawyers whenever someone in the Capitol in Washington D.C. whispers about redirecting funds or subsidies away from the military, the police, private correction facilities, the fossil fuel-industry, or the pesticides-addicted agricultural sector and towards sustainable energies and farming, social services, or public education.

To "deny" big corporations, conglomerates, and industry-players with their CEOs, department managers, and middle-managements their annual profit of tens of millions to billions of Dollars and the expected bonuses has become synonymous to being *"socialist"*, *"communist"* or plainly *"anti-American"* in the minds of a certain type of Americans. Ironically, the around 35% of Americans sharing this mindset consist in large parts of the same Americans who suffer most from toxic living- and working environments, inadequate schooling of their children, meagre salaries in outdated industries, insufficient health insurances, cheap-diet related diseases, and the underfunding of life-saving social services.

While clearly dissatisfying, progressives in America and other Western countries need to consider this generation of wilfully ignorant reactionaries as a complete write-off without realistic prospects of recovery. Providing the textbook-example for the only viable way of dealing with this *"basket of deplorables"* are in fact none other than the Catholic and Evangelical churches, who now practice for centuries already the age-old scheme of *"Getting to the children when they are still young"*. Other than the churches, however, a robust, well-equipped, public education system can offer children a comprehensive education based on facts, reason, and independent thinking to convey a morale founded on universal human rights and on practical examples of benevolence, plurality, and equality, and to instil furthermore curiosity about the world beyond their parents' horizon as well as an affinity to science, the arts, philosophy, and literature.

Already on January 6, 2012, the linguist "Johnson" wrote in his column for *The Economist* with the title, "*The failure of American political speech*", that, *"Socialism is not "the government should provide healthcare" or "the rich should be taxed more" nor any of the other watery social-democratic positions that the American right likes to demonise by calling them "socialist"—and granted, it is chiefly the right that does so, but the fact that rightists are so rarely confronted and ridiculed for it means that they have successfully muddied the political discourse to the point where an awful lot of Americans have only the flimsiest grasp of what socialism is."*

Over eight years later and millions of Americans are still following a president who rode down a golden elevator and on to victory on the exact same ticket of demonizing this obscure notion of *"socialism"*. Many of these Trumpists are parents of children who will never have a chance to make up their own minds, instead being raised with the same fear-based belief that an American society without endemic racism, bigotry, and misogyny, a two-lane justice system for whites and "others", a militarized, systemically violent, racist, and in large parts unchecked police force, and without an oligarchic class of 1%ers controlling 80-90% of all market capital would be nothing short of Hell on Earth for the little *"Youth for Trump"*-members Ned, Chet, Bret, Ted, Susan, and Claudette. After all, their parents said so and they in turn heard it from the man who finds himself by all accounts so deep in the pockets of the oligarchs running the show that he couldn't find his way out even if he wanted to.

> *Pandering to the Poor: A Global Success Story*

Like most well-working scams developed in the course of human history the *Appeal to Poverty*-scheme looks back on a centuries-spanning successful run. Befuddlingly, though, humankind appears to have learned fuck all from this history, despite the undeniable fact that the same script – *"Aspiring autocrat associates himself with the unemployed, poor, and working poor and abuses their support to his advantage"* – lies at the heart of entire bloody revolutions and long-lasting dictatorships sparingly disguised as "the people's rule" as well as of the creation of populist-nationalistic parties on at least four continents in the past ten decades alone.

The modern age of the *Appeal to Poverty*-scheme began with three genuine monsters on the humanity's long list of inhumane and utterly callous dictators whose names have become synonymous with some of the worst atrocities ever committed in the "name of the people".

Against the backdrop of extremely different political, historical, and social circumstances in their respective countries of Germany, Russia, and China, the three hellraisers Hitler, Stalin, and Mao Zedong each crafted their very own trademark-variation of the *Appeal to Poverty*-tool to manipulate the destitute masses, while still all based on the same scheme of appropriating the struggles of the downtrodden, exploited, and discarded poor. Brandishing the people's plight as their own fight, the three dictators solemnly promised to deliver the yearning masses from their squalor and lead them to a golden future in a land of plenty.

Nowadays, the general belief prevails that a repetition of events like the ones in Hitler's Nazi-Germany, Stalin's Soviet Union, or Mao's China would be impossible in any modern, civilized and democratic society. If anything, so the popular opinion, an *Appeal to Poverty* might perhaps still work in such dictatorships and autocratic regimes as North Korea's Kim-dynasty, whose latest scion is the third absolute ruler in the family but first of his line who can brag about being a U.S.-President's openly confessed love-interest. ("*We fell in love!*", Donald J. Trump, 09/30/2018).

Other notable examples of dictators harnessing the poorest and most desperate part of the population to their cart in the few decades between the end of WWII in 1945 and the end of communism in Europe in 1989/1990 include Cambodia's Pol Pot, he of the *Killing Fields*, the complete line of General Secretaries of the USSR from Khrushchev to Brezhnev, Andropov, and Chernenko, as well as the late Fidel Castro and his brother Raúl Castro, and any number of former and present-day Arabic potentates from Iraq's Saddam Hussein to Egypt's Hosni Mubarak, Tunisia's Zine el-Abidine Ben Ali, Libya's Muammar al-Gaddafi, or Saudi-Arabia's King Abdullah, not to forget Iran's Ruhollah Khomeini and his successors.

Yet, prior to the fall of the iron curtain also the North and West had no lack of dictators with a penchant for *Appeal to Poverty*-rhetoric. East-Germany's Walter Ulbricht and his only successor, Erich Honecker, kept for instance the entire GDR-population imprisoned in their own state while praising the glorious achievements of their "Worker's Paradise", while the communist dictators of Warsaw Pact-states during the Cold War era are best summarized by their probably most evil representative, Romanian dictator Nicolae Ceausescu who, in a crude kind of poetic justice, found his end with his back to a bullet-riddled wall of a dilapidated apartment block in Bucharest, facing a revolutionary execution squad next to his equally despised wife.

As a side note, in contrast to the above oppressors most African and South American dictators in the cold war-era of 1945-1990 did not bother overly much with appealing to the destitute working class and the poor in their own countries. Having the full power of the military on their side did the trick apparently well enough.

A quick glance at the political preferences of 20th century dictators reveals their political positions to have been almost exclusively of the extreme left, viz communist or proclaimed socialist, with the exception of military dictators in South American countries such as Argentina under Jorge Rafael Videla, Paraguay under Alfredo Stroessner, or Bolivia under Hugo Banzer, all having leaned far-right towards fascism and pure military dictatorship. African dictators, on the other hand, proved to be predominantly *kleptocrats* who filled their bottomless pockets with any coin they could press out of the impoverished citizenry. Aside from these exceptions though, the second half of the 20th century almost exclusively saw communist and pseudo-socialist strongmen employing the *Appeal to Poverty*-strategy. Giving the impression of the *Appeal to Poverty* as a tailor-made scheme perfectly fitting far left and communist populists whose focus lies on the "liberation" of the suppressed working class and disenfranchised poor.

A notion that just a few decades ago would have been correct, with the period between the end of dictatorships in the Western and South-American political hemisphere in 1983 and the beginning of the "War on Terror" in 2001 having given every indication that far-right authoritarian regimes were finally gone for good and with no neo-fascist dictator left on the world-stage to employ propagandist schemes, leaving only Eastern European and Asian communist dictatorships to uphold the charade of the *Appeal to Poverty*.

In the wake of the collapses of the last neo-fascist dictatorships, in Spain with dictator *Caudillo* Franco's death in 1975 and in Argentina with the end of the military Junta dictatorship in 1983, a global political vacuum on the far-right emerged that appeared to remain safely unfilled for quite a while. When the Eastern European revolutions of 1989 and 1990 brought about relatively stable democratic systems in the former communist-ruled European states a few years later, very few political experts were envisioning the fascist-authoritarian regime-model returning any time soon to pose a serious threat to humanity's future.

Of course, the three decades following historian Francis Fukuyama's optimistic declaration in 1989 of *"The End of History"* have since then proven once again that history always finds new ways to keep the world on its toes. In hindsight, the return of the radical right to the political world-stage appears to have been rather inevitable, considering the old school-axiom that nature abhors a vacuum.

In accordance to this basic fact, the beginning of the new millennia saw a new breed of de facto dictators entering the geopolitical arena with autocratic despots and strongmen like Recep Tayyip Erdoğan of Turkey (in office since 2001), Vladimir Putin of Russia (since 2000), Viktor Orbán of Hungary (since 2003), Rodrigo Duterte of the Philippines (since 2016), or Jair Bolsonaro of Brazil (since 2019). Sharing a taste for pomp and circumstance and personal enrichment combined with an uncanny appeal to the lower classes, the anti-social and anti-democratic strongmen quickly rendered the notion obsolete that the *Appeal to Poverty*-scheme constitutes a propaganda-tool exclusively suited for the extreme left. While Bolsonaro and his autocratic colleagues enjoy the support of a small group of old money-elites and *nouveaux riches* owing their ill-gotten gains to their Leaders' predator-capitalistic policies, the likes of Erdoğan, Duterte, and Orbán all lean heavily on the undying support of an ill-educated, poor, rural population desperately feeding on the *Appeal to Poverty*-rhetoric of their rulers if not on much else.

At the same time, European far-right parties like Spain's *Vox*, Germany's *Alternative für Deutschland*, France's *Front National*, Great Britain's anti-European *Brexit Party*, Italy's populist *Lega*, Austria's *Freiheitspartei*, or the anti-immigration *Sweden Democrats* are all seeing their last chance having come for an ultimate reactionary revision of the last seventy-plus years that saw Europe rising from the ashes and transforming into a peaceful, social-minded, multi-cultural, and fundamentally social-democratic continent.

To date, however, far-right populists in most European countries have only managed to throw the ever same, simplistic bogeymen as convenient hate-objects at the feet of their followers. According to the fear-mongers, this "mortal enemy" comes with brown or black skin, an odd name, and a different monotheistic religion, and buys, cooks, and eats unusual food, listens to alien-sounding music, and talks in an *"unintelligible, uncivilized, horribly sounding gibberish*". In short, these "Others" don't fit the stencil of traditional Caucasian norms, turning them automatically into a threat to *"law-abiding, natural citizens who were born and raised in this sacred land and can speak our fucking language, for fucks sake!"*

While approximately 95% of these god-fearing, xenophobic, wilfully ignorant *"good people"* have yet to properly meet and talk to, any of these "nation-destroying enemies", let alone invite them to their homes or for a coffee at the next Café, they are nonetheless convinced that it is *"high time to do something drastic about them before it's too late!"*, since in their opinion they will otherwise be unavoidably marginalised and lose not only their jobs but also their wives and daughters to Musliminism, (*"or whatever that false religion is called"*). Moreover, the billions of dollars which rightfully should be spent on *"the real citizens of this nation"* are being *"wasted on feeding and accommodating these scroungers, serial rapists, plague-carriers, drug-lords, muscled thugs, terrorists, and other cowards who ran away from a war in their own country for which any real American would've stayed to fight!"* Clearly it is an invasion! A veritable flood, if not even the end of Western civilization. Get my rifle, Doris!

> The Modern American Poor

With every Trumpist interview, every trumpist show-caller on talk-radio, and every YouTube-video of Trumpnatics hollering racist slogans, the evidence piles further up that in later stages of the Trump presidency roughly 99% of Trumpists are in complete Reality-Denial Mode, fully taken in by the

Trumpministration's *Appeal to Poverty*-strategy targeting the modern poor.

However, this new class of poor Americans has nothing to do anymore with the old-fashioned kind of poverty that often comes to mind in sepia-colored pictures of half-starved children dressed in rags, posing with their joyless little faces in front of a dilapidated wooden hut in the mud. Instead, modern poor Americans might drive the newest GM-truck and live in a 3-bedroom house with garden while still being financially crippled by three mortgages on the house, monthly leasing-rates for the neat truck, exorbitant hospital-bills and drug-costs due to illness or accident, extensive credit card-debts, and on top of it all a depressingly high college-debt.

Moreover, financial poverty in the sense of the inability to afford bare necessities like regular meals, a home with a roof, a functioning car, public transportation, and basic health care coverage, constitutes not the only type of poverty making people feel excluded from society. A lack of basic education or professional training as well as less than rudimentary communication-skills and insufficient literacy levels, a self-imposed or by no fault of their own existing ignorance of fundamental social and political procedures, rules, and regulations, and a lack of good manners all contribute to an altogether different type of poverty, making it almost impossible for *"undeservedly marginalised"* Trumpists to participate in and profit from the dealings and doings in 21st century society, where specialised knowledge represents the fuel that drives the engine of an increasingly well-trained and specialized workforce.

In a country where high school-graduates and college-students cannot point at the USA on a world-map, are unable to solve simple math-subtractions, do not know who fought whom in the American Civil War, and genuinely believe Africa to be a country, it is easy to assume that large employers in the fields of science, production, engineering, finance, et.al. will have lowered their employee-standards accordingly by now, hence giving even the bible-thumping, home-schooled offspring of die-hard Trumpists a realistic chance in corporate America.

Alas, this Trumpist pipe dream will not come true, no matter how often Donald J. Trump promises *"great jobs for everyone"*. In reality, there exists still an admittingly declining percentage of young Americans who come from open-minded, educated parental homes, have educated themselves and attended the appropriate college courses, and possess a reality-based, rational understanding of the world, who together represent a large enough pool for modern companies to choose from while leaving the fiction-over-facts believing part of the population deservedly in the dust.

Nonetheless, many envious *American Dream*-dreamers still believe to deserve the same new and shiny GM truck and the elegant 3-bedroom house as the Doctor of Literature on the brighter side of town, accordingly sinking themselves into debts to their hairlines only to wail and gnash their teeth subsequently and to pray to an ex-reality show host to relieve them from their "unfair" burden.

But aside from these perpetually whining, poor Trumpists there naturally exists also a large number of modern poor who have fallen victim to a system that has been assiduously established by the Republican Party under the guidance of their financial backers over the last four decades. Due to the ever increasing gap between the group of the fortunate and/or felonious few and the group of the miserable and/or mistreated many "the poor" demographic has long since outgrown its traditional definition of being solely comprised of "trailer park trash", inner city derelicts, unskilled laborers, the uninsured, chronically ill, and long-time unemployed.

Rather, today's modern poor include such formerly unlikely candidates as the once traditional middle- and lower middle-class family with parents working 2-4 jobs and still hardly making ends meet, but also many young, single mothers and fathers, as well as college-absolvents, teachers, veterans, municipal workers, nurses, public services employees, and really anyone who got fucked sideways by the system of turbo-capitalism where the minimum wage of $7.25 remained constant since 2009 while the average compensation for CEOs in the 350 largest U.S.-firms has reached $14 million per person in 2018, constituting an increase of 29.4% since 2009.

Despite this gigantic writing on the wall concerning them more than most, it was nonetheless the demographic of white men (with 34% of all voters in the 2016 election) who voted for Trump by an almost two-thirds majority (62%), providing an overwhelming confirmation of the effectiveness of Trump's *Appeal to Poverty* strategy.

Additionally, of the 37% of American white woman who voted in 2016, more than half (52%) cast their ballot for Trump.

Their vote against their own fundamental interests becomes even more flabbergasting when considering that the group of white voters consists predominantly not of CEOs, lawyers, doctors, and investment-bankers, but already in 2018 contained a total of 9%, viz almost 1 in 10 white Americans who live below the poverty threshold of $20,212, (*for a family with two adults and one child, 2018. Source: Henry J. Kaiser Family Foundation*).

Believing in rabid fox Trump's honey-laced protestations to be "one of them", the frightened white rabbits invited the predator willingly into their burrow to take good care of them, hoping that the flea-ridden carnivore will improve their dismal living-conditions as farm-helpers, office cubicle-worker, phone-support, assistant secretary, foreman, sales-rep, waiter, clerk, factory-worker, coal-miner, and other employees whose whole existence is at the mercy of an exclusively profit-oriented management.

After decades in which the wolves of Wall Street and the vultures of Big Business had backed the weasels in the Republican Party to transform a cooperating, caring society into a Zero Sum-game playing pack of scared individuals, in 2016 the time had come to send the rabid fox into the rabbit-hole to collect. In conditions where millions are living with the constant background-fear of losing their jobs and subsequently health insurance, means of transportation, and their home inside of a month, it was one of the fox's easiest tricks to make the white rabbits believe in him as their savior delivering them from evil.

From Ronald Reagan to George Bush Sr., George W. Bush, and Donald J. Trump, the *Gang of Plunderers* (GoP) has shown extreme tenacity in reshaping American Society, once a role-model for prosperity and democracy, into a predator-capitalistic jungle where the delusional prey believes to have a chance of joining the predators' side, if they *"just work hard enough"*. In consequence, the trembling rabbits reconcile themselves to 50, 60, or 70-hour weeks and working 2 or 3 jobs simultaneously, with an average of a ridiculous 9.7 days of paid annual leave for full-time employees.

In comparison: *Australia* has a minimum of 4 weeks and for shift-workers 5 weeks of annual paid leave. The *United Kingdom* has a minimum of annually 28 days paid leave. *Iceland* has a minimum of 24 days paid leave per year plus 12 paid public holidays. Employers in *Germany* provide an average of 30 days paid leave per year plus up to 10 paid public holidays annually. In *Italy* employees have at least 20 days paid leave annually plus 12 paid public holidays plus one town/city specific "patron saint day" plus a right to 15 days of paid leave for a wedding plus the legal right to receive paid leave for up to 3 years to take care of sick children. In the *European Union* (all 27 countries) the law demands a minimum of 20 days of paid leave annually. *New Zealand* has no less than 4 weeks of paid annual holiday plus 11 paid public holidays. And employees in *Russia* get between 38 and 56 days of paid leave depending on the region. In contrast, to repeat, the annual average of paid leave days in the United States is 9.7, i.e. less than 10 days per year.

Additionally, American workers also put up with 0 (zero) days of paid maternity- or parental leave. In comparison: *Estonia*: 62 weeks with 100% pay; *Germany*: 14 weeks with 100% pay; *Italy*: 22 weeks with 80% pay; *Norway*: 35 or 45 weeks, with 100% pay for 25 weeks or 80% pay for 45 weeks; *Spain*: 100% pay for 16 weeks mandatory for the mother, another 10 weeks can be transferred to the father; *Israel*: 14 weeks with 100% pay with an additional 12 unpaid weeks; China: 128 days with 100% pay; *Mongolia*: 120 days with 70% pay.

And, of course, U.S.-law does not require for employees to have access to any paid sick days in case of short-term illnesses either affecting oneself or a family member, for instance a young child. In comparison, *Sweden* demands a minimum of 80% of one's income to be paid for 364 sick-days, with 75% salary-payment for a further 550 days. In *Germany* employers are legally required to provide at least 6 weeks of sick leave per illness with 100% of the salary paid during that time. In *Australia* 10 days of 100% paid sick/carer's leave per year are mandatory, to be carried over to subsequent years if not used. Or in more general terms: *"At least 145 countries provide paid sick days for short- or long-term illnesses, with 127 providing a week or more annually. 98 countries guarantee one month or more of paid sick days."* – (Source: Jody Heymann, Alison Earle, and Jeffrey Hayes, The Work, Family and Equity Index: *How*

Does the United States Measure Up? - Institute for Health & Social Policy, 2007).

To put it bluntly, these exceptionally bad work-conditions make the United States unique not only among industrialized first-world countries but worldwide. Yet, in year four of Trump's occupation of the White House there are no signs for a change to the better despite Trump's ceaseless assurances that he will *"make America great again"* for the average, white, male American worker. Half stroke of luck and half the result of a decades-long preparation by the Republican establishment, the demographic of the white, middle-aged, ill-educated American wo/man keeps swallowing the false narrative of social security-, civil rights-, consumer and environmental protection-, and basic welfare-benefits all being evil inventions of *"socialists and communists"*.

For 40 years, from the days of old warhorse and communist bane Ronald Reagan onward, the fearmongers on the right are creating terrifying bogeymen out of any politician with concepts and solutions carrying even the slightest whiff of *"left-wing ideology"*. And until 1990, the horror-vision of the Soviet Union's "evil empire" played additionally into the hands of conservative ideologues who did not miss a beat to link the indubitably inhumane regimes in communist states to general concepts of *socialism*, social justice, and *social democracy*. Several generations of ill-educated and ill-informed Americans later, the deliberately disseminated fallacy of *"Democratic Socialism = The Death of America"* has taken deep roots in the minds of conservative, evangelical, and alt-right sections of society. When Donald Trump entered the stage, this notion had been already so deeply ingrained in the minds of the conservative rank and file outside of big cities that even a former TV show-host had no problem to utilize the mortal fear of *socialism* prevalent in the low-skilled, tradition-bound, god-fearing, and predominantly white workforce. Consequentially, Trumpists remain ignorant to even the most blatant inconsistencies between Trump's promises of *"getting jobs back to America"* and *"winning the trade war with China"*, *"health care for all"* and *"cutting health care costs"*, or, *"a tax cut for all"* and *"a tremendous tax cut for the super-rich"*, to name but a few.

Hence, the orange handmaid of the U.S.-oligarchy simply sticks the label *"socialist"* on any policy presented by Bernie Sanders, Alexandria Ocasio-Cortez, Elizabeth Warren, or Andrew Yang, making Trumpists shudder with fear while never realizing that these *"unamerican"* ideas would quite likely benefit them personally as well as their families, friends, and colleagues. Duh.

> *Plain Common Sense*

The very first fallacy any Trumpublican fearmonger commits when crying *"Socialism!"* consists of crying *"Socialism!"* when any European conservative politician could readily tell them that *socialism* comes in numerous varieties with no single definition of the term covering all types at once.

The one element common to all types, however, is the notion of *social ownership*. Yet, this notion does *not* correlate with some communistic pseudo-equality where *"all means of production belong to the workers"* or *"the proletariat"*. Instead, modern *socialism* represents a policy centered on the well-being of the individual as an integral part in the larger framework of a just and fair society.

Modern socialism sees for instance certain elementary functions such as universal health care, free education, supervised free markets, et.al., which are essential for a society supporting equal justice and opportunities for all, to be ideally managed by elected representatives instead of by a tiny number of oligarchs and their minions. The simple reason being, of course, that history has abundantly proven that people whose prime objective it is to maximize their private wealth will usually achieve this objective by exploiting the state and its tax-paying population, regardless whether from outside the political arena or from within.

Corruption, nepotism, insider-dealings, quid-pro-quos, cronyism, and a culture of concealment, systemic lies, and pretend-outrage, are all inherent to a government led from behind by a syndicate of so-called "best people" who never stood for election and are still tasked with supervising essential government-services like the national postal service, the department of justice, the intelligence community, or the stock market. *Democratic socialism* in action means to strengthen the positions of independent supervisors, investigator generals, and supervisory committees by protecting them from government-interferences, by appointing elected and thoroughly vetted officials to these offices and by implementing strict laws and rules to prevent outside meddling with the duties of these guardians of proper official conduct.

Moreover, the frequently conservative nightmares-inducing notion of *social ownership* does not denote any "communist dictatorship" in which all private property gets distributed among the masses and will henceforth become illegal. On the contrary, *social ownership* pertains to the protection of individual rights to private and public ownership, tasking the government with curbing any unjust and illegal excesses of individuals and legal entities resulting, for instance, in faux universities, price-controlling cartels, market-dominating monopolies, awarding of contracts to government-cronies, misappropriation of government-funds, stock market Ponzi schemes, or the unimpeded exploitation of natural resources and natural preserves owned by the people.

Additionally, *social ownership* tasks officials with closing loopholes enabling tax-evasion, disguise of bribery, evasion of personal responsibility, benefitting from insupportable working conditions, or profiteering from another's financial plight. Make no mistake, most European *Democratic Socialists* (or *Social Democrats*) consider themselves strong proponents of capitalism, albeit of a capitalism with strict and strongly enforced boundaries in place, minimizing the possibilities of financial, physical, or mental exploitation of employees and workers.

Regardless, Trumpists consider the term *"socialist"* to be an insult on a par with words like *"rapist"*, *"atheist"*, *"lesbian"*, or *"vegan"*, while simultaneously chuckling good-naturedly when watching the latest news about another large-scale tax-evader, a crime still considered to be a trivial offense committed by "gentlemen" and ungrudgingly applauded by these "real patriots" who laughingly admit that they would do just the same if they only had this much money. Naturally without realizing that the "gentleman"-fraudster's filched loot has in fact been *his* money in the first place, while angrily labelling Democrats attempting to stop such raiders in the future as *"anti-American socialists and communists"*. Go figure.

This limited mindset of the typically white, middle-aged, male Trumpist raising his beer-can to the news of some *"clever bastard"* defrauding society of millions of dollars, ultimately bears a large part of the responsibility for his own, precarious work-situation. While up until the late 1990s, most job-positions suitable for the insufficiently or ill-educated American worker had neither demanded professional communication-skills, nor quick reaction times, mental and social flexibility, continuous improvement of skills and job-specific knowledge, on the spot adaptation to rapid changes, or constant readiness to face new challenges, in the ever faster turning, global job-market of the 21st century, these abilities are usual preconditions for any well-paying and secure job.

Unsurprisingly, the archetypical American worker toiling in a job that pays just about enough to cover monthly bills and debt-payments hence believes himself under attack from all sides, with threats seemingly coming from a young, well-educated, and highly skilled next generation of specialists just as much as from managers and CEOs trained in regarding employees as mere "human resources". Even the former Republican establishment had not been on their side, having for decades failed to improve their lot while paving the way for a profit-oriented world where the

American worker needs to compete with Chinese factory-workers, Indian call-center agents, and Eastern European commodities-producers with monthly salaries that in the United States would not even pay for a family-night at Chick-fil-A®.

Alone in his car while stuck in traffic on his commute, *Joe Blue-Collar* from Anywhere, USA, ponders his suspicion that he might in fact be somewhat inadequately prepared for the fast-paced technologization of today's working world as well as for the growing demands on his skill-set coming with globalization, often including bilingualism, continuous further education, and ongoing self-improvement. And on top of this already giant albatross around Joe's neck comes the current cultural upheaval to also turn his traditions-based private life and beliefs violently on their heads.

Curtesy of the *"feminazi-controlled #MeToo-movement"*, Joe is suddenly not anymore allowed to good-naturedly slap that juicy ass of the tasty secretary in accounting or of the pretty waitress at his diner! Even worse, these *"bull dykes"* have taken down some of Joe's greatest heroes on television and in politics and show no signs of stopping with their *"purge"* anytime soon. *"Seriously"*, Joe thinks, *"they should be glad that they even get noticed by real men! I mean, why make such a fuss about some harmless, good-natured teases, what? Am I right or am I right?"*

Moreover, Joe is seriously worried about this uncontrollable, unreal, and *unrelenting Black Lives Matter*-movement, led by a horde of anarchic Blacks and brutal Antifa-terrorists who show no respect for the proper order of things and its enforcers in blue. Millions of white-faced, blue-collared, and red-capped Joes continue to passionately believe, "if you do nothing wrong, the police won't come along". Surely, George Floyd must have done something wrong to deserve such special attention from America's heroic fighters for law and order, no?

A simplistic worldview that carries over to all other areas of social life, from healthcare, (*"Universal health care? You mean, free health care for the scroungers? And I have to pay for it? That's pure communism!"*), to the *Black Live Matters*-movement, [*"Democratic politicians don't fear the mob. Noticed that? Why? Because they don't need to. They control the mob! The mob operates with their permission. These are their foot soldiers. This is their militia!"* – Tucker Carlson, June 23, 2020].

Boxed-wine moms and Cheetos jumbo-pack dads on their sofas watching FOX News know to fear this *"mob"*, as Sean, Tucker, Laura, and Jeanine love to unironically label the peaceful protests against systemic racism and police brutality at any opportunity. No matter that this *"mob"* at the *Black Lives Matter*-protests consisted of a small fraction of knuckleheads who show up at any demonstration with violence on their minds. Putting these deeply disturbed youths front and center in the midst of millions who peacefully protest against abundantly proven police-brutality and systemic racism constitutes merely one of the oldest propaganda-tricks in the book and at that being as transparent to any level-headed citizen as it is effective on Trumpists, one third of whom excitedly slurp their cheap wine and stuff their face with Cheetos while worrying that a horde of black-clad vandals will storm their triple-mortgaged house to kill them in their wine- and fat-induced slumber.

Another third fears less any personal consequences from the *"raging mob"*, regarding the apocalyptic fantasy-scenario on FOX News rather as the beginning of the end of civilization with police forces as the last bastion of order against the all-encompassing chaos, alternating between horror and elation in jittery expectance of the forthcoming Rapture.

The final third, however, while knowing full well that Tucker Carlson's *"mob"* makes up merely 1% of demonstrators is nonetheless gleefully watching Carlson's, Ingraham's, and Hannity's demonization of the nationwide movement against racism and violent police forces, in the hope that the FOX-demagogues will spur on many more Kyle Rittenhouses to take to the streets and fire supersonic pieces of metal into the unprotected heads, limbs, and organs of innocent fellow Americans since in their view the United States could very well use some more racist violence and police-brutality.

However, all three thirds agree on the point that Donald J. Trump constitutes the only chance to stop those terrifying masses of anarchists, socialists, communists, illegal immigrants, gang-members, *bad hombres*, Chinese *"Kung Flu"* disseminators, virus-alarmists, facemask-wearing anti-Americans, disloyal ex-officials, lying enemies of the people, SJWs, *#Me Too* witches, *Squad* terrorists, *Greta*-worshipping weather-pussies, *Sandy Hook Promise* brats, *Black Lives Matter* looters and thugs, and Democratic deep state-operatives, from utterly destroying this good, old America exclusively existing in Trumpists' regressive fantasy.

A mindset that also prompted those 6,200 Trumpists who made it to Trump's rally on June 20, 2020, at the "re-opening" of the Trump-campaign in Tulsa's 19,000-seating *Bank of Oklahoma* Center to go berserk when the President labelled COVID-19 with the racist term *"Kung Flu"*. The small crowd of predominantly unmasked Trumpists cheered for each one of Trump's attacks on anyone not agreeing with his racist, misogynistic, and reality-distorting assertions, once again confirming the *Appeal to Poverty*-tactic of *"We against them!"* to work flawlessly with the remnant of medieval peasantry in the 21st century.

There are exactly two reasons why this millennia-old trick still works so smoothly on some 21st century-adults. For one, any autocratic ruler's golden rule purporting that nothing will close the ranks tighter than the threat of an outside enemy.

For another, the lesser known autocrat-rule implying that throwing a juicy bone of "enemies" to the people on the lowest ladder-rung will instil a sense of faux pride and self-esteem and further deepen their loyalty.

Tossing stereotypical figures like the *"malicious illegal immigrant"*, the *"violent Antifa-activist"*, the *"unpatriotic mask-wearer"*, or the *"looting Black protester"* to the autocrat's unskilled, ill-educated, overweight, and underpaid disciples allows the "poor victims of circumstance" to find themselves suddenly not anymore at rock bottom to be trampled on by everyone above their social rank but instead in a new position giving them the opportunity to finally kick down on people who have officially been declared to constitute the lowest scum of the earth.

To the underprivileged masses this new constellation appears to be the long-awaited elevation to a well-deserved higher social status, while in reality they remain of course on exact the same rung as before, with the only difference of now being allowed to treat even more vulnerable and desperate people in the same manner they are treated by the rest of society. With the instigator meanwhile watching the cruel game unfold in the safe knowledge that the feral pack of followers at the ladder's base will be too busy maltreating their newest, frequently changing hate-objects for getting any ideas about closing in on him and his multi-millionaire and billionaire clientele.

> *The Hero They Do Not Need but Deserve*

Donald John Trump may be late to the modern autocrats' party compared to his fellow Pied Pipers in Russia, Hungary, Poland, Turkey, or the Philippines, let alone to such veteran party-animals as the ones in Saudi-Arabia, Iran, Syria, Nigeria, Vietnam, China, or North Korea.

But the former TV-show host and life-long racist, (*see*: Central Park Five, 1989), Donald Judas Trump has been quite busy making up for his late start with ever-escalating racist, misogynistic, homophobic, and below-the-belt *ad hominem*-attacks going as far as verbally assaulting four U.S.-Congresswomen of color, (three born in the USA with the fourth naturalized in 2000), in a tweet on June 14, 2019, thusly: *"Why don't they go back and help fix the totally broken and crime-infested places from which they came.*

Then come back and show us how it is dome. These places need your help badly, you can't leave fast enough."

Predictably, the achromatic Trump-base did not question the verisimilitude of Donald Jezebel Trump's allegations, let alone criticise his racist insinuations. What had been unthinkable before 2017, viz an all-out racist *"Go back to where you come from!"*-attack on duly elected, honorable members of Congress by the actual President of the United States of America himself, has become just a few, short years later *"the new normal"* in the USA, constituting a new state of *"normalcy"* long in the making and eagerly awaited by roughly 35% of Americans, if the raunchy cheers of Trumpists prompted by his tweet are any indication.

Future generations, provided there will be any future generations of course, will no doubt have little difficulties to pass their own judgement on the conduct of the 45th American President. After all, *Sir Liesalot* is not hiding most of his unlawful actions all that well. On the contrary, in his assumed safe knowledge that he has *"Article II of the Constitution"* on his side, *"where I have the right to do whatever I want as president"* - (Donald J. Trump, July 23, 2019), he busily continued to add new impeachable offenses to his long list of improper and allegedly illegal acts and freely admitted them either on national television, *("When you do testing to that extent, you're going to find more people, you're going to find more cases. So I said to my people, slow the testing down, please."* – Donald J. Trump, June 20, 2020, Tulsa, Oklahoma), or to renowned Pulitzer-journalist Bob Woodward on tape, (*"You just breathe the air and that's how it's passed"*, Trump said in a

February 7, 2020, call with Woodward. *"And so that's a very tricky one. That's a very delicate one. It's also more deadly than even your strenuous flus. This is deadly stuff."* – *"I wanted to always play it down. I still like playing it down,"* Trump told Woodward on March 19, 2020. *"Because I don't want to create a panic."*)

This level of audacity displayed by *Fuckface von Clownstick*[1] has also been exemplified by his firing of three high-ranking government-officials a mere two days after his foreseeable acquittal in the Trumpublican-led U.S.-Senate's impeachment trial. Trump's son *Donny Douchebag Jr.*[2] downright admitted in a tweet that the reason for having Alexander Vindman, a Purple Heart-decorated United States Army Lieutenant Colonel and (former) Director for European Affairs for the United States, humiliatingly escorted from his office at the White House by security personnel, came down to an act of pure vindictiveness against Vindman for his role as witness in the House impeachment inquiry. Additionally, the *Corn Husk Doll Cursed by a Witch*[3] in the White House fired also Vindman's twin-brother Yevgeny, a military officer and (former) attorney on the United States National Security Council. The third official who got the axe was big-time 2016 Trump-donor ($1 million) and subsequently Trump-appointed ambassador to the EU, Gordon Sondland. Sondland is going to be remembered particularly for his statement at the House inquiry that, *"everyone was in the loop"*, including *Flat Top*[4] himself.

---

[1] curtesy of former *Daily Show* host Jon Stewart
[2] curtesy of *Real Time* host Bill Maher
[3] curtesy of Chris Hardwick of @MIDNIGHT
[4] one of Trump's boyhood nicknames

Although red-headed and -hatted Trumpists demanded the head of a decorated, law-abiding Lieutenant Colonel rolling in the dust, however, in contrast to the private sector where a CEO can easily fire employees disagreeing with his shady dealings and gag them with an NDA, the public sector's regulations are better equipped to protect brave whistle-blowers, the natural antibodies of the political system. Hence, for instance *18 U.S. Code §1513* - Retaliating against a witness, victim, or an informant, states: "(e) *Whoever knowingly, with the intent to retaliate, takes any action harmful to any person, <u>including interference with the lawful employment or livelihood of any person</u>, for providing to a law enforcement officer any truthful information relating to the commission or possible commission of any Federal offense, shall be fined under this title or imprisoned not more than 10 years, or both.*"

Any first semester law-student must therefore conclude that the sacking of Ltd. Col. Alexander Vindman, let alone of his uninvolved brother, constitutes a violation of 18 U.S. Code §1513. A fact that the constitution-loving experts in *Lord Dampnut's*[5] government conveniently overlooked.

Nonetheless, a part of the guilt lies demonstrably also on the doorstep of the judiciary, having largely remained silent in the face of the numerous violations of laws and regulations committed by *Mr. Meticulous*[6] since January, 2017. District Attorneys in hot pursuit of the *Peripatetic Political Showman's*[7] breach of numerous regulations on the executive branch's powers are presumably well advised

---

[5] anagram of 'Donald Trump
[6] military academy nickname given to Trump for folding all his underwear into neat squares
[7] coined by *The Fiscal Times*

to let the American public in on their findings, whether before or after the 2020-elections. While the 35% of MAGA-hatters remain to hold considerable sway over the political landscape in *Teflon Don's*[8] America, this cannot be the reason for allowing Trump to get away with his allegedly illegal and certainly immoral actions.

Including, for instance, pardoning convicted and confessed criminals like *First Lieutenant Michael Behenna* [sentenced in February 2009 to 20 years in prison plus dismissal from the Army for assault and premeditated murder - pardoned by president Trump in May 2019], or *Major Mathew L. Golsteyn* [pardon issued by Trump in November 2019 before [*sic*] his trial for his confessed, premeditated murder of a *suspected* bomb-maker in Afghanistan, 2010]. Or issuing commutations for people like *Ronen Nahmani* [sentenced to 20 years in prison for conspiracy to distribute synthetic drugs in October 2015 - commutation issued by Trump in February 2020], or *Judith Negron* [sentenced in December 2011 to 35 years imprisonment for healthcare fraud, money laundering, and defrauding the United States - commutation issued by Trump in February 2020].

In February of 2020 alone, the *Maladroit Savage Spiralling Out of Control*[9] in fact granted executive clemency to 11 convicted criminals, leading to immediate speculations whether *John Miller*[10] is actually paving the way for an even bigger round of pardons in the near future benefitting imprisoned Trump-cronies like former Trump-campaign manager Paul Manafort, Republican spin-doctor Roger Stone,

---

[8] curtesy of Michael R. Burch
[9] curtesy of Charles M. Blow
[10] one of the pseudonyms Trump uses for anonymously bragging about his feats

or former National Security Advisor General Michael T. Flynn. Yet, even the granting of clemency to 11 convicted criminals by *Herr Lügenpresse*[11] did not stir up the slightest ripple on the surface of the leaden sea that is the collective consciousness of the Trump-base.

No one but *#DishonestDonald*[12], having lived his whole adult life in a world with literal golden toilets to plonk his flabby ass on, would be narcissistic enough to choose as his "natural" target-group the rural lower middle-class, the disenfranchised, and the working poor. The *Failed Mail-Order Meat Salesman*[13] presented himself to this demographic from day one as their *"man of the people"*, at the same time unironically stating that paying for grocery-shopping demands the showing of an ID-card to the cashier. In fact, very few are further removed from the daily grind of the average American worker than *Silver Spoon Donald*[14]. Yet, on November 8, 2016, another date that might well be living in infamy, all prognoses by polling-experts proved to be grossly incorrect, with parties and pollsters alike having severely underestimated the raw power of persuasion and entrapment of the *Human Bullhorn's*[15] expertly use of the *Appeal to Poverty*. Ironically, a strategy once perfected by infamous communists Mao and Stalin, had helped the *Screaming Carrot Demon*[16] to win over the one group of Americans previously been believed to be

---

[11] *Mr. Lying Media"*, curtesy of Dan Rather
[12] trending on Twitter
[13] curtesy of Ashley Feinberg, satirizing Trump Steaks
[14] curtesy of Don C. Reed
[15] curtesy of Jim Newell, *Slate*
[16] curtesy of Samantha Bee, *Full Frontal*

utterly immune to communist propaganda methods, aka white, ill-educated, male Americans.

See, it is funny because whenever Trump panders to his devout Trumpists' tastes by referring to these self-declared underdogs and grit-eaters as *hard-working Americans, honest workers, true patriots,* or, *the greatest workforce on Earth,* their *Poster Child of American Decline*[17] utilizes the exact same *Appeal to Poverty*-rhetoric as the demagogues in communist Soviet Russia and Mao's China, as well as in the Nazis' "Third Reich". Trump's flattered base thus remains loyal to a conman who once said *"the point is that you can't be too greedy"* and keeps clinging to the lips of the *Orange Manatee*[18] just as tightly as his straw-like hairpiece is clinging to the bone-white dome of the *Boiled Ham in a Wig*[19]

Together with a number of further psychological, rhetorical, and mass-manipulating propaganda-schemes laid us in Vol. 1 and Vol. 2 of this book, the *Appeal to Poverty* constitutes an essential chapter in Trump's playbook, providing one major reason for the often unfathomable willingness of Trumpists to swallow whole shitloads of *Diaper Donald's*[20] rhetorical manure and to applaud their *God*[21].

In the eye of a storyteller, the astonishing success-story of Trump's *Appeals to Poverty*-strategy seems less the result of a comprehensively structured script, sharing instead rather uncanny similarities with a failing screenwriter's convoluted

---

[17] curtesy of Robert Spencer
[18] curtesy of Stephen Colbert, *The Late Show*
[19] curtesy of Jon Stewart
[20] curtesy of Kevin Cavanaugh
[21] curtesy of Jay Leno

screenplay conceived in a drunken fever-dream and roundly rejected by Hollywood-executives for its unbelievably nonsensical plot.

Prior to the 2016 election and with the eerie exception of *Simpsons*-creator Matt Groening, even in one's wildest dreams nobody could have imagined the reality of a Trump-presidency. Not that long ago it would have been impossible to find a single professional author, screenwriter, late show-host, journalist, or political commentator who would have dared to insult their audience with a scenario even half as outlandish, crazy, and horrifying as the years under Trump have unequivocally proven to be, for fear of accusations of simply ripping off *Twilight Zone, Game of Thrones*, and *House of Cards* and mixing them into a surreal and unbelievable polit-horror story. No doubt an unfair accusation, considering a reality in which ...

- ... a spray-tanned, septuagenarian porn-star afficionado with a penchant for having his ass spanked, a decades-long history of alleged women-molestation and known adultery, and a patently obvious ignorance of the Bible's content can become *the revered champion of the most rigorously bible-abiding Evangelicals.*

- ... an obese, germophobic real-estate developer who lives in a golden penthouse, swindles construction-suppliers and -workers out of their money, dodged the Vietnam-draft with a fake diagnosis, and calls on U.S.-companies to bring manufacture back to the United States while having his own merchandise made in China can become *the acclaimed idol of millions of hard-boiled blue-collar workers.*

- … a former TV-show host, nepotist, obstructionist, and open opponent of the Framers' system of checks and balances and the co-equal branches of government can with greatest ease persuade the highest-ranking leaders of the Republican Party to fight tooth and nail for pole-position to *crawl as deeply as possible into his gaping posterior hole.*

Despite the persistent suspicion that somewhere along the timeline the world must have been nudged into an alternate reality in which some failed polit-horror-story writer's ludicrously dark fantasies have become reality, some rays of hope have recently begun to emanate from several corners of the political and social landscape.

Such lights cutting through the trumpist darkness include Democrats in Congress like Adam Schiff, Bernie Sanders (ind.), Elizabeth Warren, Eric Swalwell, Ted Lieu, Ayanna Pressley, and Alexandria Ocasio-Cortez, as well as journalists shining their flashlights at the rotten underbelly of the Trumpministration like Lindsay Gellman, Ronan Farrow, Bob Woodward, Louis Theroux, Diane Sawyer, Rachel Maddow, Chris Hayes, Jake Tapper, Stephanie Ruhle, Brianna Keilar, and dedicated editorial teams at the *Washington Post, New York Times, Los Angeles Times, Boston Globe,* and *New York Daily News.*

Moreover, several exceptionally competent and dedicated YouTube-channels continue to hold the torch high for democracy, justice, equality, humanism, and an impartial justice-system, among them *The David Pakman Show*, *The Ring of Fire*, *The Young Turks*, *Democracy Now!* with Any Goodman, *The Majority Report* with Sam Seder, and *Brian Tyler Cohen*. Not to forget the late show-hosts currently manning the media-frontline in the battle against an increasingly authoritarian government, with Stephen Colbert, Trevor Noah, Bill Maher, John Oliver, Jimmy Kimmel, Samantha Bee, and Seth Meyers on the ramparts.

Prominent activists like Jane Fonda, Daniel Ellsberg, Charlize Theron, Joaquin Phoenix, Martin Sheen, Sally Field, Alyssa Milano, and many others use their popularity to raise awareness for the impending danger of an all-out authoritarian regime in the United States while last but by no means least, brave men and women inside the U.S.-administration regarded it their duty to pull the curtain back, open a window, and blow the whistle on the dealings of the *Fascist Carnival Barker*[22] and his gang of unfunny clowns. Whistle blowers like Ltd. Col. Alexander Vindman as well as other, unnamed guardians of democracy who contributed to the exposure of *Donald the Deadbeat's*[23] Mafia-methods, represent genuine role models for future generations of government employees, state officials, public servants, and representatives of the people.

Decidedly and unfortunately missing from this list are any practicing district attorneys, civil rights lawyers, and representatives of big non-profit organizations such as the *American Center for Law and Justice*, the *Natural Resources Defense Council*, the *Humane Society of the United States*,

---

[22] curtesy of Martin O'Malley
[23] curtesy of Dan Rather

the *American Association for the Advancement of Science*, the *NARAL Pro-Choice America Foundation*, the *Southern Poverty Law Center*, or the *American Civil Liberties Union* ACLU.

While these and other organizations certainly do not sit idle while the democratic framework of the nation rapidly erodes all around them, a large majority of Americans would nonetheless be unable to identify any of their representatives by name. In times when it is all but impossible to ignore the omnipresent *"black mirrors"*, i.e. the ubiquitous screens providing every citizen 24/7 with information, the literal facelessness of well-established civil rights-, watchdog-, and protectionist organizations and absence of any recognizable and recurring spokesperson from the hundreds of millions of screens will likely contribute to their growing irrelevance, since a message without a face promulgating it must fall flat in its attempt to raise awareness, ultimately resulting in a dwindling of public support.

A person who understands this equation perfectly is, of course, *Dangerous Donald*[24], who often works overtime to flood as many media-channels as possible with his face, voice, and tweets. The fact that even a Donald J. Trump cannot completely dominate the airwaves and the web does not mean he is not trying. Still, when even 10-hour long tweeting-frenzies, daily chopper-talk "press conferences" and further rambling monologues to TV-cameras, as well as weekly barnstormer-rallies in the boonies and occasional public appearances with foreign dignitaries, government officials, or "exalted artists" like Kid Rock and Kanye West prove insufficient in gaining Trump total on-air supremacy, the

---

[24] curtesy of Hillary Clinton

Terroristic Man-Toddler[25] nonetheless rests assured that one loyal ally will trustfully impart his daily *Appeal to Poverty* to the hooked honkeys in Hometown, USA, viz his media-megaphones.

> A Mass-Manipulator's Must-Have: The Matching Megaphone

Donald Trump's undeniably shrewd understanding of television and social media as perfect multipliers for his rhetorical flytraps compels inevitably the comparison with another masterful exploiter of the primary information-source of his time. As rightfully uncomfortable as it feels and as cockeyed as the references are often enough, there is no avoiding the obvious similitudes between the 21st century-style populist in the White House and the inventor of modern propaganda, in cahoots with his ingenious right-hand man *Reichspropagandaminister* Joseph Goebbels.

As most Americans are at least superficially aware of, the origins of the name *"Volkswagen"* (VW) for the 1937-founded German car-manufacturer had been the result of a project Hitler instigated to mass-produce an affordable *Volkswagen* (people's car) for every German family, marking the beginning of German mass-motorisation in combination with the construction of the original *Autobahn*-network.

Considerably less Americans might know though, that Hitler applied the same principle of cheap mass-production also to the so-called *"Volksempfänger"* (people's receiver; people's radio). Modern historians regard the affordable and robust *Radio VE 301*, complete with its standardly embossed swastika, as one of the most important instruments of the all-

---

[25] curtesy of Charles M. Blow

pervasive Nazi-propaganda, also because no "reputable" German family could be seen without this pinnacle of German technology and symbol of state- and party-allegiance in their living room. With the *VE 301* Hitler created an inescapable "megaphone", allowing him to put one of his core propaganda-strategies optimally into practice that derived from his perception that, *"the broad masses of a population are more amenable to the appeal of rhetoric than to any other force"*.

A lesson seemingly wholeheartedly embraced by the *Trumpet*[26] and his Trumpaganda-brigade around Stephen Miller and formerly Kellyanne Conway, just as another infamous "wisdom" of Nazi-Germany's *Führer*, stating that, *"the great masses of the people will more easily fall victim to a big lie than to a small one."*

Unquestionably, there are some exceptionally good reasons why it remains more than problematic to compare any person, living or dead, to Adolf Hitler or any political organisation to the Nazi-party NSDAP for that matter. For one, such a comparison constitutes an inexcusable insult to literally everyone, except the most gruesome dictatorial monsters in history who can be counted on two hands tops. More importantly, however, any comparison will inevitably relativize the incomparable atrocities and horrors committed by Hitler and his helpers, in consequence diminishing the unimaginable sufferings of millions of innocents who died in or lived through a literal hell on earth established, expanded, operated, and "efficiently" administrated by the *Nationalsozialisten*.

---

[26] another of Trump's boyhood nicknames

On the other side, to completely ignore the situation in Germany between 1933 and 1945 and to remain mum regarding the devilish methods of the proverbial epitome of totalitarianism and his evil henchmen out of a false or even fake sense of considerateness, (e.g., *"let bygones be bygones"*, *"don't wallow in history's mud"*, *"give the victims a rest"*, *"we need to look forward, not backwards"*, et.al.), would also mean to ignore some of the most important lessons history can teach mankind. Even a determinately right-winged historian would presumably be hard pushed to deny for instance certain obvious parallels between the Nazis' use of *Appeal to Poverty*-propaganda in combination with modern media (radio) and the constant *Appeals to Poverty* by the *Tiny Fisted Emperor*[27] on FOX News and Twitter.

History-buffs who are familiar with Hitler's *"Third Reich"* [with the First *Reich* (i.e. Empire) having been the *Holy Roman Empire of the German Nation,* 962–1806, and the Second *Reich* the *German Empire* under the Hohenzollern monarchy with *Kaiser* (i.e. Emperor) Wilhelm I. and *Kaiser* Wilhelm II., 1871–1918], will have probably succumbed at least once to the temptation of drawing comparisons between the hellish creatures once squirming and scheming in Hitler's inner circle and their current pale imitations in the service of America's *Two-Bit Caesar*[28] in the White House since 2017.

It certainly is a blessing in disguise that authoritarian rulers appear to surround themselves instinctively with people cut from their own cloth, viz the type of narcissistic, egomaniacal, greedy opportunists who believe themselves far above their

---

[27] curtesy of Murfster35 on *DailyKos*
[28] curtesy of Bill Kristol

genuine capabilities. Moreover, the world can count itself lucky that Hitler's score of plain stupidity in his henchmen has been easily surpassed today by Donald Trump's pack of out-of-their-depths minions. While Hitler's inner circle, from Rudolph Hess (second-in-command) to Heinrich Himmler (SS-chief) to propaganda-warlock Joseph Goebbels, had shown an uncanny level of devious intelligence and manipulation-skills, the current clowns in the employ of *Rome Burning in Man-Form*[29] can be generally found several Grand Canyons-depths below the competence-level of the Nazis and their infamous mastery of state-propaganda.

Stephen Miller, (Kellyanne Conway), and former and present Lying-to-the-Press Secretaries Sean Spicer, Sarah Huckabee Sanders, Stephanie Grisham, and 1988-born Kayleigh McEnany in the White House Bunker as well as Ingraham, Pirro, Coulter, Hannity, and Tucker over at Trump-TV assumedly wish to possess just a sliver of the evil genius once having distinguished Hitler's clubfooted chief-propagandist Joseph Goebbels, knowing that their mediocre manipulation-skills have little to no effect on the U.S.-population beyond the 35% of Americans who also give *Corona Beer* a wide berth since the Corona-Virus outbreak.

In the lasting absence of an ingenious, media-manipulating mastermind like Joseph Goebbels, Trumpublican backroom-plotters calling the shots on the *Golden Wrecking Ball*[30] obviously changed tactics after Sarah *"Smokey Eyes"* Sanders' demise, having given up on a single, effective human megaphone and leaving the field instead

---

[29] curtesy of John Oliver, *Last Week Tonight*
[30] curtesy of *the* Sarah Palin

exclusively to *Creep Throat*[31] and his tweeting thumps, *chopper-talk* ramblings, and grandstanding announcements at the Oval Office, Cabinet room, or rally-podium. Meanwhile, the actual *War on Truth* wages on thousands of online-battlefields where *Captain Chaos*[32] plays merely the role of a ventriloquist's dummy with the hands of far-right Super PACs and the Russian government up his backside while aiming at undermining permanently the American people's trust in their Constitution, civil rights, democratic system, and public institutions.

A similar course-correction took place on national television where initial Trumpagandists of the first generation turned out to be anything but emotionally stable, let alone professionally or intellectually up to the job. Prime examples being Paris Dennard, Jeffrey Lord, blonde dumbshell Scottie *"Riots aren't necessarily a bad thing"* Nell Hughes, or erstwhile official Trump-spokeswoman Katrina Pierson who back in 2016 appeared no less than 3-6 times per day on television while being in 2020 just as obscure as Donald J. Trump's tax-returns.

Mercifully, in later stages of the Trump-era broadcasters like CNN, MSNBC, and ABC realized the futility of inviting Trump-stooges to mindlessly unreel rhetorical schemes like the *3 Steps Argument from Authority*, *Circular Reasoning*, or plain *Bullshitting,* in turn leading to the Trumpaganda-division's decision to replace their ferociously screaming, incoherently rambling, or mind-numbingly chattering spokesfailures with more stable and streamlined mouthpieces.

---

[31] curtesy of Seth Meyers, *Late Night with Seth Meyers*
[32] curtesy of NBC News

The importance of such human propaganda-megaphones for the Trumpministration was made obvious at the latest when *Boldfinger's*[33] erstwhile campaign communications-director and Trumpist eye-candy Hope Hicks declared in 2016, according to *TIME Magazine*: *"We are extremely grateful to those who appear on TV to voice their support of Mr. Trump and his candidacy, especially given the totally biased media and so called pundits who routinely malign Mr. Trump."*

Compartmentalizing and outsourcing day-to-day *Appeals to Poverty*-work from the very beginning with the purpose of keeping a perpetually angry, frustrated, and malcontent Trump-base at operating temperature allowed the Trumpaganda-division to present the public with a wide variety of once believed impossible to be real characters, each covering distinct target-groups. With members of the well-paid Trumpaganda-militia regularly found on FOX News and other TV-networks, as well as on YouTube, Facebook, Instagram, and Twitter, including individuals like Trump's fourth *Lying-to-the-Press* Secretary and former *National Press Secretary for the 2020 Trump-campaign,* the perpetually caterwauling spitfire Kayleigh McEnany, the *Women for Trump* co-founder and *Karen*-embodiment Amy Kremer, in 2020 gone off the radar *Blacks for Trump* leader and token Black behind Trump at rallies Maurice Symonette, aka Mikael Israel, and 1993-born *Turning Point USA*-founder Charlie Kirk who praised in his book explicitly former *TPUSA* national field-director Crystal Clanton, who in turn purportedly wrote in a text-message to a fellow *Turning Point*-employee: *"I hate black people. Like fuck them all ... I hate blacks. End of story."*

---

[33] curtesy of Michael R. Burch

> *The Lahren- & Karen-Conundrums*

Whether unceremoniously thrown back into oblivion by 2020 or still actively around, Trump's cardboard cut-out conservatives McEnany, Kremer, Symonette, Kirk and others like Instagram-"star" Tomi Lahren, LGBTQ-demonizer Kaitlin Bennett, or OANN's bubblehead Liz Wheeler, all have been individually aligned to target their characteristic subgroups inside the trumpist base to disseminate anti-social, elitist, evangelical, reactionary, and zero-sum policies embodied by the *Barrel-Shouting Meatbal*[34]*l* whose slurred statements serve as their directives.

However, the Miller-Conway chimera and their boss appeared to have a preference for the type of peroxide-blonde, female high school-bully that is long since overrepresented on TV by the likes of Megyn Kelly, Kayleigh McEnany, Tomi Lahren, Lauren Southern, Katherine Timpf, or Ainsley Earhardt and their botoxed grannies Laura Ingraham and Ann Coulter, in the transparent attempt to assign them the double role of far-right poster girl whose pictures hang metaphorically or literally above the beds of horny 16-26 year-old Trumpboys in the Bible belt, while on the other hand functioning as *"The Intelligent yet Beautiful Face of Conservatism"* to be secretly admired by frustrated, middle-aged Trumpboy-fathers.

In stark contrast, rotund and rosy-cheeked *Women for Trump* co-founder Amy Kremer had been poised to skim off the equally large target-group of proverbial *Karens*, that wobbly mass of white, middle-aged, suburban housewives, stay-at-home mothers, part-time real estate agents, anti-

---

[34] curtesy of Chris Hardwick, @MIDNIGHT

vaxxers, essential oils-hawkers, Ponzi-scheme hucksters, anti-abortionists, bible group participants, anti-facemaskers, morning-wine drinkers, town-gossips, and busybodies demanding to speak to the manager the moment they detect an apparently grave violation of their "rights" as white, Christian, American women.

For perfect *Karen*-decal in appearance and demeanor Amy Kremer, netting this demographic for her adored *Cinnamon Hitler*[35] must have appeared to resemble shooting fish in a barrel. Indeed, Kremer's *Appeal to Poverty* variation – with her target-group's *"poverty"* constituting an inner emptiness preferably filled by wine and interfering in the lives of others – has been extremely successful, mainly because of one notion that appeals to Kremer's army of *Karens* even more than racist, homophobic, and bigoted attacks camouflaged as *"holding up traditional Christian, American values"*, viz to dedicate their life to the support of a larger-than-life, manly superman with stamina, virility, handsomeness, and power, who will make their fantasy-vision of America *"great again"*.

Their mediocre to low intelligence quotient coupled with reactionary upbringing lets most *Karens* yearn for a never having been real version of America with a Dear Leader enforcing traditionalist, hidebound values and rules showing non-whites "their place" and reverting women to their "hereditary roles" as pleasure-providing birthing machines, happy housekeepers, and obedient servants to an all-round superior, male head of the household. *Karens* strongly tend to admire men in the role of protector and usually love themselves *"a dashing man in uniform"* like the

---

[35] curtesy of Trevor Noah, *The Daily Show*

gallant police officers who keep the yellow, black, and brown riffraff "so heroically off our streets".

No wonder, therefore, that Kremer's message appeals more to the upper middle-class WASP wife and less to the hard working, lower-class American woman. Long-term boyfriends, fiancées, and husbands of a *Karen* generally support their poppet's infatuation with the *Groper-in-Chief*[36], since both intuitively identify with the conman's *Appeal to* their own, specific brand of *Poverty*, the bankruptcy of the soul.

> *Blacks & Boogaloo for Trump*

Not so much a crippling need for filling an inner void has been characteristic for the juvenile fans of *Turning Point USA*-youngster Charlie Kirk, but rather a burning desire to be on the seemingly "winning" side. From covert Nazi-admirers to self-proclaimed future business-tycoons and Wall Street-legends, the predominantly male *Turning Point USA*-clientele worships the zero sum-mentality of their *Mogul*[37] and found in Kirk the high priest of their cult. Like most cults, however, *TPUSA* experienced its share of dissidents and rejections, apparently because there seems to have been not enough violence and "action" to be had. For people thus inclined, the pro-gun, anti-government *Boogaloo movement* has offered the perfect alternative, particularly white supremacist and neo-Nazi sub-groups inside the movement believing in a coming race war to be fought in Hawaiian shirts.

---

[36] curtesy of Nicholas Kristof
[37] Trump's Secret Service code name

Lastly and unlike his fellow Trump-megaphones, *Blacks for Trump*-leader Maurice Symonette, born Maurice Woodside and also known as Mikael Israel, did not incite anyone with his shenanigans, whether in the background of Trump's televised rally-speeches or off-camera. Symonette, who has called himself *Michael the Black Man* when rallying for Trump, has been reported to have played a considerable role in the rise and fall of the *Yahweh Ben Yahweh* cult, a part of the *Black Hebrew Israelites* movement, and had often been seen at Trump's 2016-election rallies in the crowd behind the podium with his *"Blacks for Trump"*-sign.

Presumably, it will remain one of history's great mysteries whether Symonette has appealed to any demographic at all, at least until today no one has been coming forth declaring allegiance to *Michael the Black Man* about whom not much more is known, hence leaving it up to speculation whether Symonette's personal lowlight in his one-man crusade for Trump had come during Trump's 2016-rally in Redding, California, when *America's Black Mole*[38] passed him over, pointing instead at a certain Gregory Cheadle and yelling: *"Oh, look at my African American over here! Look at him! Aren't you the greatest?"*

Considering the 2020 *Black Lives Matter*-protests, the countless racist comments of the 45th American president, and his incessant support for the violent conduct of America's police forces, even Maurice will not have been surprised that according to *a NPR/PBS NewsHour/Marist* Poll on June 2-3, 2020, the disapproval-rate for *Genghis Can't*[39] among all non-white voters had reached new heights with 67% disapproving

---

[38] curtesy of John Oliver, *Last Week Tonight*
[39] curtesy of Michael R. Burch

(55% *"disapprove strongly"*) of Donald Trump's job as President. A safe indication for the non-white American electorate to have proven the most immune to Trump's *Appeal to Poverty* strategy among all social sub-groups, which may also be partly explained by this demographic's internally spread historical experience and the painful lessons learned. With another part certainly owing to a general open-mindedness, tightly knit relations, and strong solidarity permeating Black and Hispanic communities, together resulting in strong "auto-immune" traits, in fact constituting already the first half of the only effective defense a population can successfully muster against an autocrat's *Appeal to Poverty*.

> *Repulsing the Populist Appeal*

The second half of a population's successful defense against populists and their *Appeal to Poverty*, *Circular Reasoning*, *Ipse Dixit*-argumentation, *Bullshitting,* or other populistic parodies, constitutes a comprehensive humanistic education for every young member of society.

No one is born as a racist, bigot, zealot, or misogynist. And while today's generation of adult Trumpublicans and Trumpists must be regrettably regarded as a lost cause, many young Americans are not yet beyond being open to reason. In order to avoid a repetition of the Trumpastrophe with potentially worse consequences, the next government succeeding the *King of the Oompa Loompas*[40] will need to declare it a top priority to comprehensively educate all American children on topics of racial, gender, and universal

---

[40] curtesy of Justin Baragona

equality, the foundations of humanity and social-mindedness, curiosity, scientific principles, culture, and rational thought.

The appalling circumstance of having a large number of adult Americans seriously refusing to wear a facemask during the worst pandemic in 100 years with more than 190,000 dead compatriots after a mere six months allows objective observers only to come to the conclusion that American education has reached abysmally insufficient rock bottom. Even more so when considering that no other country worldwide experienced anything coming close to the irrational, deranged, and outright crazy behaviors displayed by America's "anti-facemask"-movement. With YouTube providing ample examples of adult Americans lambasting city councils and officials for making facemasks mandatory while citing as reasons for their refusal to protect fellow Americans among other points their *"Freedom"*, (although one person's freedom ends where it infringes on the freedom of another, for instance the freedom to be alive), as well as *"Breathing in poisonous air" and "Suffocation"*, (although nurses and doctors wear facemasks daily for hours on end), and being subject of *"Discrimination"*, (although the same people discriminate openly against topless sun-bathing and would be appalled by anti-discrimination laws allowing shopping in the nude despite being far less health-endangering than shopping without a mask), and finally that, *"God doesn't want us to cover our faces"* (although –. No, clearly there is such a thing like an ultimate excess of stupidity, making any kind of rational argument an utter waste of potentially infectious breath.)

Unfortunately, America's "anti-mask" morons have been from the very beginning marching in lockstep with *"Socialism kills!"*-, and *"No healthcare for all!"*-blockheads, anti-vaxxer children-tormentors, flat-earther lunatics, micro-penis-compensating gun-nuts, *QAnus*-asshats and *"Pizzagate"*-putzes, chemtrail cretins, *"deep state"*-dimwits, 5G-conspiracy chumps, and all the other half- and nitwits flooding the internet, airwaves, and streets in 2020 across the United States.

That these groups overlap considerably with the Trump-base will only surprise people who have lived in North Korea for the last ten years. Everybody else will be by now acutely aware of the fact that wilful ignorance paired with a blooming *Dunning-Kruger Effect* and a toxic dose of *Circular Reasoning-, Bullshit-, Argument from Authority-,* and *Appeal to Poverty*-gullibility are by no means restricted to only one idiotic belief-system. And to be clear, no amount of enlightened education will be able to completely eradicate America's presently most common illness, since a die-hard core-demographic of utterly obstinate dimwits with elemental fears easily to be exploited by confidence tricksters appears to be present in all current and historic societies. The decisive difference between a stable community and one ruled by retards therefore lies first of all in the percentage of dimwits present in any given community.

A community build on the solidarity of a well-educated citizenry goes a long way in reducing this percentage from a toxic and almost lethal 35% to the global and historic average of a healthy and manageable 5-10%, making *Appeal to Poverty*-susceptible fools a negligible minority without influence or power to speak of. Any attempts by such morons or their media-outlets to disseminate crude conspiracy theories on behalf of a chief-manipulator are then quickly dragged into the light, ridiculed, and dismissed as the empty gibberish they are while the few remaining, adamant zealots whose foolishness can seriously endanger the lives and well-being of others, e.g., anti-vaxxers, "pro-lifers", facemask-rejecters, gun-barrel suckers, etc. are going to experience the full vigor of the law that puts the right to an unthreatened and state-protected life over any childish and selfish cries *"FoH maH FreEdOm!"*.

Finally, the insufferable trend of *"alternative facts"* and *"equally valuable counter-truths"* that has taken root in U.S.-society long before the *World's Greatest Troll*[41] came along, for instance by allowing so-called creationists any say in school curriculums, certainly would wither and die in the face of an educated public not suffering any more fools. As the great former Secretary-General of the United Nations, Kofi Annan, once said: *"Knowledge is power. Information is liberating. Education is the premise of progress, in every society, in every family"* – and the premise of a future worth fighting for.

O

---

[41] curtesy of Nate Silver, Five ThirtyEight

Author's note

Thank you so much for reading this book, Volume I of two volumes making up the complete *"Mega MAGA Mind Meltdown"*-experience. I hope you enjoyed your read and consider continuing your wild ride across the decidedly alien landscape of the Trumpist mind in the next volume.

Please check out my author's page on kindle for other highly biased and deeply offensive books like, *"Eristic Dialectic - Arthur Schopenhauer's School of Verbal Combat"*, *Surfin' in Nebraska – A Fool's Take on Idiots, Imbeciles & The Idiosyncrasies of American Insults*, and *"Authoritarianism - Everything You Need to Know about The Hot New Trend in Governance"*.

Finally, a personal note.

Doubtlessly, the year 2020 will go down as a dark and pivotal moment in history, looked back at in wonder and horror alike by future generations with the final verdict much depending on a certain election on November 3, 2020. But regardless of whether the orange Emperor will have won on this day and liberty died with thunderous applause or whether the light side will have ultimately prevailed, the battle for the future of the United States and in certain aspects of the world will not just have been over the next day. The 35% responsible for the gigantic clusterfuck representing the Trumpministration will not simply have crawled back into its holes and shut the lids but instead will continue its destructive work with new vigor.

This book was written for several reasons, with the most important one always having been the hope that it might help readers a wee bit better understanding the "other side" in order to deal with Trumpists, their mental processes, arguments, and modes of reasoning in a most effective manners. While arguing with Trumpists generally feels like hacking away at a granite wall with a sewing-needle, Volume I and Volume II of this book may provide some ideas on how to effectively attack and widen the cracks in Trumpists' rigid but brittle defenses. And as Edmund Burke said, *"Nobody made a greater mistake than he who did nothing because he could only do a little."*

S.J. Brede, September 2020